THE HUNGER GAMES

by
Suzanne Collins

Literature Guide Developed by Mary Pat Mahoney
for *Secondary Solutions*®

ISBN-13: 978-0-9845205-6-5

Secondary Solutions
THE *FIRST* SOLUTION FOR THE SECONDARY TEACHER®
WWW.4SECONDARYSOLUTIONS.COM

The Hunger Games Literature Guide

About This Literature Guide

Secondary Solutions is the endeavor of a high school English teacher who could not seem to find appropriate materials to help her students master the necessary concepts at the secondary level. She grew tired of spending countless hours researching, creating, writing, and revising lesson plans, worksheets, quizzes, tests and extension activities to motivate and inspire her students, and at the same time, address those ominous content standards! Materials that were available were either juvenile in nature, skimpy in content, or were moderately engaging activities that did not come close to meeting the content standards on which her students were being tested. Frustrated and tired of trying to get by with inappropriate, inane lessons, she finally decided that if the right materials were going to be available to her and other teachers, she was going to have to make them herself! Mrs. Bowers set to work to create one of the most comprehensive and innovative Literature Guide sets on the market. Joined by a middle school teacher with 21 years of secondary school experience, Secondary Solutions began, and has matured into a specialized team of intermediate and secondary teachers who have developed for you a set of materials unsurpassed by all others.

Before the innovation of Secondary Solutions, materials that could be purchased offered a reproducible student workbook and a separate set of teacher materials at an additional cost. Other units provided the teacher with student materials only, and very often, the content standards were ignored. Secondary Solutions provides all of the necessary materials for complete coverage of the literature units of study, including author biographies, pre-reading activities, numerous and varied vocabulary and comprehension activities, study-guide questions, graphic organizers, literary analysis and critical thinking activities, essay-writing ideas, extension activities, quizzes, unit tests, alternative assessment, online teacher assistance, and much, much more. Each Guide is designed to address the unique learning styles and comprehension levels of every student in your classroom. All materials are written and presented at the grade level of the learner, and include *extensive coverage of the content standards.* As an added bonus, all teacher materials are *included!*

As a busy teacher, you don't have time to waste reinventing the wheel. You want to get down to the business of *teaching*! With our professionally developed teacher-written literature Guides, Secondary Solutions has provided you with the answer to your time management problems, while saving you hours of tedious and exhausting work. Our Guides will allow you to focus on the most important aspects of teaching—the personal, one-on-one, hands-on instruction you enjoy most—the reason you became a teacher in the first place.

Secondary Solutions—The *First* Solution for the Secondary Teacher!®
www.4secondarysolutions.com

How to Use Our Literature Guides

Our Literature Guides are based upon the *National Council of the Teachers of English* and the *International Reading Association's* national English/Language Arts Curriculum and Content Area Standards. The materials we offer allow you to teach the love and full enjoyment of literature, while still addressing the concepts upon which your students are assessed.

These Guides are designed to be used in their sequential entirety, or may be divided into separate parts. Not all activities must be used, but to achieve full comprehension and mastery of the skills involved, it is recommended that you utilize everything each Guide has to offer. Most importantly, you now have a variety of valuable materials to choose from, and you are not forced into extra work!

There are several distinct categories within each Secondary Solutions Literature Guide:

- *Teacher's Guide*—A variety of resources to help you get the most out of this Guide as well as the text you are teaching. The Teacher's Guide includes a sample Teacher's Agenda, Summary of the Play or Novel, Pre-and Post-Reading Ideas and Activities and Alternative Assessment, Essay and Writing Ideas, Rubrics, complete Answer Key and more. Look for the Teacher's Guide at the end of this Guide. Pre-Reading Ideas and Activities are located at the beginning of the Guide.

- *Exploring Expository Writing*—Worksheets designed to address the exploration and analysis of functional and/or informational materials and of the historical aspects of the text
  - ✓ *Author Biography* including heritage, beliefs, and customs of the author
  - ✓ *Historical Context,* including allusions and unique diction, comparison of situations across historical eras, analysis of theme relevant to the historical era
  - ✓ *Biographies of relevant non-fictional characters*
  - ✓ *Relevant news and magazine articles, etc.*

- *Comprehension Check*—Similar to *Exploring Expository Writing*, but designed for comprehension of narrative text—study questions designed to guide students *as they read the text.*
  - ✓ Questions focus on *Reading Comprehension and Analysis* and cover a wide range of questioning based on Bloom's Taxonomy

- *Standards Focus*—Worksheets and activities that directly address the content standards and allow students extensive practice in literary skills and analysis. *Standards Focus* activities are found within every chapter or section. Some examples:
  - ✓ *Literary Response and Analysis,* including *Figurative Language, Irony, Flashback, Theme, Tone and Mood, Style,* and *Aesthetic Approach, etc.*
  - ✓ *Writing Strategies,* including developing thesis statements, audience and purpose, sentence combining, concise word choice, developing research questions, etc.

- *Assessment Preparation*—Vocabulary activities which emulate the types of vocabulary/ grammar proficiency on which students are tested in state and national assessments. *Assessment Preparation* activities are found within every chapter or section. Some examples:
  - ✓ *Writing Conventions,* including Parts of Speech, Precise Word Choice, Punctuation
  - ✓ *Vocabulary and Word Development,* including Context Clues, Connotation/ Denotation, Word Roots, Analogies, Literal and Figurative Language

- *Quizzes and Tests*—Quizzes are included for each chapter or designated section; final tests as well as alternative assessment are available at the end of each Guide.

Each Guide contains handouts and activities for varied levels of difficulty. We know that not all students are alike—nor are all teachers! We hope you can effectively utilize every aspect our Literature Guides have to offer—we want to make things easier on you! If you need additional assistance, please email us at customerservice@4secondarysolutions.com. Thank you for choosing Secondary Solutions—The *First* Solution for the Secondary Teacher®!

The Hunger Games

Pre-Reading Activities and Ideas

The following are suggested activities to supplement the study of *The Hunger Games prior* to the reading the novel:

1. What is a sponsor? Have students discuss the advantages to athletes in having sponsors.

2. Have students research who sponsors their favorite athletes, and the perks that go along with being sponsored.

3. Have students research the history of sports arenas from the Colosseum in Rome to present-day sports arenas.

4. Have students take a class, grade-level, or school-wide survey of students' favorite games. Students can post survey results in a hall display using a graph.

5. How familiar are students with reality TV shows? Hold a class discussion on what they are and why students think they are popular.

6. Discuss the term "voyeurism" and how important it is in our society. Have students consider the YouTube phenomenon and the prevalence of camera phones. Is it a good thing or a bad thing to watch so much of what's going on in our world? You may want students to take sides to debate the issue, or more simply, create a pro and con chart.

After completing the author biography, pp. 9-11:

7. Have students compile a list of their favorite books. Consider having a vote and displaying a chart of votes for their favorites.

8. You may want students to view and discuss some of the video interviews of Suzanne Collins. Videos are available through the Scholastic website.

9. In the interview, Suzanne Collins talks about reading books about surviving in the wild. Provide students with a collection of survival skills books. Allow students to peruse the books with the question, what skills would they need to survive in the wild?

After completing the pre-reading activity about Theseus, pp. 12-14:

10. Have students choose a scene from the story to illustrate.

11. Have student research the history of labyrinths and mazes.

12. Have students find out what Theseus's adventures are after he returns to Athens.

After completing the dystopia/utopia activity, pp. 15-17:

13. Have students write a description of their utopian society, complete with an illustration.

14. Provide other dystopian novels and stories for students to sample. You may want to create a display of these novels on a bulletin board or on a special shelf. Some novels to include: *The Giver, A Wrinkle in Time, Animal Farm, Among the Hidden, 1984, Brave New World, The Handmaid's Tale, A Clockwork Orange, The Time Machine, Anthem, Fahrenheit 451, The Running Man*, and *Oryx and Crake*.

After completing the pre-reading activity about propaganda, pp. 18-19:

15. Have students design their own public service announcement.

16. Have students contrast propaganda with persuasive language. They could create a Venn diagram to show the similarities and differences.

17. Have students find out about using *logos, pathos, ethos* in argument.

18. Students may be interested in learning about the film version of the novel, which at the time of this printing, is still being cast.

19. Have other titles written by Suzanne Collins available to students. The *Gregor* series is geared for a younger reader, but it is an excellent series.

The Hunger Games

Exploring Expository Writing: Author Biography
Internet Activity—Suzanne Collins

What is your favorite novel of all times? In the space below, write the name of the novel and a one-sentence explanation telling why you love it.

Share what you wrote with a classmate. What do your answers have in common?

Perhaps you picked your favorite book because it is surprising or unusual. Maybe the author came up with a new idea, clever characters, or amazing events that made this book a "must read" for you. Where do these great ideas that authors get come from and what can you learn from them? If only it were as easy as turning on a light bulb the way we see in cartoons! Novelists come up with original ideas the same way everyone else does – by thinking creatively, putting ideas together in new ways, drawing on past experiences, and looking at the world differently.

> Your teacher may want to post your favorite book title in the classroom. Using book recommend-ations from classmates is a great way to find new books to read and different genres that you might not otherwise try.

Suzanne Collins's Novel Idea

As a child, Suzanne Collins loved myths – in particular, she loved the myth of Theseus. In this myth, as a punishment for past wrongdoing, the citizens of Athens are forced to send their children as tributes to Crete. There they will fight the Minotaur – a monster they had no hope of defeating.

Collins was fascinated by the idea of a society so powerful and cruel that it could force another society to give up its children, sacrificing them as retribution for past crimes. Her fascination with the myth helped shape her idea for the novel *The Hunger Games.*

The idea came about one evening as Collins was "channel surfing." She switched between two programs: one was about a group of teenagers competing for prizes, and the other program was about teenagers fighting in a war. As Collins flipped from one channel to the other, she asked a question many great writers ask: what if? What if children competed in games to the death like Roman gladiators did? What if a government controlled citizens by randomly selecting their children to participate in a brutal game that could only have one winner? What if a girl took her little sister's place in this fight to the death; could she survive?

By combining her channel surfing experience and her childhood fascination with the Theseus myth, Suzanne Collins created a story idea that has captured the interest of many, many readers.

Collins's writing career began in 1991 when she started writing for children's television shows. She had been working on TV scripts for several years when a fellow writer encouraged her to try writing a novel. Her first book was *Gregor the Overlander*. It's the first book in a series of five novels that tell the story of a boy who discovers a world underneath the streets of New York City.

Themes

Both *The Underland Series* and *The Hunger Games* deal with themes of war. Perhaps that is because Collins's father was in the Air Force, and he fought in the Vietnam War. As a child, Collins was aware of the war; she sometimes saw scenes of it on the evening news. Although she was a young child at the time, those images and thoughts stayed with her and influenced her ideas while she was writing *The Hunger Games.*

In the novel, the citizens of the fictional North American country of the future called Panem are forced to watch the scenes of the Hunger Games on TV as the contestants battle to the death. The theme of TV as entertainment, regardless of what is on the TV is something Collins finds troublesome. She is concerned that TV viewers may be becoming "desensitized" to the horrors of war that they see on television. In *The Hunger Games*, death becomes entertainment. Today, it is easy to think that all TV is entertainment and forget that some things, like wars and starvation, are real events that happen to real people. The problems those people face don't go away once the television is turned off.

As you read *The Hunger Games,* notice how television is used in the Games and by the government.

The "What If" Factor

Look back at the favorite book you wrote about at the beginning of this activity. Why is it your favorite? Is it because of memorable characters, an exciting plot, or a surprising chain of events? What is the "what if" question the author considered in writing the book?

As readers, we enjoy the "what if" questions because we know the answer is going to be complex and interesting. We're never sure which way a story will turn or how it will end – just like in real life.

Name_____ Period_____

Comprehension Check: Exploring Expository Writing

1. How did Suzanne Collins's reading interests as a child influence her writing as an adult?

2. Explain how an experience watching TV influenced her idea for writing *The Hunger Games*.

3. What do you think Collins means when she states she's worried that people have become "desensitized" by what they see on TV?

4. Do you agree that TV desensitizes people? Why or why not?

5. How might her father's experiences with the Vietnam War influence how Suzanne Collins writes about war?

6. What inferences can you make about what type of person Suzanne Collins is? Give examples to support your answer.

7. What do you think might be some differences between writing a novel and writing for television?

8. What questions would you ask if you were granted an interview with Suzanne Collins?

The Hunger Games

The Myth of Theseus

Myths are stories that are passed down from generation to generation. Often they answer questions about the world. For instance, the myth of Pandora explains why there is evil in the world.

Myths also often contain heroes who overcome obstacles by using superhuman strength or skill. Some, like the Greek and Roman myths, are thousands of years old. The popularity of books like *The Lightening Thief* is proof that even today people are captivated by the drama and adventure of myths.

The characters and events of the myth of Theseus are easy to imagine and difficult to forget. As you read the story, ask yourself what makes Theseus's adventures memorable.

The Myth of Theseus: Hero and Adventurer

Aethra had a darling little boy named Theseus. He was growing into a strong, smart young man, and Aethra knew that she would soon need to tell him about his father, Aegeus the king of Athens. Theseus had never met his father and didn't even know who he was. But Aegeus had planned for his son. Before he left Aethra and returned to Athens, Aegeus placed a sword and a pair of sandals under a boulder. Aegeus told Aethra that if their son could lift the boulder and retrieve the items, he should come to Athens and claim his inheritance as the heir to the throne of Athens.

The day arrived for Aethra to tell Theseus about his father and the boulder. *Would he be strong enough to lift it? He was.* He retrieved the sword and sandals and was ready to go to Athens to meet his father. Theseus could travel by land or sea. The journey to Athens over land was dangerous; the countryside was full of murderers, robbers, and villains. It would be much safer for Theseus to travel by sea. But in spite of advice to do otherwise, Theseus decided to take the more dangerous route and travel by land, to test his heroism and rid the countryside of evildoers.

Theseus didn't have far to travel before he came across his first challenge, Periphetes. Peripetes was a vicious man who used a club to kill anyone he met along the road. Theseus turned Periphetes's own club against him. As a trophy for his first victory, Theseus took the club. Next, Theseus met Sinis who was extremely strong. His nickname was "pine bender" because he liked to bend two pine trees down to the ground and tie his victim to the two trees. When he let go of the trees, the victim was ripped in two. Theseus defeated Sinis by using his own pine tree trick against him.

Theseus traveled on and encountered a giant sow that was terrorizing the countryside. He killed it and then traveled along a narrow coastal road where he met Sciron. Sciron like to stop travelers and force them to wash his feet. While they were on their knees at his feet, Sciron shoved the travelers over the cliff where they fell into the sea and were eaten by a giant turtle. Theseus, *as you may have already guessed*, tricked Sciron. It was Sciron who ended up falling over the cliff into the sea.

Theseus's next encounter was with Cercyon, the king of Eleusis. Cercyon challenged travelers to a wrestling match. If they lost, Cercyon killed them. Theseus defeated and killed Cercyon and became king of Eleusis.

Finally, Theseus was nearing Athens, but there was still one more obstacle for him to overcome: Procrustes. Procrustes offered travelers a bed for the night, which seemed nice, but there was a catch. Procrustes wanted to make sure his guests fit in the bed, so if guests were too short, he stretched them to make them longer. If guests were too tall, he'd cut off their limbs so they'd fit. Theseus used the bed against Procrustes and defeated the last villain on the way to Athens.

When Theseus arrived in Athens, he was a hero. People were happy he'd rid the countryside of its terrible inhabitants. Theseus went to see Aegeus and his wife Medea. Medea was a sorceress and she controlled Aegeus through magic. She realized that Theseus was Aegus's son, and knew that if Aegeus accepted him and took him in, Medea would lose her power over the king. To turn Aegeus against Theseus, Medea convinced Aegeus that Theseus could not be trusted, and that Theseus was only there to overthrow the King.

Medea and Aegeus planned to give Theseus poisoned wine at a banquet. However, as Theseus was about to drink the poison, Aegeus recognized the sword Theseus was carrying as the one Aegeus had placed under the boulder. Aegeus knocked the poisoned wine away from Theseus and accepted him as his son. Medea, seeing her plans were foiled, left the kingdom.

Now that Theseus is accepted as Aegeus's son and wicked Medea is gone, the story should have a happy ending, right? Not so fast. Theseus then learns that the Athenian people have been forced to pay Minos, the king of Crete, an annual tribute. They must send seven boys and seven girls to Crete where they will be sent into the labyrinth. The labyrinth is a maze that is impossible to escape, but the worst part is the Minotaur that inhabits the labyrinth. The Minotaur is a creature that is half man and half bull. It feasts on the fourteen tributes.

When Theseus hears this, he is determined to go into the labyrinth and defeat the Minotaur. He volunteers to be one of the tributes to Crete. Aegeus begs him not to go, but Theseus is determined. Before setting sail, he promises his father that on his way back to Athens, he'll change the ship's sails from black to white as a sign that he's defeated the Minotaur. And so Theseus begins his next challenge.

Once they arrive in Crete, the tributes are paraded before King Minos. Minos' daughter Ariadne sees Theseus and falls in love with him. Before the tributes are sent into the labyrinth, Ariadne goes to Theseus and gives him a spool of thread. She tells him to tie the spool of thread to the gate of the labyrinth and unroll it as he walks through the maze so that he will be able to find his way back out again. Theseus enters the labyrinth and follows Ariadne's advice. He slays the Minotaur and escapes from Crete with Ariadne and the other tributes.

On their way back to Crete, they stop at the island of Naxos. There are different versions of the story of what happened next and why, but Theseus left Ariadne on the island and then traveled on to Athens. He forgot to change the sail from black to white, and when Aegeus saw the ship traveling back with a black sail, he thought his son was dead. In his grief, Aegeus hurled himself off a cliff and into the sea – which from then on was called the Aegean Sea.

Theseus returned to Athens and became king. *You might think that this is the end of the story, but it isn't either. Theseus went on to have more adventures. But then, that's to be expected when you're the hero of a myth.*

Name_____ Period_____

Comprehension Check: The Myth of Theseus

Directions: *After reading the article on The Myth of Theseus, answer the following questions in complete sentences on a separate piece of paper.*

1. What is a myth?

2. What did Theseus's father do to ensure Theseus could one day claim his inheritance?

3. Recall the adversaries (enemies) Theseus must face on the journey to Athens.

4. Summarize the types of challenges Theseus faces on the road to Athens.

5. Infer the type of skills Theseus needs in order to defeat his adversaries.

6. What evidence do you find in the story that shows Theseus is a hero?

7. What conclusions can you draw about King Minos?

8. Why do you think Minos demanded that the tributes were children?

9. Why do you think Theseus didn't relax and enjoy being a king after he returned from Crete?

10. What part of the Theseus myth do you like best? Explain your answer.

The Hunger Games

Exploring Expository Writing: Genre—Fantasy, Sci-Fi, and Dystopia

Part One: Create a World

If you could design a perfect world, what would it be like? Use the graphic organizer in the space below to jot down some ideas of your ideal society.

My world is governed by…	School is…	Some of the best jobs are…
When I look outside, I see…	Daily life for kids includes…	For fun, we…
For dinner we eat…	The most important law is…	On vacation, I …
My favorite part of the day is…	People of this society most value …	My hobby is…

What kind of world did you create? Compare your ideas with your fellow students. What ideas did you have in common? How was your world different from your classmates'? Was your world fictional or nonfiction? If it wasn't the real world we're living in today, your world was *fictional*.

There are several sub genres that are used to further classify fiction books. Look at your ideal world again. Does it contain magical animals like unicorns or flying dragons? Is the world governed by a magic elf? For fun, do you play a game on a broomstick? If your world includes magical elements like talking animals, mythical creatures, witches, or dragons, your world is a *fantasy.* The fantasy genre contains "fantastic" elements that could not happen in the natural world. One of the joys of reading fantasies includes imagining a world where these kinds of events can occur.

Perhaps your world is based on events that could possibly happen at some time in the future like flying cars, synthetic foods, purple trees, or computers that finish homework. In this case, the world you created is *science fiction*. Books written in the science fiction genre include things that really could happen in the future. In the future, computers *could* take over the world, cars *could* fly, and you *could* live on a colony on the moon. People enjoy reading science fiction because the events of the story could actually happen – perhaps in a future time.

Think about some of the books you've read. Have you read some fantasy and science fiction? Write the titles in the graphic organizer below. Next to each title, give a piece of evidence as to why it is fantasy or science fiction. You may want to work with a partner or a group. Some examples have been given.

Fantasy	Science Fiction
Example: *Harry Potter* – there are wizards and magic wands *Cloudy With a Chance of Meatballs* – food falls down from the sky	Example: *A Wrinkle in Time* – the characters have the ability to travel through time *Among the Hidden* – the government has made rules about how many children a family can have

Part Two: The Perfect and Imperfect Worlds of Fiction

Whatever kind of fiction story a writer is working on, he or she must create the fictional world in which the characters live. In a *realistic* fiction story, the world might be like your life. In a *historical* fiction story, a writer wants to create a historically accurate world. Realistic and historical fiction novels are based in our imperfect world. However, the genres of science fiction and fantasy don't have to follow the rules of our real world.

In fact, a writer could create a perfect world. That is what Sir Thomas More did when he wrote a book in 1516 that he entitled *Utopia*. He made up the title by combining the Greek words *outopia* which means "no place" and *eutopia* which means "a place where all is well." Today we use the word *utopia* to mean a perfect place.

Sir Thomas More wasn't the first person to write about a perfect society. In 380 B.C., Plato wrote *Republic,* which discusses the meaning of justice, and whether man is happier under his own rule or the rule of others. Since Sir Thomas More's time, many other writers have tackled the question of what makes a perfect society.

But what about a fictional world that isn't perfect? The term *dystopia* is used to describe a sub genre of science fiction in which a futuristic world is far from perfect. The prefix *dys* means "bad" (think *dysfunctional*). Most dystopian fiction includes a repressive government that restricts individual rights. Like other science fiction books, readers can see the "seeds" of the development of a dystopian society in real life. For example, readers know how important computers are, so a sci-fi novel about computers replacing bus drivers or pilots might not seem so far-fetched.

> The term **anachronism** refers to something or someone that is not in the correct historical time period. If you read a historical fiction book that takes place during the Revolutionary War and a character looks at her wristwatch, that's an anachronism.

As you read *The Hunger Games*, you will quickly see what kind of society Suzanne Collins has created – utopian or dystopian. Look for evidence to support your belief.

Comprehension Check: Genre—Fantasy, Sci-Fi, and Dystopia

Directions: *After reading the article about Fantasy, Sci-Fi, and Dystopia answer the following questions using complete sentences on a separate piece of paper.*

1. What is meant by a "sub genre" of fiction?

2. What is the difference between fantasy and science fiction?

3. What is "dystopia"?

4. Identify some additional elements of fantasy that aren't mentioned in the article. (Think about some fantasy books you are familiar with.)

5. Identify some additional elements of science fiction that aren't mentioned in the article. (Think about some science fiction books you are familiar with.)

6. Analyze the word "utopia." Look at the definition of the two Greek words Sir Thomas More used to create the word. What do the definitions tell you about what he thought of the possibility of a utopian society?

7. Look at the world you created in Part One of this activity. What changes would you make to solve any problems you might have in your society?

8. Do you think your perfect world would work? Explain your answer.

9. Do you think it's possible for a perfect society to exist? Explain your answer.

10. What type of fiction do you prefer, science fiction or fantasy? Why?

The Hunger Games

Historical Context: Who's In Control? A Look at Propaganda

What is persuasion and how do you persuade someone?

Think about the last time you were able to persuade someone. What did you persuade them to do or think? How did you do it? Did your efforts work? Why or why not? Share your response with a classmate.

Nearly everyone has tried to convince someone to think or act in a different way. An effective persuasive argument is based on evidence in the form of facts, logic, and examples. However, not all persuasive arguments are constructed the same. Skilled writers can persuade readers by using emotions, incomplete facts, generalizations, and faulty reasoning. A particular form of persuasion that uses faulty arguments is called *propaganda.*

Propaganda is the intentional spread of true or false information to the public with the goal of influencing public opinion and behavior. It is intentional, widespread, purposeful, powerful, and *biased. Biased* means it presents only part of an argument; it is one-sided. Propaganda simplifies complex issues, uses symbols, and is emotional. Often propaganda will have a slogan or saying that is easy to remember.

Propaganda can be used for good or bad. A public service announcement can be an example of good propaganda. The goal of a public service announcement is to influence the public to act in a certain way. It might be to get a flu shot, buckle seat belts, or recycle.

From the National Highway Traffic Safety Administration www.nhtsa.gov

Propaganda can also be used to promote bad government policies. In history class, you may have learned about the Nazi party that came to power in Germany in 1933. Hitler wrote, "Propaganda is a truly terrible weapon in the hands of an expert." Indeed, the Nazis used propaganda skillfully as they tried to influence how citizens felt about and treated Jews. Propaganda based on rumors, fears, and prejudices encouraged the discrimination and persecution of the Jews. By persuading citizens that eliminating Jews from Germany was a good thing, the Nazi party and its allies were responsible for the deaths of six million Jews. Of course, propaganda wasn't the only way the Nazi's influenced the public, but it certainly had an important place in shaping attitudes and encouraging discrimination.

As a reader, you must be thoughtful about what someone is trying to persuade you to do or think; a good reader asks questions and makes sure arguments are presented in a logical, balanced manner so that an informed decision can be made. Today, we have many ways to check on the accuracy of information we receive. We can watch several different news shows, we can check online for facts about an event. We can read different newspapers. It is always important to question sources and consider where your information comes from.

When you read *The Hunger Games,* you'll notice that the government has its own "spin doctors" who analyze the Games and players. They decide what the public will and won't see in an effort to create a message that will control the audience. You'll also notice how the government uses propaganda to instill fear into the citizens in an effort to control their behavior. By controlling the accuracy and type of information the citizens receive, the government can maintain its power and control over the public.

> Have you ever heard the term "spin doctor"? Today, we use this term about the people who create a story around high-profile events such as a political scandal or a company that has done something wrong. The "spin" around an event is the bias someone creates to influence how the public views the scandal or wrongdoing. This is a form of propaganda.

Comprehension Check: Who's In Control? A Look at Propaganda

Directions: After reading the article "Who's In Control? A Look at Propaganda," answer the following questions using complete sentences on a separate piece of paper.

1. What is propaganda?

2. Explain how the Nazi party used propaganda in World War II.

3. Compare propaganda with other forms of persuasion. How is propaganda different?

4. Evaluate why propaganda can be such a powerful way to persuade people.

5. Analyze the "Buckle Up America" poster. What elements of the poster categorize it as propaganda?

6. Infer why a government might want to use propaganda to promote something good like wearing seat belts.

7. Propose some other positive issues that could be promoted through propaganda.

8. How can you determine if something is propaganda?

The Hunger Games

Historical Context: Roman Influences
"Friends, Romans, Countrymen"

As you are reading *The Hunger Games*, you'll begin to notice Roman names. Why might an author include names and references to another culture – especially an ancient one?

There is no doubt that our lives today are greatly influenced by Roman culture. Greek and Roman civilizations are often referred to as "classic," meaning something that holds its value throughout time. Indeed, much of our architecture, art, calendar, language, and even our numbers echo ancient Rome. Many civilizations have looked to ancient Greece and Rome as cultures to be emulated. A modern civilization that incorporates some Greek and Roman words, practices, and culture into its own gives the ancient culture special importance and makes the modern culture appear to be part of a classic world. As you read the novel, decide if this is true of Panem, the "imaginary" location where *The Hunger Games* take place. Did Panem copy only the best of the Roman civilization?

Suzanne Collins isn't the first author to want to use Roman names and influences. One famous playwright, William Shakespeare, used many Roman names in his plays. Look at the character names from *The Hunger Games* listed below and their Shakespearean counterpart.

Caesar Flickerman – The name Caesar refers to Julius Caesar, emperor of Rome. Shakespeare wrote the play *Julius Caesar* about his assassination. While Caesar Flickerman isn't an emperor in *The Hunger Games*, he is a powerful public personality.

Cato – This is the name of a soldier in *Julius Caesar*. It makes sense that Cato in *The Hunger Games* has a very soldier-like temperament. He is focused, determined, and has a mission – to win.

Cinna – In the play *Julius Caesar*, there are two characters named Cinna. One is a poet, and the other has plotted against Caesar. The crowd captures and murders Cinna the poet – not caring that they've caught the wrong person. In *The Hunger Games* is Cinna a "poet" of sorts? He certainly is an artist and his costumes are symbolic.

Claudius Templesmith – In the play *Hamlet*, Claudius is the name of Hamlet's uncle and stepfather. Hamlet believes that Claudius has murdered his father. In the play *Julius Caesar*, Claudius is a guard. In *The Hunger Games* Claudius Templesmith is the announcer of the Games.

Flauvius – This name appears in both *Julius Caesar* and *Timon of Athens*. In *Julius Caesar,* Flauvius is disappointed about the support Caesar is receiving. In *Timon of Athens*, Flauvius is a servant. As a stylist in *The Hunger Games*, Flauvius is similar to a servant. The name actually means "golden haired."

Octavia – In the play, *Mark Antony and Cleopatra*, Octavia marries Mark Antony.

Portia – This name appears in two plays. In *Julius Caesar*, Portia is Brutus's wife who commits suicide by eating hot coals. In *The Merchant of Venice*, Portia disguises herself as a lawyer. Portia and Cinna are responsible for the fiery costumes Peeta and Katniss wear.

Other Roman "influences" you'll find in the novel:

The Arena – The area in which the Games will be held is called the arena. An arena is similar to the Colosseum used to host gladiator games during the Roman times.

A battle to the death – In ancient Rome, gladiators fought to the death for the public's entertainment. Gladiators were usually slaves that were given special housing, food, medical care, and training. Sponsors invested in the gladiator as a way to gain public status and prestige.

Capitol excesses – The residents of the Capitol all appear to lead extravagant lives of wealth. Their excesses in fashion and food are similar to the wealthy ancient Romans.

Chariot – The tributes ride to City Center on a chariot – a two-wheel, horse-drawn wagon. Ancient Romans used chariots as well.

Cornucopia – This word comes from the goat horn that was used to feed the Greek god Zeus as a baby.

Slaves/Avox – The Romans had slaves who were often captured in wars and brought back to Rome. In *The Hunger Games* the Avox is a slave of sorts. Certainly, the Avox is not given any rights and is physically mutilated for a crime.

Tribute – The idea of a tribute comes from the story of Theseus and the Minotaur.

Weapons – Isn't it interesting that in the technologically advanced world of Panem the tributes are given primitive weapons? Bows, arrows, spears, and knives were the weapons of choice in ancient Roman times.

**Research Panem – Find out the meaning of Panem and see if you can figure out why Suzanne Collins chose that name for the location of the novel. Once you finish reading the novel, decide if your answer was correct.

The Hunger Games

Standards Focus: Allusions, Unique Terminology, Sayings

The Seam – nickname for District 12, population 8,000. The term "seam" actually refers to a geological formation. Just like a seam in a garment is where two pieces of fabric are joined, a geological seam is a thin layer or vein of a mineral that can be mined. In the case of District 12, the seam is a layer of coal.

Katniss plant – a flowering plant of the genus Sagittaria; found in ponds, canals, and slow rivers, but never in abundance. They bear an edible tuber, sometimes cultivated as food in North America and East Asia. Its leaves are arrow-shaped.

The arena – similar to the Roman Colosseum

Reaping – the ceremony in which one boy and one girl aged 12–18 is chosen from each district to participate in the Hunger Games

Peacekeepers – the police force that keeps law in District 12 and other districts

Panem – the name of the fictional country that was once North America; the name is part of a phrase, "panem et circenses" which means "bread and circuses," and is representative of ancient Rome.

Hob – the place in District 12 where they hold the black market

Tesserae – a year's supply of grain and oil for one person; received in return for the additional entry of a child's name into the reaping (singular form: tessera)

Apothecary – similar to a pharmacist; one who heals with herbs and potions

The Hunger Games – in punishment for an uprising (the Dark Days) each of the twelve districts of Panem are required to provide two tributes, one boy and one girl, to fight to the death in an artificially created arena.

District 13 – destroyed as a result of the uprising

Muttations, also called **mutts** – Capitol-bred, genetically-altered animals used as weapons

Mockingjay – a cross between the genetically altered jabberjay and the mockingbird. The bird is able to mimic human songs and cries. Madge has given Katniss a mockingjay pin to wear in the Games.

Avox – a criminal whose tongue has been cut out and who is a servant

Hovercraft – a helicopter-like vehicle

Gamemakers – those responsible for the environment and rules of the Hunger Games.

Star-crossed lovers – a phrase coined by Shakespeare in the play *Romeo and Juliet,* meaning a couple whose love is doomed from the start.

Career Tributes – "Careers" are tributes who've been trained to participate in the Games.

The Hunger Games

Standards Focus: Elements of Fiction
Literary Terms to Know

In the study of literature, it is important to remember that a story consists of several elements: plot, characters, setting, point of view, conflict, symbol, and theme. In the realm of fiction, the author can place an emphasis on any one or more of these elements, or conversely, de-emphasize any one or more of these elements. For example, some authors may want the reader to focus on the plot, so the setting of the story may not be a major focus. It is important when analyzing a piece of literature that you look at all of the elements and how they work together to create an entire story.

❖ **Plot** - the related series of events that make up a story
  ▪ Exposition - the beginning of a story in which the main characters, conflicts, and setting are introduced
  ▪ Rising action - the action that takes place before the climax; the plot becomes more complicated, leading to the climax
  ▪ Climax - the turning point of the story; emotional high point for the protagonist
  ▪ Falling action - the action that takes place after the climax, leading to the resolution
  ▪ Resolution - the end of a story; problems are solved, and characters' futures may be foreshadowed
❖ **Conflict** - the struggle(s) between opposing forces, usually characters
  ▪ Internal conflict - a character's struggle with himself or his conscience
  ▪ External conflict - a character's struggle with an outside force, such as another character, nature, or his environment
❖ **Characters** - the individuals involved (directly or indirectly) in the action of the story
  ▪ Protagonist - the central character in a story; struggles against the antagonist
  ▪ Antagonist - the conflicting force against the protagonist; can be another character, a force of nature, or the protagonist struggling against himself
❖ **Setting** - the time and place, or where and when, the action occurs
  ▪ Physical - the physical environment in which a story takes place; this includes the social and political environment
  ▪ Chronological - the time in which a story takes place (includes the era, season, date, time of day, etc.)
❖ **Point of View** - the perspective from which a story is told
  ▪ Narrator - the "voice" that tells a story; may or may not reflect the opinions and attitudes of the author himself
  ▪ First person - a narrator who uses the first-person pronouns (I, me, my, myself, etc.) when telling the story; focuses on the thoughts, feelings, and opinions of a particular character
  ▪ Third person limited - a narrator who uses the third-person perspective with the third person pronouns (he, she, it, they, etc.); observes the action as an outside observer, revealing the thoughts, feelings, and opinions of *only one* character
  ▪ Third person omniscient - like third-person limited, the third-person omniscient narrator uses the third-person perspective with the third person pronouns (he, she, it, they, etc.); this type of narrator observes the action as an outside observer, however, revealing the thoughts, feelings, and opinions of *several* characters
❖ **Theme** - the main idea behind a literary work; the message in the story

The Hunger Games
Vocabulary List

Directions: *Use a dictionary or the author's words to find the meanings of the following words from **The Hunger Games**. Your teacher will direct you to do this lesson either as you read each chapter, or as a pre-reading activity. Whatever method your teacher chooses, be sure to keep this list and your definitions to use in vocabulary exercises and to study for quizzes and tests.*

Chapter 1
1. reaping (3)
2. deterrent (4)
3. poaching (5)
4. maniacally (7)
5. preposterous (9)
6. haggling (10)
7. adjacent (17)

Chapter 2
1. protocol (22)
2. dissent (24)
3. plummets (24)
4. radical (26)
5. predicament (27)

Chapter 3
1. disastrous (35)
2. intensity (35)
3. insurmountable (36)
4. gratified (40)
5. sniveling (41)
6. replicate (43)
7. disgruntled (46)

Chapter 4
1. mentor (48)
2. pondering (49)
3. inexplicable (51)
4. gnarled (53)
5. deteriorated (54)
6. substantial (55)
7. detest (56)

Chapter 5
1. vulnerable (62)
2. affectations (63)

3. flamboyant (64)
4. sustenance (65)
5. despicable (65)
6. tangible (71)

Chapter 6
1. exclusively (73)
2. barbarism (74)
3. ironic (74)
4. adversaries (79)
5. mandatory (81)

Chapter 7
1. amiable (92)
2. demean (93)
3. oblivious (93)
4. surly (99)
5. sever (101)
6. fixated (101)

Chapter 8
1. impulsiveness (103)
2. leniency (104)
3. sic (104)
4. irredeemably (104)
5. potential (104)
6. defiantly (106)

Chapter 9
1. ludicrous (114)
2. banal (115)
3. intrigued (116)
4. sullen (116)
5. hostile (116)
6. prestigious (124)
7. unrequited (130)

Chapter 10
1. assent (133)
2. breached (134)
3. entourages (134)
4. aghast (134)
5. perceived (135)
6. reenactments (145)

Chapter 11
1. adversaries (149)
2. condenses (150)
3. void (151)
4. botched (151)
5. rejuvenating (152)
6. dispersed (152)

Chapter 12
1. lapdogs (161)
2. gall (162)
3. hoist (163)
4. imprudent (164)
5. dynamic (165)
6. scarcity (167)

Chapter 13
1. quell (173)
2. abate (176)
3. stupor (180)
4. incompetent (182)
5. conspiratorially (183)
6. bravado (183)

Chapter 14
1. precariously (187)
2. persevere (187)
3. sated (187)
4. balm (188)
5. honing (190)
6. mayhem (190)

Chapter 15
1. onslaught (195)
2. wracked (195)
3. noxious (197)
4. prominent (198)
5. tentatively (200)

Chapter 16
1. ordeal (210)
2. rations (211)
3. forages (211)
4. obliging (211)
5. rendezvous (213)
6. copse (214)

Chapter 17
1. doggedly (223)
2. subsequent (225)
3. fractured (227)
4. fragmenting (227)
5. subtly (228)
6. vulnerable (229)
7. decadent (230)

Chapter 18
1. fretful (234)
2. audible (235)
3. inadequate (236)
4. inflict (236)
5. despondency (238)
6. lethargy (240)

Chapter 19
1. dissipate (247)
2. pariahs (247)
3. loathe (247)
4. evade (248)
5. scrupulously (249)
6. ruse (250)
7. peruse (252)

Chapter 20
1. tethered (263)
2. potent (266)
3. ratcheting (266)
4. wheedles (268)
5. incoherence (276)

Chapter 21
1. arduous (278)
2. asset (279)
3. infusion (279)
4. emanating (281)
5. irreparable (281)
6. ominous (282)
7. staunch (289)

Name _____ **Period** _____

Chapter 22
1. vaguely (290)
2. plaintively (294)
3. famished (294)
4. irreverent (296)
5. tirades (296)
6. exorbitant (299)
7. exasperated (302)

Chapter 23
1. savoring (303)
2. surly (306)
3. noncommittal (308)
4. peevishly (308)
5. surreal (318)
6. extricating (312)
7. emaciated (318)

Chapter 24
1. sustained (322)
2. oblige (323)
3. mesmerized (329)
4. dissonant (329)
5. wielding (329)

Chapter 25
1. inadvertently (332)
2. glowering (333)
3. purchase (333)
4. callously (334)
5. avenging (334)
6. stalemate (336)
7. tourniquet (338)

Chapter 26
1. feverishly (347)
2. garish (354)
3. contrived (355)
4. arbitrary (355)
5. sophisticated (355)
6. benign (355)

Chapter 27
1. keen (360)
2. debut (360)
3. berserk (361)
4. disproportionate (362)
5. linger (362)
6. insidious (365)
7. segue (368)

The Hunger Games

Character List

Katniss Everdeen – main character and narrator; nicknamed "Catnip" by her best friend Gale. Sixteen years old and has been responsible for providing for her family ever since her father was killed in a mine accident five years ago. Expert with bow and arrow. Lives in the Seam in District 12.

Prim – nickname for twelve-year-old Primrose Everdeen, Katniss's little sister. She is good with animals and at treating sick or injured people.

Mrs. Everdeen – Katniss and Prim's mother; lost her husband, Mr. Everdeen, in a mining accident; went into a deep depression and had to be taken care of by Katniss; a healer

Gale Hawthorn – eighteen-year-old best friend to Katniss, the only person Katniss feels she can be herself around. Hunts with Katniss. Expert with traps and bow and arrow.

Effie Trinket – the overly cheerful escort for District 12. She's come from the capital and reads the names for the reaping.

Greasy Sae – a buyer of Katniss and Gale's poached animals. She makes and sells soup in the Hob.

Madge – the mayor's daughter who goes to school with Katniss. She gives Katniss the mockingjay pin that she wears in the Games.

Mayor Undersee – the mayor of District 12

Haymitch Abernathy – the only victor of the Hunger Games from District 12 who is still living. He's the mentor to the current tributes. He's a middle aged alcoholic who is generally drunk and obnoxious.

Peeta Mellark – the boy tribute from District 12. Son of a baker – he once gave Katniss bread for her family and saved them from starvation. He is in love with Katniss.

Cinna – Katniss's stylist in the Games. He is the most normal looking stylist of the group – this is his first Hunger Games and he asked for District 12. Katniss always feels she can somehow trust Cinna.

Portia – Peeta's stylist in the Games

Venia – another stylist with aqua hair and gold tattoos above her eyebrows

Flauvius – a stylist with orange corkscrew hair and purple lipstick

Octavia – a stylist whose body is dyed pale green

President Snow – president of Panem; has snake-like eyes and white hair

Caesar Flickerman – host of the tribute interviews for the last forty years though he looks as if he's never aged. Friendly, and tries to help out tributes so they do their best during the interview.

Claudius Templesmith – the announcer for the Games; the voice the tributes hear in the arena

Rue – the tribute from District 11 who reminds Katniss of Prim; twelve years old, dark skin; can "fly" through the trees

Thresh – the boy tribute from District 11 who is big and quiet

Cato – a Career Tribute from District 2; large and strong

Clove – a Career Tribute from District 2 who excels at knife throwing; also large and strong

Foxface – the nickname Katniss gives the tribute from District 5. A red-headed girl with a foxlike face. She is clever and resourceful.

Glimmer – a Career Tribute from District 1; blond and sexy

Name _____   Period _____

The Hunger Games

Part One: Chapters One – Nine
Standards Focus: Note-Taking and Summarizing *Sample*

To help you keep track of the novel's events as they occur, you will be keeping notes using a chart similar to the one below. For each set of chapters as indicated, fill in the chart with the necessary information. Directions for completing the chart are in the boxes below. See the next page for an example using Chapter One.

Main Events of the Chapters	In this space, write a brief summary or bulleted points of the action that takes place in this section.
Characters	In this space, list and describe important characters in this section. Be sure to include details on how or why they are important to the plot at this point in the story.
Setting	In this space, write a description of where and when the action occurred.
Primary Conflict	In this space, detail the primary conflict(s) and which characters are involved in the confict(s).
Thoughts, Feelings or Predictions	In this space, write your prediction of what you think will happen in the next section.
Possible Thematic Issues Being Raised	In this space, detail the important themes or ideas that have been raised in this section.

Name _____ Period _____

The Hunger Games

Part One: Chapters One – Two
Note-Taking and Summarizing: Chapters One-Two

Directions: *To help you keep track of the novel's events as they occur, you will be keeping notes using the chart below. For each set of chapters as indicated, fill in the chart with the necessary information. Refer to the example Note-Taking and Summarizing Chart on page 27 for help for completing the chart. If you need more room, attach a separate piece of paper.*

Main Events of the Chapters	
Characters	
Setting	
Primary Conflict	
Thoughts, Feelings or Predictions	
Thematic Issues Being Raised	

The Hunger Games

Part One: Chapters One – Two
Comprehension Check

Directions: *To help you understand all aspects of the novel, answer the following questions for Chapters One – Two. Write your answers on a separate piece of paper using complete sentences.*

Chapter 1

1. Where is Katniss going this morning?

2. What kind of place is District 12?

3. What is the reaping?

4. What are the Hunger Games and how did they come about?

5. Theorize how the tessera is another type of punishment.

6. Analyze why Katniss is confused when Gale says they could run away and live in the woods.

7. Predict what Katniss will do when she hears Prim's name called at the end of the chapter. Explain your answer.

8. Based on what you know so far, draw a conclusion as to what kind of government runs Panem. Explain how you came to your conclusion.

9. Look up the word "seam" in the dictionary. Look for the geological meaning of the word. Based on what you discover, why is this an appropriate name for the area?

Chapter 2

1. What does Katniss do in response to Prim's name being drawn?

2. Why does Katniss insist that she not cry or respond emotionally?

3. How is television an important factor in the reaping?

4. Infer what the reaction of the crowd means when Katniss volunteers to take Prim's place. Explain your answer.

5. What is Katniss's connection to Peeta Mellark?

6. Formulate a theory about the bread incident and Peeta's behavior toward Katniss on the stage. Why do you think he behaved as he did? What might Peeta's behavior tell you about him?

7. How was the bread incident a turning point for Katniss?

8. Explain the importance now of Katniss feeling like she owes Peeta something as they plan to compete in the Games.

The Hunger Games
Part One: Chapters One – Two
Standards Focus: The Cast of Characters

Directions: *Fill in the characters' names as you read The Hunger Games. Include descriptions of the characters. Some descriptions and names have been filled in for you.*

	Character Name	Character Description
Everdeen Family	Father	Killed in a mining accident when Katniss was eleven.
	Mother	Seriously depressed after the death of her husband, she is unable to care for her children.
	Katniss	
		Twelve-year-old sister of Katniss. She is the one person Katniss knows she loves.

Character Name	Character Description
Gale	
	The boy tribute from District 12. His family works in a bakery. Katniss remembers him because he gave her bread when her family was starving.
Haymitch Abernathy	
	The Capitol representative for District 12. She is overly happy and chipper.
Madge Undersee	

Although the Capitol and District 12 aren't characters, you'll want to make some notes about where they are located, what kind of cities they are, and what happens there.

District 12	
The Capitol	

Name _____ Period _____

The Hunger Games

Part One: Chapters One – Two
Assessment Preparation: Verb Tenses & Moods

Part I: Verb Tenses
You already know that we can use verbs show *when* an action occurs. In English, we show that through the verb tenses – past, present, future.

1. Look through the first chapter of *The Hunger Games*. In what tense is the novel written? _____

2. How do you know? Use an example from the book to help support your answer.

_____

_____

_____

3. As a reader, how do you feel about the way the tense is used to write the novel? Did you notice the tense? Does it make the novel "sound" different to you? Explain your answer. _____

_____

_____

4. What is the point of view of the novel? How do you know? _____

_____

_____

5. Why do you think Suzanne Collins chose to write the novel in the present tense rather than the past? Compare the difference between a book written from the first person point of view in past tense and the first person point of view in the present tense. How do you think the verb tense and the first person point of view will affect the tension in the novel? _____

_____

_____

_____

Part II: Verb Moods

When you think about verbs, your first concern probably isn't that it will be in a good mood! But verbs do, in fact, have "moods." That doesn't really mean the verb is happy, grumpy, or bored, though. The mood of a verb tells the listener or reader what the speaker or writer's attitude is toward the subject.

The moods (sometimes called modes) of English verbs are:

    1. Indicative – states a fact, expresses an opinion, or asks a question
For example: *Harvey made dinner last night. It was Lima Bean Surprise.*
                    I don't like lima beans.
                    Would you pass the bowl of Lima Bean Surprise and the ketchup?

    2. Imperative – gives a command
For example: *Don't ever invite Harvey over for dinner again!*

        When writing in the *imperative* mood, the subject of the sentence is "you," but it is implied rather than directly stated. "You" are the subject of the sentence since "you" are being given a command.

    3. Subjunctive – makes a suggestion or requirement; states a wish or desire
For example: *When Harvey brings over dinner, I wish I were a lima bean enthusiast.*

        Of these three moods, the subjunctive mood is one where writers are most likely to make mistakes. If you are writing about something that might happen, you wish would happen, or that is a hypothetical situation, you are using the *subjunctive* mood.

Some writers have difficulty when writing in the subjunctive mood because they're not sure whether to use *was* or *were.* In the sentence: *"When Harvey brings over dinner, I wish I were a lima bean enthusiast,"* you are not enthusiastic about lima beans but you wish you were. Consequently, you use *were* rather than *was* to indicate the verb is the *subjunctive* mood.

Directions: *Read the following sentences from The Hunger Games. In what mood is each of them written? Write the mood on the line following the statement and explain your choice.*

1. "I prop myself up on one elbow." (3) _____

_____

2. "He [Buttercup] hates me." (3) _____

_____

3. " 'It's to the Capitol's advantage to have us divided among ourselves,' he might

say if there were no ears to hear but mine." (14) _____

_____

4. " 'Wear something pretty,' he says flatly." (14) _____

_____

5. "People file in silently and sign in." (16) _____

_____

6. " 'And may the odds be *ever* in your favor!'" (19) _____

_____

7. " 'Let her come forward.'" (23) _____

_____

8. "Haymitch is whisked away on a stretcher, and Effie Trinket is trying to get the

ball rolling again." (25) _____

_____

9. "I kept telling myself if I could only hold out until May, just May 8th, I would turn

twelve and be able to sign up for the tesserae and get that precious grain and oil to

feed us." (28) _____

_____

10. "Feed it to the pig, you stupid creature!" (38) _____

_____

Part III: Vocabulary
Directions*: Imagine the news report that would have been broadcast all over
Panem after the unusual events during District 12's reaping. Using the vocabulary
words from Chapters 1 and 2, write a short television news report about the reaping.
Include important details in your report. You may use the vocabulary words in any
order, and you may change the form of the word if necessary. Present your news
report to your class. Your teacher **may** choose to allow you to work with a partner.*

reaping	adjacent
deterrent	protocol
poaching	dissent
maniacally	plummets
preposterous	radical
haggling	predicament

Name _____   Period _____

The Hunger Games

Part One: Chapters Three – Four
Note-Taking and Summarizing: Chapters Three-Four

Directions*: To help you keep track of the novel's events as they occur, you will be keeping notes using the chart below. For each set of chapters as indicated, fill in the chart with the necessary information. Refer to the example Note-Taking and Summarizing Chart on page 27 for help for completing the chart. If you need more room, attach a separate piece of paper.*

Main Events of the Chapters	
Characters	
Setting	
Primary Conflict	
Thoughts, Feelings or Predictions	
Thematic Issues Being Raised	

The Hunger Games

Part One: Chapters Three – Four
Comprehension Check

Directions: *To help you understand all aspects of the novel, answer the following questions for Chapters Three-Four. Write your answers on a separate piece of paper using complete sentences.*

Chapter 3

1. Who are the guests that come to say goodbye when Katniss goes to the Justice Building?

2. What does Katniss fear is going to happen to her mother?

3. What gifts does she receive?

4. Why is Katniss so concerned that she must not cry?

5. Explain why Effie Trinket's comment, "At least, you two have decent manners" (44) offends Katniss. How does she respond?

6. What does the term "mentor" mean? Explain why a mentor is important in the arena.

7. Imagine what a sponsor might do for a tribute in the arena.

8. Predict some problems Katniss and Peeta might have with their mentor Haymitch.

Chapter 4

1. Why does Peeta's offer to clean up Haymitch change the way Katniss feels about Peeta? What does she plan to do?

2. How did seeing the dandelion in the schoolyard set off a chain reaction that saved the Everdeen family?

3. What do Katniss and Peeta do that surprises Haymitch?

4. Explain why Haymitch's decision to help them is a big step.

5. Do you agree with Katniss's evaluation of Peeta's behavior as the train pulls into the Capitol?

6. What inferences can you already make about the differences Katniss will see between the Capitol and District 12? Explain your answer.

The Hunger Games

Part One: Chapters Three – Four
Standards Focus: In Media Res

Imagine you are going to school and you see a clown standing at the bus stop. She has a monkey dressed like a penguin perched on her shoulder. When you get to school, you can't wait to tell your best friend about what you saw. Do you start your story at the beginning of your day when your alarm went off to wake you up? Do you start your story on the day you were born? Where would you start telling your story. Why? _____

_____

_____

When creating a fictional world, an author has to figure out when to start the story. The author could begin the novel on the day the main character is born, but what would be a disadvantage of doing that? _____

_____

Many novels begin in the middle of some action. The reader is dropped right into the start of something interesting or exciting that is about to happen – or is even happening right now. This writing technique is called *in medias res.* It means "in the middle of things." What is an advantage to beginning a novel this way?

_____

_____

How do you know *The Hunger Games* is written *in medias res*? _____

_____

Think back to the story of the clown with the monkey at the bus stop. Where does the story get interesting? Is it when you see the clown or when the clown sits next to you on the bus and the monkey hops into your backpack? The monkey climbing into your backpack is action! Now you've got a story to tell.

In a novel, the story begins to take off when there is an *inciting moment.* This is the event that triggers the other events of the story. What do you think is the inciting moment of *The Hunger Games*? _____

_____

Once the author starts the novel in the middle of exciting events, things are going to start happening, and this is going to be a great book, right? It's not that easy. Since the author has started the novel in the middle of the action, the reader will feel left out or confused if there isn't any background information. The writer could still lose the reader if there isn't enough information about who the characters are, where they came from, and what problems they're facing. The novelist will probably use *flashback* to fill in information for the reader. A flashback recalls events that occurred before the current plot of the novel. In order for the reader to understand the novel, he or she needs background knowledge.

Directions: *Use information from the novel to identify flashbacks and how they may be important to the plot of the novel. Then make predictions about what you think will happen in the future plot. Some of the events have been filled in for you.*

Past	Present	Future (predictions)
Peeta gave Katniss bread	Katniss feels indebted to Peeta	Katniss will want to make that up to Peeta in some way
Katniss learned to hunt to save her family from starvation		
Katniss loves Prim more than anyone in the world		
Haymitch won the Hunger Games		
Peeta might have burned the bread on purpose		
	It bred with the mockingbird and became the mockingjay	
Katniss's mother has a book of edible plants		
Katniss finds the katniss plant that grows in water – it's edible		
	Katniss has plenty to eat on the train as they go to the Capitol	

Look at the beginning of a novel you are currently reading or have recently read. How did the author begin the novel? What is the title of the novel? What was the inciting incident? _____

_____

_____

The Hunger Games

Part One: Chapters Three – Four
Assessment Preparation: Coordinate and Cumulative Adjectives

You probably are familiar with many rules for using commas. Some of the rules are easy to remember, like putting commas between items in a series. Other rules are not as easy to remember. When you are writing a description and you have more than one adjective in front of the noun, do you need a comma between adjectives? There are a few rules you can follow that will help you decide how to punctuate your sentence.

Coordinate adjectives modify a noun separately.
You'll know the adjectives are coordinative if:
1. you can replace a comma with the word "*and*"
2. you can mix the adjectives around and the meaning doesn't change

"Once inside, I'm conducted to a room and left alone. It's the richest place I've ever been in, with thick, deep carpets and a velvet couch and chairs."

The adjectives that describe the carpet can be separated with the word *and*: "thick *and* deep carpets." The adjectives can be switched around as well "deep, thick carpet" and the meaning of the phrase doesn't change.

Cumulative adjectives, on the other hand, do not need a comma between them. Cumulative adjectives rely on each other in order for the phrase to make sense.

"Blossoms with three white petals."

The adjectives that describe the petals can't be connected with *and* "three *and* white petals" and they can't be switched around "white three petals." This phrase contains cumulative adjectives that do not need a comma to separate them.

Directions: *Analyze the following sentences. Explain why they have either coordinate or cumulative adjectives. The adjectives have been underlined.*

1. "Prim named him Buttercup, insisting that his <u>muddy yellow</u> coat matched the bright

flower" (p. 3). _____

_____

2. "His eyes land on a <u>small, circular</u> pin that adorns her dress" (p. 12). _____

_____

_____

3. "I slept in the <u>elaborate braided</u> hair my mother did for the reaping" (p. 55). _____

_____

_____

4. "I take a sip of the <u>hot, sweet, creamy</u> liquid and a shudder runs through me" (p. 55).

_____

_____

Directions: *Practice writing and punctuating using coordinate and cumulative adjectives. Use the vocabulary word given in parentheses as one of your adjectives. You will need to add at least one more adjective to the sentence. An example has been done for you.*

Example: Cumulative adjective: (substantial) <u>*The substantial wool blanket covered the shivering child.*</u>

1. Coordinate adjectives: (disastrous) _____

_____

_____

2. Coordinate adjectives: (gnarled) _____

_____

_____

3. Cumulative adjectives: (disgruntled) _____

_____

_____

4. Cumulative adjectives: (insurmountable) _____

_____

_____

5. Choose either cumulative or coordinate adjectives. Identify which type you've written: (inexplicable) _____

_____

Vocabulary: Antonyms and synonyms
Directions: *Write an **antonym** for the following words. Remember that an antonym is a word that means the opposite. Your antonym may be more than one word or a phrase.*

1. pondering _____   4. substantial _____

2. sniveling _____   5. detest _____

3. deteriorated _____

Directions: *Choose a **synonym** for the following words. Remember that synonyms are words that have the same meaning. Your synonym may be more than one word or a phrase.*

1. intensity _____   3. replicate _____

2. gratified _____   4. mentor _____

The Hunger Games

Part One: Chapters Five – Six
Note-Taking and Summarizing: Chapters Five-Six

Directions: To help you keep track of the events as they occur in Chapters 5 – 6, fill in the chart with the necessary information. If you need more room, attach a separate piece of paper.

Main Events of the Chapters	
Characters	
Setting	
Primary Conflict	
Thoughts, Feelings or Predictions	
Thematic Issues Being Raised	

The Hunger Games
Part One: Chapters Five – Six
Comprehension Check

Directions: *To help you understand all aspects of the novel, answer the following questions for Chapters Five – Six. Write your answers on a separate piece of paper using complete sentences.*

Chapter 5

1. What is the purpose of the Remake Center?

2. What are some of Katniss's worries about what she'll be wearing for the opening ceremonies?

3. Why is the costume so important?

4. Contrast Cinna to Flavius and Octavia. How is he different from them?

5. What is the reaction of the crowd to Peeta and Katniss?

6. What does Katniss mean at the end of the chapter when she says, "two can play at this game"? Why does she kiss Peeta?

7. Do you agree with Katniss's interpretation of Peeta's words? Why or why not?

Chapter 6

1. Why is the roof of the Training Center a safe place for Peeta and Katniss to talk?

2. Contrast the Training Center to Katniss's home in District 12.

3. What kind of person is Effie Trinket?

4. What is an Avox?

5. How does Katniss know the Avox?

6. Why do you think Peeta helped Katniss at dinner by saying the Avox reminded him of Delly Cartwright?

7. Explain Katniss's feelings about the redheaded Avox.

The Hunger Games

Part One: Chapters Five – Six
Standards Focus: Building a Fictional World

Have you heard of Newton's Laws or laws of the universe? These aren't laws that prevent speeding or make people pay taxes; they're laws that are constant elements that make our world function the way it does. Take the law of gravity for example. If things suddenly started to float around, our world would certainly experience a crisis!

Can you think of another law of nature that we rely on?

When an author is going to write a science fiction or fantasy novel, he creates a world for his stories. The world must be believable and feel real to the reader. If the fictional world doesn't make sense to the reader, the reader isn't going to continuing reading.

In a science fiction book like *The Hunger Games*, Suzanne Collins has to create a world in which the government is cruel enough to send children to their deaths in battle. In order for the reader to believe the world, he or she needs to make connections that make sense. Readers look for things that we already know from our real world and connect those ideas with the fictional world.

Some of the characteristics of Panem are listed in the chart below. Using that information, make connections to the fictional world of *The Hunger Games.* Analyze your connections in the last column. Some of the information has been started for you.

Facts about Panem	What connection can you make with our world today? How is this different or similar to the world we live in today?	What conclusions can you draw from this information? Why this is this important in building the fictional world of the story?
It came from a place once called North America. Panem is a Capitol surrounded by thirteen districts.	We are familiar with North America. The United States originally started with thirteen colonies.	We are already familiar with North America. We know the country. It's important because I'm familiar with it.
During the "Dark Days," the districts rebelled and District 13 was destroyed.	It could be similar to the Civil War when the South rebelled – or the Revolutionary War.	

Name _____ Period _____

Facts about Panem	What connection can you make with our world today? How is this different or similar to the world we live in today?	What conclusions can you draw from this information? Why this is this important in building the fictional world of the story?
As a result of the rebellion, the districts must participate in the Hunger Games.	We have games like the Olympics, but nothing like the Hunger Games. I'm also familiar with the story of the Minotaur, which is similar to the tributes being sent to battle.	
The Hunger Games are treated like a celebration.		
People in District 12 are very poor and starving, but people in the Capitol are rich.		
District 12 is a mining area.		
Children can receive tesserae which allow them to get food in exchange for entering their names another time in the reaping.		
Everything that happens with the Games is televised.		
High speed trains can travel at 250 miles per hour.		
Certain places, like the woods, are restricted with electrified fences.		
People from the Capitol have a strange way of talking; they wear bright makeup and wigs.		

After looking at the world of Panem, do you believe a world like this could really exist? Explain your answer, using a separate sheet of paper.

The Hunger Games

Part One: Chapters Five – Six
Assessment Preparation: Etymology

Where do words come from? The history of a word, where it came from, and how its meaning has changed over time is called its *etymology*. When linguists trace the meaning and usage of a word through time, they often discover that the meanings of the word has changed. Words like "cool," "wicked," "sick," and "bad" have meant different things to different generations of English speakers.

What are some words or phrases you and your friends use that might mean something different to your parents or grandparents? What are some words your parents or grandparents use that don't mean the same thing to you?

English is a very welcoming language; new words are constantly added to our lexicon. Some words come from other languages, and some words are made up, like "duh" or "email."

Most words are absorbed into our language because they fill a need. There was no word "email" before computers were invented because we didn't need it. During the Renaissance though, scholars thought Latin was a better language than English. Scholars thought Latin words should replace English words. Many of those words were used in science, which helped to standardize terms and allow scientists to use universal names for plants, animals, and elements. Over time, some of the non-scientific words were forgotten, but some of them stuck around and are still used today. We can thank sixteenth-century scholars for these words: monopoly, lexicon, thermometer, autograph, crisis, vacuum, and explain.

> **Words to Use When Talking About Words**
> - **Etymology** – the study of the history of a word
> - **Linguist** – a person who studies words
> - **Lexicon** – a collected vocabulary
> - **Neologism** – a new word. The prefix *neo-* means "new" and *logos* means "word"

Directions: Using the selected vocabulary words below, find their etymology. You should be able to find the information in a dictionary (in a book or online).

Word	Where it came from	What it originally meant
vulnerable	Latin	able to wound
flamboyant		
sustenance		
despicable		

Word	Where it came from	What it originally meant
tangible		
barbarism		
exclusive(ly)		
ironic		
adversary (ies)		
mandatory		
affectation(s)		

Why is it important to know where a word came from? Many roots, prefixes, and affixes of English words come from Latin and Greek. Being familiar with these parts of words can help you understand new vocabulary.

Directions: *Complete the chart below using the vocabulary words from Chapters One – Six. You may need to do a bit of digging to find the root word of words with prefixes. Take off the prefix, and look up the root. Then write the dictionary definition of the word in the last column. If you already checked the etymology of the word, add the information from that chart.*

Affix	Meaning	Vocabulary Word	Root or other information about the word	Definition
in-	not	insurmountable	insurmountable – the root means "to rise above"	unable to overcome
		inexplicable	inexplicable – the root "explicate" means to "unfold"	unable to explain
dis-	not, apart	dissent	dissent—	
		disaster	disaster –	
		disgruntled	disgruntle –	
-ment	act of, state of, result	predicament	predicate –	

Affix	Meaning	Vocabulary Word	Root or other information about the word	Definition
-ous	full of, having	preposterous disastrous (see dis-)	preposterous –	
-ity	state of, quality	Intensity	intense –	
-able/ -ible	able, capable	insurmountable, inexplicable (see in-) vulnerable despicable tangible	vulnerable – despicable – tangible –	
-ance	action, process, state	sustenance	sustain –	
-ism	system, manner, condition, characteristic	barbarism	barbarian –	
-ic	nature of, like	Ironic	irony –	

Directions: Look over the chart you completed above. What etymologies surprised you? Why? _____

_____

How does understanding the etymology of a word like disaster or barbarian help you understand the meaning of a word? _____

_____

The Hunger Games
Part One: Chapters Seven – Nine
Note-Taking and Summarizing: Chapters Seven-Nine

Directions: For Chapters 7 – 9, fill in the chart with the necessary information. If you need more room, use an additional sheet of paper.

Main Events of the Chapters	
Characters	
Setting	
Primary Conflict	
Thoughts, Feelings or Predictions	
Thematic Issues Being Raised	

The Hunger Games

Part One: Chapters Seven – Nine
Comprehension Check

Directions: *To help you understand all aspects of the novel, answer the following questions for Chapters Seven – Nine. Write your answers on a separate piece of paper using complete sentences.*

Chapter 7
1. What is the training and how does it end?
2. What does Haymitch tell Katniss and Peeta to do during the training?
3. What do you think Peeta meant when he said of Katniss, "She has no idea. The effect she can have"?
4. Why is Peeta good at camouflage?
5. What problem does Katniss face when it's her turn to perform for the Gamemakers?
6. Do you think Katniss's actions toward the Gamemakers were a good idea? Why or why not?

Chapter 8
1. Why is the Gamemakers' score on Katniss's performance important?
2. What is Haymitch's reaction to Katniss's behavior toward the Gamemakers?
3. What is surprising about Katniss's score?
4. Now that the training is complete, what is the next event?
5. Contrast Katniss's relationship with Peeta and her relationship with Gale. How are they different?
6. Compare Katniss's relationship with Peeta and her relationship with Gale. How are they similar? Explain your answer.
7. What might Peeta's motivation be for asking to be coached separately from Katniss?

Chapter 9
1. What problem does Katniss have with her training with Effie?
2. What problem does she have with training with Haymitch?
3. What is Katniss's response to the negative day with both Effie and Haymitch?
4. What strategy does Katniss eventually use during the interview? Does it work for her?
5. How does Katniss's personality differ from usual during her interviews?
6. What does Peeta reveal in his interview?
7. What evidence do you have so far in the novel that would verify what Peeta says is true?
8. What evidence do you have so far in the novel that would verify that Peeta is lying?

The Hunger Games

Part One: Chapters Seven – Nine
Standards Focus: Character Analysis
Close Up on Katniss and Peeta

If you could meet a character from any book, who would it be? Why?

The characters from books that we find interesting and want to meet are often like people from real life. They are unpredictable, funny, smart, curious, daring, or silly. They have negative qualities as well. They might be short-tempered, liars, procrastinators, or unkind at times.

A character from a book that seems so real to us that he or she feels like a real person is referred to as a round or *dynamic* character. A dynamic character has a personality and, just like a real person, has good and bad qualities. Dynamic characters are able to learn, change, and grow throughout the plot of a book. That's another reason why the character seems real to us.

What can we learn about Katniss's personality traits through what she says and does?

Directions: Review the passages listed in the table below. Infer what you think the reader learns about Katniss from the passage. Some of the answers have been started for you.

Chapter & Page	Event or description	What does that tell us about Katniss?
Chapter 1, p. 7	Katniss killed a lynx because he scared off game. *"... he wasn't bad company. But I got a decent price for his pelt."*	
Chapter 1, p. 8	*"But to be honest, I'm not the forgiving type."*	
Chapter 1, p. 14	*"But what good is yelling about the Capitol in the middle of the wood? It doesn't change anything. It doesn't make things fair."*	
Chapter 2, p. 32	*"I feel like I owe him something, and I hate owing people."*	Katniss doesn't like to be in debt to others. She likes her independence.
Chapter 4 p. 49	*"A kind Peeta Mellark is far more dangerous to me than an unkind one. Kind people have a way of working their way inside me."*	

Chapter 3, p. 35	*"There's no me to keep you both alive. It doesn't matter what happens. Whenever you see on the screen. You have to promise me you'll fight through it!"*	She is determined that her mother not fall into a depression like she did when Katniss's father died.
Chapter 4, p. 51	*"The woods became our savior, and each day I went a bit father into its arms. It was slow-going at first, but I was determined to feed us."*	
Chapter 5, p. 72	*"Peeta is planning how to kill you…He is luring you in to make you easy prey."*	
Chapter 6 p. 85	*"That I'm ashamed I never tried to help her in the woods. That I let the Capitol kill the boy and mutilate her without lifting a finger."*	
Chapter 7, p. 102	*"I pull an arrow from my quiver and send it straight at the Gamemakers' table…Everyone stares at me in disbelief."*	
Chapter 9 p. 124	*"I can feel my pulse pounding in my temples. It's a relief to get to my chair, because between the heels and my legs shaking, I'm afraid I'll trip."*	

Directions: *What makes Katniss a dynamic character? List the qualities you've discovered about Katniss.*

Positive qualities	Negative Qualities
She looks out for her family	She is suspicious

Directions: What do you learn about Peeta's personality? Since the story is told through Katniss's point of view, we only know what Katniss tells us. Use the chart below to list your thoughts.

Positive Qualities & Evidence	Negative Qualities & Evidence
He is generous – he gives Katniss bread when her family is starving	He has a temper – he smashes the glass out of Haymitch's hand

Based on your analysis, do you think Peeta is a dynamic or static character? Why?

_____

_____

The opposite of a dynamic character is a flat or *static* character. This is a one-dimensional character. While this character may seem real, when you look carefully, you notice that the character doesn't have enough varied qualities to make him or her seem like a real person.

Take a look at the characters Effie Trinket and Cinna. Both characters are interesting, but do you know enough about them to understand why they act the way they do and what they think about the world?

Directions: Use the chart below to analyze these two characters. You may not be able to fill in each spot in each column.

Effie Trinket		Cinna	
Positive qualities	Negative qualities	Positive qualities	Negative qualities
She really likes the Hunger Games	She doesn't think of the tributes as real people		

Based on your analysis, do you think Effie is a dynamic or static character? What about Cinna? _____

_____

Why do you think an author would write a book in which some of the characters are dynamic and some characters are static? _____

_____

The Hunger Games

Part One: Chapters Seven – Nine
Assessment Preparation: Author's Purpose – Greek Themes

As you have been reading *The Hunger Games,* you've probably come across words that sound Roman. Many of those words are names. List some of the names you think have a Roman "sound" to them. What are some things you already know about Greek or Roman civilizations that you've also noticed in *The Hunger Games?*

_____

_____

_____

Why might Roman or Greek names appeal to the residents of the Capitol? What Roman or Greek qualities might the residents of the Capitol be trying to imitate?

_____

_____

The name of the fictional country Panem is based on the Roman phrase *panem et circenses.* This phrase means "bread and circuses." It refers to the ancient Roman government's way of controlling the people. By keeping citizens happy with food and entertainment, they weren't interested in politics, citizen's rights, or making the world a better place.

You are probably familiar with the Roman gladiator games where soldiers would fight in an arena. The arena also hosted theater, chariot races, wild animal displays, public executions, and even reenactments of sea battles. These events took place in coliseums that were similar to the stadiums of today.

In *The Hunger Games*, how do you think the Capitol used *panem et circenses* to control the citizens? _____

_____

Why do you think Suzanne Collins picked Greek and Roman influences for her novel? _____

_____

Directions: *Some of the meanings of the names of characters in The Hunger Games fit their personality and others do not. Analyze whether the name fits the character. Some of the answers have been started for you.*

Name	Meaning of name	Does this name fit the character? Why?
Euphemia (Effie)	Melodious talk	It fits her because she talks a lot and her voice is described as cheerful
Flavius	Golden or yellow haired	

Venus (Venia)	Goddess of love	
Caesar	Ruler of the Roman empire	
Octavia	Female version of Octavius which means eighth	Not really – it says she's plump
Portia	Roman family name meaning pig	

Find out the meaning of the word *Avox* by looking up the prefix a- and the root vox. Why is *Avox* an appropriate name for the servants? _____

_____

Part II: Denotation/Connotation. The definition of a word is called *denotation*. It is the meaning of the word you'll find in a dictionary. But many words have feelings attached to them. That is called *connotation*.

Directions: *Use a dictionary, and check the etymology of the following words. Then, describe the image or feeling you get from each word. Is the word positive, negative, or neutral? Some of the answers have been started for you.*

	Denotation	**Connotation**
chariot	A carriage drawn by horses	I think of something fast and sleek – used by gladiators. The word feels positive to me.
tribute		
sponsor		
arena		
game		

Why do you think many of these words have positive connotations? Why would the Capitol choose these particular words to describe the events of the Hunger Games?

_____

_____

Choose one or two of the words from the chart that have positive connotations. Find a synonym for them that has a negative connotation. _____

_____

Name _____   Period _____

The Hunger Games

Part One Activity: What's in your backpack?
Research / Internet – *Individual or Group Activity*

At the end of Part One, the tributes are nearly ready to go into the arena for the competition. They're not sure what the environment will be, and they will travel into the arena without any supplies.

Suppose you are going on a weeklong wilderness survival trip, what would you take if you could only bring a backpack? Unlike Katniss's trip into the arena, on your trip, you'll only be surviving the elements – you won't be fighting other kids. What *items* and *skills* would you need to survive?

1. First choose the environment you'll be traveling to from the list below. Your teacher may assign you an environment; like Katniss, you'll have to learn about your terrain and survive!

Florida Everglades	Sahara Desert	The Grand Canyon
The Artic Circle	Devon Island Canada	a raft in the Pacific Ocean
Antarctica	The Amazon Rainforest	Great Smoky Mountains

2. Find out about the location. Use the graphic organizer below to organize your research.

Location	Temperature during the day	Temperature at night	Animals that live in this location
Sources for clean water	Ground conditions that may affect the shelter you'll build	Natural resources that could help you survive	Natural resources that could harm you
Plants that could be eaten	Weather that might affect your chances of survival	The terrain	What skills do you already know that could help you survive?

Name _____ **Period** _____

3. Decide what skills you need. Suppose that, like the tributes in the Hunger Games, you'll be able to learn some new skills. Which skills would you need? Create your list using the chart below.

Skill	Reason I'll need it

4. Pack your backpack. Draw, use clip art, or include a photograph of each of the items you'll be bringing along.

5. Create a display. Use a poster board or large piece of construction paper to display your backpack and the items you'll be taking on your trip. Create a caption for each item explaining why you need it and what it's for. Include a title for your poster, where you are going, and some of the challenges you'll be facing to survive in your environment. Include a menu for one day's meals you'll have that uses items you'll find in your environment.

Checklist for your poster:

☐ Includes a title

☐ Includes some of the challenges you'll be facing on your trip

☐ Menu

☐ Backpack

☐ Items you'll be taking with you

☐ Caption for each item

☐ Neat, attractive, and easy to read

☐ No grammatical or spelling errors

The Hunger Games

Part Two: Chapter Ten
Note-Taking and Summarizing: Chapter Ten

Directions: For Chapter 10, fill in the chart with the necessary information. If you need more room, use an additional sheet of paper.

Main Events of the Chapter	
Characters	
Setting	
Primary Conflict	
Thoughts, Feelings or Predictions	
Thematic Issues Being Raised	

The Hunger Games
Part Two: Chapter Ten
Comprehension Check

Directions: *To help you understand all aspects of the novel, answer the following questions for Chapter Ten. Write your answers on a separate piece of paper using complete sentences.*

1. Why is Katniss upset by Peeta's proclamation of love?

2. Why does Haymitch think Peeta's proclamation is good for Katniss?

3. What is Haymitch's last piece of advice to Peeta and Katniss?

4. On the rooftop, Peeta and Katniss talk. How are their attitudes toward the arena different? Explain how they differ in what they expect to happen.

5. Can you relate to Katniss's inability to sleep the night before the Games? When was a time you were anxious about something and couldn't sleep? How was your experience similar to Katniss's? How was your experience different?

6. What is the tracker?

7. How does the Capitol treat the arena after the Games are over? What does that tell you about the Capitol?

8. What is Katniss's token?

9. What can you infer about the token the girl from District One wanted to take into the arena?

10. Can you relate to Katniss's anxiety as she waits to enter the arena? Explain your answer.

Name _____   Period _____

The Hunger Games

Part Two: Chapter Ten
Standards Focus: Star-crossed Lovers and Other Archetypes of Literature

"You're all they're talking about. The star-crossed lovers from District Twelve!" Haymitch tells Katniss after the interview. What do you think Haymitch means when he uses the term "star-crossed lovers"? _____

_____

Go back to the section in the chapter where Katniss is thinking about how the viewers perceive them: *"I...cannot avoid seeing that every screen is now dominated by a shot of Peeta and me, separated by a few feet that in the viewers' heads can never be breached. Poor tragic us" (134).* What does Katniss mean in the next paragraph: *"But I know better"*? Is she right in her thinking? _____

_____

The term "star-crossed lovers" comes from long ago when people believed that the stars controlled the events of life. If something was meant to be, it was "written in the stars." They believed there was nothing that could be done to change the course of events.

In 1623, William Shakespeare coined the phrase "star-crossed lovers" in the prologue of the tragic play *Romeo and Juliet.* If you are familiar with the play, you know that both Romeo and Juliet die at the end of the play. Their love is "star-crossed" because their families hate each other and have had a long-standing feud. Neither set of parents wants their child to befriend a child from the other family—let alone fall in love! But that is exactly what happens, and the love affair ends tragically in their deaths.

In *The Hunger Games*, the audience of the televised interviews recognizes the tragedy of Katniss and Peeta's situation as being "star-crossed." Even though *The Hunger Games* is set in a time in the distant future, the audience understands the tragedy of this kind of love.

How do you think they know this?

One way the audience may know about star-crossed lovers is through *archetypes*. An archetype is an image, pattern, or character type that is often found in literature. Archetypes have been repeated in books, plays, songs, poems, and movies for many, many years – so much so, that readers are familiar with them. For example, we are familiar with the archetype of the hero. We expect a hero to act a certain way when we encounter him or her in a novel.

When the audience of the Capitol recognizes the star-crossed lovers of Katniss and Peeta, they understand what that means – doomed love.

Often one piece of literature will have multiple archetypes. A writer may add a twist to the archetype like making a hero in a novel a vampire or space Jedi.

Name _____ **Period** _____

Directions: *Read the description below of the archetyped character. 1) Identify a character from The Hunger Games who fits that archetype and explain why. Then 2) identify a character who also fits that archetype from another novel, story, TV show, or movie you're familiar with. Be sure to identify the character and where the character came from. The first one has been done for you.*

Star-crossed lovers: two people whose love is destined to fail.

1. From *The Hunger Games*: Katniss and Peeta because they are supposedly in love, but cannot be together	
2. Other character/s: Edward and Bella	From: *Twilight*

Villain: an evil character who is opposed to the hero of the story. The villain can also be called the *antagonist*.

1. From *The Hunger Games*:	
2. Other character/s:	From:

Hero: the central character. A true heroic character is different from a *protagonist*. The hero must show extreme bravery and courage. A hero may have great physical strength. The *protagonist* is another term that is used to describe the main character who may or may not be a hero.

1. From *The Hunger Games*:	
2. Other character/s:	From:

Scapegoat: a character or characters that must be sacrificed for the greater good of a society or for real or imagined sins.

1. From *The Hunger Games*:	
2. Other character/s:	From:

Name _____ **Period** _____

In addition to characters being archetypes, a plot can be an archetype. The hero's journey or quest is another example of archetype. Another kind of archetype can be the task or job that must be completed by the protagonist or hero of the story.

Remember *The Wizard of Oz*? What is the task the Dorothy and her three companions must complete in order for Dorothy to go home? _____

_____

What trials does Dorothy go through in order to complete her task? _____

_____

_____

Think about the "task" Katniss has as she enters the arena. How will she know she's completed the task? _____

_____

Make some predictions about the trials she may face as she tries to complete her task. _____

_____

Colors, as well, can be archetypes. What is the color of love? If you said "red" you were thinking of the archetypal color. What are some of the ideas you associate with these colors?

White: _____

Black: _____

Blue: _____

Purple: _____

Green: _____

Images can also be archetypes. What are some ideas you associate with these images?

Fire: _____

Water: _____

Like many readers, you may wonder if authors intentionally use archetypes in their writing. Only the writers can answer that question, but some psychologists believe that human beings were born understanding archetypes that they are part of our collective unconscious.

The Hunger Games

Part Two: Chapter Ten
Assessment Preparation: Writing with Purpose/ Concise Word Choice

What is the general purpose of writing? If you think "communication," you are correct, but the type of communication depends on the purpose for your writing. Think about the following scenarios and decide the purpose of the writing. Write your answer in the box.

Type of Writing	Purpose
Sending a text message to a friend about where to meet at the mall.	inform
Writing an email to a company to ask for a refund.	
Writing a book report for your English class.	
A note to Granny for the birthday present.	
A message to your dad about a phone call he received.	
Directions to your house.	
Your name and address for a school form.	

When your writing has a purpose, you know why you're writing and what you want your reader to understand.

As you read *The Hunger Games*, you may have noticed that in Part I of the novel, Suzanne Collins spent a lot of time explaining the events of the Games, the history of Panem, and how the reaping worked. Why do you think that was necessary? _____

_____

_____

Part I: Concise words
Concise word choice helps writers write with purpose. To be concise means to say a lot but with few words. This means the writer chooses each word carefully, so it has the precise effect the writer wants. Suzanne Collins fills *The Hunger Games* with concise language that vividly describes events of the novel.

Concise words help readers imagine and connect with what is being read. Just as the word "giggle" has a different image than "snort" or "laugh," the writer's choice of words can make a big difference in what the reader pictures as he reads. Readers can connect with concise words by imagining what they already know and picturing the scene.

Take a look at this sentence: "The roar of the crowd is deafening" (133).
- What makes it concise? Three key words in the sentence "roar," "crowd," and "deafening" all have to do with noise – and a lot of it. These are specific, vivid words.
- What does the reader picture? The reader can picture a mass of people all cheering, clapping, and screaming, but the noise is so loud, it sounds like a roar.

- How can the reader connect to the writing? As readers, we can imagine this because most of us have seen a sports game on TV, and we know how loud a crowd can be. Or maybe we've even experienced it in person.

Directions: Using the sentences below, answer the three questions about concise language.

1. "He loses his balance and crashes into an ugly urn filled with fake flowers" (134).
   - What words make it concise? _____
   - What does the reader picture? _____
   - How can the reader connect to the writing? _____
   _____

2. "Haymitch turns on me" (135).
   - What words make it concise? _____
   - What does the reader picture? _____
   - How can the reader connect to the writing? _____
   _____

3. "Haymitch is right, they eat that stuff up in the Capitol" (136)
   - What words make it concise? _____
   - What does the reader picture? _____
   - How can the reader connect to the writing? _____
   _____

4. "We start the cream and rose-petal soup without them" (137)
   - What words make it concise? _____
   - What does the reader picture? _____
   - How can the reader connect to the writing? _____
   _____

5. "What traps have the Gamemakers hidden to liven up the slower moments?" (148)
   - What words make it concise? _____
   - What does the reader picture? _____
   - How can the reader connect to the writing? _____
   _____

Part II: Why is concise language important?

At the beginning of this lesson, you wrote about the purpose for writing. When you text your friend to meet you at the mall, your language needs to be more specific than "the mall," right? Specific, concise language allows to you write exactly what you mean, and it can prevent you from rambling on and on. Concise writing chooses the right word for the job.

Name _____ **Period** _____

Analyze the difference between Suzanne Collins's original sentence and a less-concise sentence.

> "The roar of the crowd is deafening" (133)
> > It was loud.

Distinguish the differences between the two sentences. How are they different?

_____

_____

> "We start the cream and rose-petal soup without them" (137)
> > We eat soup.

Distinguish the differences between the two sentences. How are they different?

_____

_____

Part III: Practice concise writing using haikus

You are probably familiar with the poetic form of haiku. A haiku is a poem that is made up of three lines. The first line has five syllables, the second line has seven syllables, and the third line has five syllables.

Directions: Think about the importance of concise language and writing with a purpose. Use the haiku form to write five haikus that explain the plot of The Hunger Games. Since a haiku limits the number of syllables you can use, you'll need to make sure each word is concise – that you'll be saying the most you can with the fewest number of words. You'll probably want to eliminate articles (the, a, an) and prepositions. Use punctuation marks to help clarify the meaning of your haiku. Your teacher may allow you to adjust the number of syllables per line.

> Every syllable has just one vowel sound. The word "heat" is one syllable because there is just one vowel sound even though there are two vowels in the word. To determine the number of syllables in a word, you may find it helpful to clap the syllables as you say the word out loud.

Haiku 1: Chapters 1 – 2
Haiku 2: Chapters 3 – 4
Haiku 3: Chapters 5 – 6
Haiku 4: Chapters 7 – 9
Haiku 5: Chapter 10

As an added challenge, incorporate one or more of the vocabulary words from Chapter 10 into your haikus. You may change the form of the word to fit into your haiku. An example for Haiku 1 has been done for you.

Vocabulary words to use:

assent	aghast
breached	perceived
entourages	reenactments

Haiku 1 Example:

Panem: deadly Games
Reaping Katniss and Peeta
Aghast – they accept

Name _____   Period _____

The Hunger Games

Part Two: Chapters Eleven – Twelve
Note-Taking and Summarizing: Chapters Eleven-Twelve

Directions: *For Chapters 11 – 12, fill in the chart with the necessary information. If you need more room, use an additional sheet of paper.*

Main Events of the Chapters	
Characters	
Setting	
Primary Conflict	
Thoughts, Feelings or Predictions	
Thematic Issues Being Raised	

The Hunger Games

Part Two: Chapters Eleven – Twelve
Comprehension Check Questions

Directions: *To help you understand all aspects of the novel, answer the following questions for Chapters Eleven – Twelve. Write your answers on a separate piece of paper using complete sentences.*

Chapter 11

1. What is the Cornucopia? How is it set up, and what does Katniss see as she looks at it?

2. Explain the conflict Katniss feels while she waits for the sixty seconds to end.

3. Briefly list the events that occur after the gong rings.

4. How does Katniss find out who has been killed on the first day? How many die on the first day?

5. Why is Katniss surprised at the end of the chapter?

6. Predict how the arena will help Katniss survive.

Chapter 12

1. What is Katniss's primary goal in this chapter?

2. Analyze the relationship between Peeta and the Careers.

3. Do you agree with Katniss's interpretation of Peeta's choice in joining the Careers?

4. Do you agree with Katniss's belief about why Haymitch doesn't send her water?

5. What is Katniss's new problem at the end of the chapter?

6. What judgment can you make about Katniss from the following quote:

   "So as I slide out of the foliage and into the dawn light, I pause a second, giving the cameras time to lock on me. Then I cock my head slightly to the side and give a knowing smile" (164).

The Hunger Games

Part Two: Chapters Eleven – Twelve
Standards Focus: Point of View – The World According to Katniss

Have you ever tried on someone else's glasses? What was your experience?
When we look through someone else's prescription glasses, we see the world in a
different way. Depending on the prescription, it may be a very different way!
Likewise, an author chooses how to tell a story by deciding on the *point of view* of
the story. You are probably familiar with *point of view*. What does it mean?

The way the author presents the story is called point of view. There are three main
types: first, second, and third person point of view.

In the first person point of view, the author tells the story by using one of the
characters as narrator. You can tell it's first person point of view because the
pronoun "I" is used in the narration.

The second person point of view uses the pronoun "you." Generally, you'll find a
second person point of view in an essay or book that explains how to do something.
A "choose your own adventure" book is written from the second person point of view.

The third person point of view uses the third person pronouns "he" or "she." The
narrator might be *omniscient*, being able to see everything that's happening in the
story, or *limited*, being able to see only a portion of the story.

Point of view is important to readers. The point of view determines how much
information you have about the story. If the novel is told from a first person point of
view, you only know and experience the narrator's thoughts and experiences. If it's
told from the third person point of view, you have more information. Why else might
point of view be important in telling a story?

Part I: Point of View

1. From what point of view is *The Hunger Games* narrated?

   _____

2. Find two examples from Chapters 11 or 12 that support your belief.

   _____

   _____

   _____

Part II: Katniss—Because the novel is told from Katniss's point of view, the reader
only learns about the world through her eyes, memories, experiences, thoughts, and
feelings. Based on what you've learned about Katniss so far, how does she view the
world? You may want to go back to the Standards Focus activity you completed for
Chapters 7 – 9 as you work on your analysis.

Name _____ **Period** _____

Directions: Use the following prompts to analyze Katniss's point of view. Write your answers on a separate sheet of paper. The first one has been done for you.

To Katniss…

The world is a hostile place. She doesn't trust anyone except for Gale. She believes she must do everything herself and can't rely on others.	cherished memories include…
the Capitol is…	feeling are …
the Games are…	the Gamemakers are…
Peeta is…	life is …
District 12 is …	family is …

Part III: Peeta—Could you answer the same questions about Peeta?

Directions: Using the same sheet of paper as you used for Katniss, answer the following questions about Peeta's point of view of the world.

1. How does Peeta feel about his family?
2. How do you know this?
3. How does Peeta feel about the Games?
4. How do you know?
5. At the end of Chapter 11, the reader learns, along with Katniss, that Peeta has joined the Careers. What else does the reader learn that Peeta probably doesn't know?

Part IV: A resident of the Capitol

Can you answer any of those questions about a resident of the Capitol? Choose one of the questions from the chart, and answer it from the point of view of a Capitol resident. Share your answer with a classmate and discuss if you've correctly depicted a resident's point of view.

Part V: Peeta's Point of View

Neither Katniss nor the reader knows what happened with Peeta at the Cornucopia. Peeta didn't run in the same directions as Katniss, but what happened? Write a paragraph from Peeta's point of view explaining what happened after the gong went off. How might Peeta have convinced the Careers to form an alliance with him, or did they ask him to join them? Write from the point of view of Peeta, and use the first person pronoun "I" to tell the story as if you are Peeta.

Name _____   Period _____

The Hunger Games

Part Two: Chapters Eleven – Twelve
Assessment Preparation: Reflective Writing

Have you ever watched a reality TV show? Many reality shows have a "video diary" that participants use to record their thoughts about what they're experiencing on the show. Rather than writing in a diary, the participant talks to the video camera.

Imagine the participants in the Games had access to video cameras and could create video diaries. After the Careers and Peeta leave at the beginning of Chapter 12, what would Katniss's diary be like? You're going to create a script for a video diary that Katniss might make about the first day in the arena.

Part I: Generating Ideas

Use the graphic organizer below to jot down some ideas about the following topics.

What she thinks about the Cornucopia	
What she worries about now	
What is she angry about	
What she feels about Peeta joining the Careers	
What her plan is	
What she feels lucky about	

Part II: Reflective Writing

How is a diary different from other types of communication? How might it be different from a formal essay? _____

_____

_____

Directions: Keeping in mind the type of writing you'd find in a diary, write a draft for Katniss's video diary. Write on a separate sheet of paper, creating a script she could use as if she were actually in front of the camera.

*Challenge: Incorporate five vocabulary words from Chapters 11 and 12 into your diary.

Name _____ **Period** _____

Part III: Reading and Listening for Understanding

Directions: Share your diary draft with a friend by reading it aloud. Remember to use expression in your voice. Have your classmate complete the following questions as you read.

Name of person who wrote the diary entry: _____

Name of person who is evaluating the entry: _____

1. The diary entry sounds like Katniss could have written it.   Yes   No

2. The biggest problem Katniss has right now is _____

_____

_____

3. The most important things to Katniss right now are _____

_____

_____

4. In the script, Katniss sounds very _____

_____

_____

Take turns, so each person has feedback on his or her script.

Part IV: Revising your Diary

Using the feedback from your classmate, revise your script.

Part V: Perform It!

Your teacher may allow you time in class to videotape your diary. You will need the help of a partner with lighting, camera angle and operation, and to provide feedback. You may also choose to work with a partner or group to combine diaries to create one video diary script.

If you are going to perform or record your diary, be sure you pay attention to the details of the scene and the costume. Video diaries on TV shows usually just focus on the person's face, but you will still want to pay attention to the scenery in which you are filming and create realistic costumes to make your video diary more realistic.

Name _____   Period _____

The Hunger Games

Part Two: Chapters Thirteen – Fourteen
Note-Taking and Summarizing: Chapters Thirteen-Fourteen

Directions: For Chapters 13 – 14, fill in the chart with the necessary information. If you need more room, use an additional sheet of paper.

Main Events of the Chapters	
Characters	
Setting	
Primary Conflict	
Thoughts, Feelings or Predictions	
Thematic Issues Being Raised	

The Hunger Games
Part Two: Chapters Thirteen – Fourteen
Comprehension Check

Directions: *To help you understand all aspects of the novel, answer the following questions for Chapters Thirteen – Fourteen. Write your answers on a separate piece of paper using complete sentences.*

Chapter 13

1. List the events that occur in the fire.

2. What are Katniss's injuries as a result of the fire?

3. Describe what happens when Katniss climbs the tree.

4. What new problem does Katniss have now that she's safe in the tree?

5. Draw a conclusion about the audience of the Hunger Games and the Gamemakers' use of a wall of fire. What does the fire tell you about the audience?

6. What prediction can you make about Rue and why she helps Katniss?

Chapter 14

1. Explain why the tracker jackers are dangerous.

2. Identify facts from Chapters 13 and 14 that show Katniss is a brave person.

3. Analyze Peeta's behavior at the end of Chapter 14. Why do you think he acts the way he does?

4. Formulate a theory about why the sponsors decided to send Katniss a silver parachute when they did. Why didn't they help her sooner? What did she do to prove she deserved their help?

5. Besides the balm, what other gift would be beneficial to Katniss at this point in the story?

6. Predict what will happen to Katniss now that the tracker jackers have stung her.

7. Evaluate Katniss's plan to cut down the nest. Was it a good plan even though she endangered herself?

Name _____   Period _____

The Hunger Games

Part Two: Chapters Thirteen – Fourteen
Standards Focus: Conflict in the Arena

As you go through life each day, what are some conflicts you might experience?

_____

_____

_____

When you think about the kinds of conflicts you experience every day, they may include things like arguments with a parent, sibling, or friend, the rivalry of a sporting event, or even being chased by a dog.

Start with Chapter 11 and list the conflicts and crises Katniss has had to battle since she stepped off the metal circle and into the arena._____

_____

_____

_____

By the time you finish reading Chapter 14, you may be wondering what else Katniss will be faced with in the arena. If you check your feelings as a reader, you may be repulsed by her experience with Glimmer when Katniss returns to retrieve the bow and arrows, you might be frightened by the advancing wall of fire, or you might be horrified by the burn on Katniss's leg. Regardless of your response, you're probably not thinking these were two boring chapters!

Conflict makes a story interesting. Good conflict allows readers to engage with the story, visualize the events, connect with the characters, and enjoy reading.

There are four basic kinds of conflict:
1. character vs. character
2. character vs. nature
3. character vs. society
4. character vs. self

Character vs. character: two or more characters in conflict. If you've ever argued with a sibling or friend, you've experienced this type of conflict.

Character vs. nature: the character is struggling with nature. Books like *Hatchet* or *The Cay* are about conflicts with nature. The character is usually trying to survive in a hostile environment.

Character vs. society: a conflict in which the character is opposed to society. A book like *Number the Stars* deals with people acting against the wishes of the government. Other Holocaust books describe characters fighting against the beliefs or actions of the government. In dystopian literature, you'll find characters who fight against society.

Character vs. self: the character has internal conflict. The character may be fighting against his or her character flaws like a short temper or bad habits. The character could also be in conflict about the loss of a parent, problems at home, or problems that he or she has caused. The novel *On My Honor* deals with the internal struggle a boy goes through when he lies about the drowning death of his friend.

Part I: Katniss and Conflict

Directions: *Look back at your list of conflicts Katniss has experienced in the arena. Categorize them in the chart below and add any additional conflicts you've discovered. Include one sentence explaining why you think this is a conflict. An example has been done for you.*

Character vs. character	Character vs. nature	Character vs. society	Character vs. self
Katniss vs. Peeta— She's convinced that he's plotting against her.			

Part II: Other Character Conflicts

Choose any other character in the novel. Choose one or two types of conflict you know the character is experiencing. Complete the information in the chart below. Be sure to explain why you think this is a conflict. An example using Glimmer has been done for you.

Name _____   Period _____

Example: Character Name: Glimmer   **My Character's name:**

Character vs. character	Character vs. nature	Character vs. society	Character vs. self
Glimmer vs. Katniss. *Glimmer tries to climb the tree to get Katniss but can't climb high enough.*	Glimmer vs the tree. *She wants to climb up the tree to get Katniss, but the tree limbs become too thin up higher.* Glimmer vs. tracker jackers. *She is attacked by the wasps and can't get away.*		

Part III: Behind the scenes with Haymitch

Haymitch must be doing his job and sponsors must be interested in Katniss because they sent her a silver parachute. Imagine that Haymitch has asked you to create an advertising campaign for Katniss. Create a poster that has a slogan, statements, and an image on it that would encourage sponsors to support her.

Directions: Use the graphic organizer below to brainstorm ideas for your advertising poster. Your teacher may allow you to work with a partner on this. Use another sheet of paper if you need more room.

Slogan ideas	
Statement ideas for the poster	
Image for the poster	

Once you've come up with a slogan, statements, and image for your poster, design your poster on a large sheet of paper. Then, share it with your classmates.

Name _____   Period _____

The Hunger Games

Part Two: Chapters Thirteen – Fourteen
Assessment Preparation: Using Vocabulary Words

You may have written an "I Am" poem. It follows a distinct pattern in which each line of the poem completes a sentence. You'll be writing an "I Am" poem from the point of view of one of the characters of *The Hunger Games* and using vocabulary words from Chapters 13 and 14. Your teacher may allow you to work with a partner.

Part I: Choose a Character - Your teacher may assign a character to you, or you might choose one of your own.

Katniss	Gale	Rue
Peeta	Mrs. Everdeen	Madge
Haymitch	Cato	Greasy Sae
Effie Trinket	Glimmer	

Part II: Review the character - Consider what the character says and does. Also think about what others say about the character. Take notes on your thoughts.

_____

_____

_____

_____

Part III: The poem - The pattern below is modified from the traditional "I Am" poem that you may be familiar with. Follow the pattern as you write your poem; be sure you are completing each sentence. Your teacher may ask you not to write the name of the character you are describing. You may want to read your classmates' poems and then guess their character.

Stanza 1
I am (2 unique or interesting qualities the character has) _____

_____

I consider the incompetent _____

_____

I persevere _____

_____

I precariously _____

_____

I will be sated when _____

_____

I am (repeat the first line) _____

_____

Stanza 2
A balm will _____

_____

I quell _____

_____

I worry I will be in a stupor when _____

_____

I conspiratorially plan _____

_____

As I watch the mayhem of the Games, I _____

_____

I am (repeat the first line) _____

_____

Stanza 3
I am honing _____

_____

I struggle to _____

_____

I show my bravado _____

_____

I plot _____

_____

I wait for things to abate as I _____

_____

I am (repeat the first line) _____

_____

Part IV: Publish your poem - Your teacher may want you to type and print out your poem with an illustration of the character, so you can share it with others.

The Hunger Games

Part Two: Chapters Fifteen – Sixteen
Note-Taking and Summarizing: Chapters Fifteen-Sixteen

Directions: For Chapters 15 – 16, fill in the chart with the necessary information. If you need more room, use an additional sheet of paper.

Main Events of the Chapters	
Characters	
Setting	
Primary Conflict	
Thoughts, Feelings or Predictions	
Thematic Issues Being Raised	

Name _____ Period _____

The Hunger Games

Part Two: Chapters Fifteen – Sixteen
Comprehension Check

Directions: *To help you understand all aspects of the novel, answer the following questions for Chapters Fifteen – Sixteen. Write your answers on a separate piece of paper using complete sentences.*

Chapter 15

1. How did Katniss and Rue become allies?

2. Identify important information Rue was able to provide to Katniss.

3. What skills and knowledge does Rue provide to the alliance?

4. Explain what Katniss discovers about Peeta.

5. Analyze why Katniss thinks Haymitch wouldn't approve of her alliance with Rue.

6. Predict how the glasses will be important to Katniss and Rue.

7. Explain why Katniss thinks it's important to destroy the Careers' supplies.

Chapter 16

1. Describe the way Katniss plans to destroy the Careers' food supply.

2. How are the mockingjays important to the girls' plan?

3. What does Katniss realize about the Careers' decision to allow the boy from District 3 to live?

4. At this point, who is the biggest threat to Katniss and why?

5. What new information does Katniss learn about Peeta?

6. Describe the Foxface girl and what she is able to do.

7. Do you agree with Katniss's decision to go on the offensive and attack the Careers? Explain your answer.

Name _____ Period _____

The Hunger Games

Part Two: Chapters Fifteen – Sixteen
Standards Focus: Character Map

At this point in the novel, you may be feeling like Katniss does at the end of the day. She's trying to keep track of the tributes who are still alive. At the beginning of Chapter 16 (page 209), Rue goes through the list of tributes.

Directions: Using Rue's list and what you already know, create a tribute list using the chart below. You may not have much information on each tribute, but as you continue to read the novel, fill in the chart. Part of the chart has been completed for you.

Tribute	District	Descriptions and your thoughts on the character
	District 1	
	District 2	He seems to be the leader of the Careers. He wants to kill Katniss.
	District 2	
	District 3	
Foxface girl	District 5	Sneaky, good at hiding
	District 10	
	District 11	Small and can jump from tree to tree
	District 11	
Katniss	District 12	
Peeta	District 12	

We know that one of the tributes dies in Chapter 16 because the cannon goes off. The tributes won't know who it is until the day is over. Use what you know to complete the alliance *groupings* in the space below.

In the forest   Near the lake

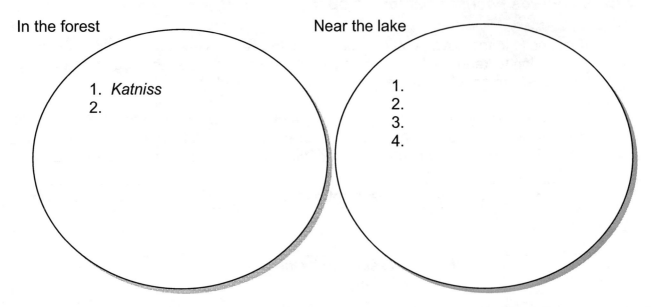

1. *Katniss*
2.

1.
2.
3.
4.

What advantages and disadvantages do the teams have? Use the chart below to analyze them. Part of the chart has been started for you.

Tribute(s)	Advantages	Disadvantages
Careers	*They have access to water and supplies (until they get blown up). They have each other, so they can protect one another. There are more of them, so each person probably gets more rest since someone can act as a guard.*	
Katniss and Rue		
Foxface		*She is alone, so she has to rely on herself for survival. Without a partner, she's probably more vulnerable.*

Name _____ **Period** _____

1. What tributes are unaccounted for? _____

_____

_____

2. Where might they be? _____

_____

_____

3. At this point in the novel, do you think it's better to be on your own or to have formed an alliance? Support your answer. _____

_____

_____

_____

_____

_____

The Hunger Games

Part Two: Chapters Fifteen – Sixteen
Assessment Preparation: Who Is the Audience?

Dystopian literature often takes place in a future that has some basis in our present day. What technology is present in Panem or in the Capitol that is also present in our world? _____

_____

_____

Is there any technology we have today that you would expect to be available in the future? _____

One piece of technology that many people think they can't live without is their phone. Texting is so predominant that there are now laws preventing people from texting while driving. What if Katniss had a phone in the arena with her? If she had a limited number of texts that she could send, who would she text? What would she say? Would a text she might send to Haymitch be the same kind of text she'd send to Prim?\

It's important to consider audience when you're writing. The tone, the word choice, and even the message itself would change depending on the audience.

Part I: Text Messaging

Directions: *Using the following scenarios, write a text message from Katniss. The first one has been done for you.*

Katniss to Prim after she awakens from the tracker jacker stings.	Hi, feeling better! Don't worry about me. Those stingers looked worse than they felt.
Katniss to Gale after Katniss realizes Peeta saved her life	
Katniss to Haymitch when she's searching for water	
Katniss to her mother after she's burned in the fire	

Describe how your message changed as you wrote each text. Explain your answers. _____

_____

_____

_____

_____

Part II: Practice writing to different audiences

Directions*: Using the vocabulary words listed below, write a letter to President Snow from Katniss's mother. She has been watching the Games and wants them to stop. She's requesting that the President end them now. Remember to use the correct format for writing a letter. Write your letter on a separate sheet of paper.*

onslaught   ordeal
noxious   forages
prominent

Using the vocabulary words below, write another letter. This time, it's a letter from Haymitch to Katniss in the arena. Write your letter on a separate sheet of paper.

rations   copse
obliging   wracked
rendezvous   tentatively

Using any vocabulary words above that you were unable to incorporate into your first two letters, write a third letter to Katniss from Rue, now that they have become allies.

Name _____   Period _____

The Hunger Games
Part Two: Chapters Seventeen – Eighteen
Note-Taking and Summarizing: Chapters Seventeen-Eighteen

Directions: For Chapters 17 – 18, fill in the chart with the necessary information. If you need more room, use an additional sheet of paper.

Main Events of the Chapters	
Characters	
Setting	
Primary Conflict	
Thoughts, Feelings or Predictions	
Thematic Issues Being Raised	

The Hunger Games

Part Two: Chapters Seventeen – Eighteen
Comprehension Check

Directions: To help you understand all aspects of the novel, answer the following questions for Chapters Seventeen – Eighteen. Write your answers on a separate piece of paper using complete sentences.

Update your Character Map from Chapters 15 – 16 with any new information about the tributes.

Chapter 17

1. Explain what happens to the Careers' supply pyramid.

2. Describe the consequences of the explosion for Katniss.

3. What happens to Rue at the end of the chapter?

4. Analyze what Cato's reaction to the explosion says about him.

5. Explain what Katniss means when she thinks "*Let the Seventy-fourth Hunger Games begin, Cato…Let them begin for real.*"

Chapter 18

1. Restate how Katniss allows Rue to die with dignity.

2. How are the rules of the Games suddenly changed?

3. Identify Katniss's actions that show she is deeply upset about Rue's death.

4. Hypothesize why the rules of the Games are changed to allow for two winners.

5. Identify what the people from District 11 give Katniss. Evaluate why they do this.

6. Why do you think Katniss calls out Peeta's name when she hears the new rule?

The Hunger Games

Part Two: Chapters Seventeen – Eighteen
Standards Focus: Map of the Setting/ Visualization

Take a few seconds to look around. Where are you? Write a short description of the setting you're currently in.

_____

_____

_____

_____

Did you remember to include information about the date and time? Did you include information about the season and about the actions of others in the room? Did you include the mood of the room that might influence the actions of others around you?

We often forget that setting means more than just the geographical placement of a story. Setting also includes the date, time of year, and can even include the philosophical make-up of the time period, for example Elizabethan England or Oklahoma during the Great Depression. Setting also includes the environment where the characters find themselves. Think about the differences in environment between the setting of a concentration camp and a Girl Scout camp.

The environment where the characters find themselves plays an important role in how the characters might act. The setting of the arena certainly influences how Katniss acts, where she goes, and how she responds to threats. At this point in the novel, you probably have an idea of what the arena looks like.

Directions: *Go back to the beginning of Chapter 11 when Katniss first sees the arena. Using a plain white sheet of paper, draw what you think the arena looks like. Use colored pencils or crayons to add color to your drawing. Label your drawing and/or create a key.*

Based on your drawing, the setting probably looks fairly harmless. Reread the end of Chapters 12 and 13. How does the setting affect the important events that happen in these chapters?

_____

_____

_____

_____

Name _____ **Period** _____

Directions: Add information that you learned about the setting in Chapters 12 and 13 to your map and label those items. Now go to Chapter 16 and reread the section where Katniss goes to the Careers' camp. Add any new information to your illustration. Skim through Chapter 17 and locate any new geographical information about the setting and include it in your illustration.

Share your illustration with a classmate and compare how they're alike and different.

Did you remember to include cameras built into the scene to pick up all the tributes' actions? Add cameras to your map. Is there a way you can illustrate the artificial sky where the dead tributes' faces are projected each night?

Add those items to your setting map. Label them or add them to your key.

After your map is finished, consider the following questions. Write a short answer for each.

1. How does the physical set up of the arena add tension to the story? _____

_____

_____

_____

_____

2. The Games are held so the tributes will kill each other as entertainment for the Capitol and create a climate of intimidation for the rest of the districts. How does this influence how the setting is created? _____

_____

_____

3. What elements of the setting do the Gamemakers have control over? _____

_____

_____

_____

4. What elements of the setting do the tributes have control over? _____

_____

_____

_____

The Hunger Games

Part Two: Chapters Seventeen – Eighteen
Assessment Preparation: Writing Powerful Sentences

Reread the last page of Chapter 18. Pay attention to the length of the sentences Suzanne Collins uses.

Part I: Analyzing sentences
Directions: Use the information from the charts below to determine the length and purpose of the sentence. Some of the answers have been started for you.

Sentence	# of words	Purpose of the sentence
"For the most part, the only communication the tributes get from outside the arena is the nightly death toll" (244).	19	*Explains the reason Katniss sits up to listen after the trumpets blare.*
"But occasionally, there will be trumpets followed by an announcement" (244).		
"Usually, this will be a call to a feast" (244).		
"When food is scarce, the Gamemakers will invite the players to a banquet, somewhere known to all such as the Cornucopia, as an incentive to gather and fight" (244).		*Explains what it means when they call the tributes to a feast.*

Generally, a long sentence is read more slowly. It may contain more information, explanation, and description. A short sentence is read quickly. It may only contain one fact or a partial explanation. Shorter sentences can be used to add emphasis, drama, or excitement to the text.

Directions: Read the following sentences and analyze the purpose of the sentence length. Some of the answers have been started for you.

Sentence	# of words	Purpose of sentence	Reason for sentence length
"Claudius Templesmith's voice booms down from overhead, congratulating the six of us who remain" (244).		*Gives information— not just congratulat- ing the six tributes, but reminding the reader that there are only six left.*	*It's longer because it has more explanation and description.*

Name _____   Period _____

Sentence	# of words	Purpose of sentence	Reason for sentence length
"But he is not inviting us to a feast" (244).			*It's shorter because it contains surprising information.*
"He's saying something very confusing" (244).			
"There's been a rule change in the Games" (244).			
"A rule change!" (244)			*She's surprised, so she repeats the information.*
"That in itself is mind bending since we don't really have any rules to speak of except don't step off your circle for sixty seconds and the unspoken rule about not eating one another" (244).			

As the chapter concludes, Katniss's heart races as she processes the news. Analyze these sentences.

Sentence	# of words	Why are these sentences so short?
"The news sinks in" (244).		*Finally, Katniss is beginning to understand the rule. She gets it!*
"Two tributes can win this year" (244).		
"If they're from the same district" (244).		

"Both can live" (244).		
"Both of us can live" (244).		

Part II: Behind the scenes with Haymitch: Holding a Press Conference

You've probably seen a press conference on television. An important person holds an informational meeting with reporters. The purpose of a press conference is to provide information to the public.

After Claudius Templesmith's announcement that the two tributes from the same district can be winners, imagine that Haymitch holds a press conference. He wants to encourage sponsors to support Peeta and Katniss. He's also competing with District 2 since they have two tributes as well.

Directions: *Write a series of questions for the press conference that a reporter might ask Haymitch. Use a variety of short and long sentences for your questions. Then trade questions with a classmate and pretend you are Haymitch answering the questions. Again, use a variety of short and long sentences to answer. Remember that the shorter sentences will give emphasis to what Haymitch says. Can you capture Haymitch's personality in his responses? An example has been done for you.*

Example:

1. What do you think Katniss will do now?

She's going to find Peeta.

2. How is she going to find Peeta?

He could be anywhere in the arena. She's a hunter. She was able to blow up supplies, cut down a tracker jacker nest, find food, and survive a fire. She can find Peeta.

> To help you formulate questions, remember the 5 W's and 1 H of questioning: who, what, when, where, why, and how.

The Hunger Games

Part Two Activity: Exploring the Labyrinth

Part I: The Labyrinth
In the myth of Theseus and the Minotaur, the tributes must go into a labyrinth. At its heart is the Minotaur who will devour them.

The form of the labyrinth has been popular for thousands of years. Labyrinths can be found as designs on floors, as garden beds, rock gardens, or hedges. Today, many people consider a walk through a labyrinth as a form of meditation. It is symbolic of a reflective journey inward into the soul or mind, and then a renewed journey outward.

Labyrinths are a bit different from mazes. A labyrinth will have one way in and one way out. There will be no dead ends or multiple paths. A maze, on the other hand, will have dead ends. It's possible to get lost in a maze, but you won't get lost in a labyrinth.

Follow the simple steps below to draw your own labyrinth.

Step 1: Create a plus sign in the center of your paper.

Step 2: Add a dot in each corner.

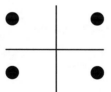

 Step 3: Moving around the design, draw a line connecting the points of the labyrinth. First, draw a line from a dot to the end of a line at the right.

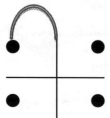

Step 4: Continue moving around the plus sign. Draw a line towards the left (counter-clockwise) from an unused dot and connecting with a line that has not been used. Next draw a line towards the right (clockwise) from an unused dot to a line on the right that isn't connected. (Note: you are moving from a dot to the tip of a line, right, left, right, left; or clockwise, counter-clockwise, clockwise, counter-clockwise.)

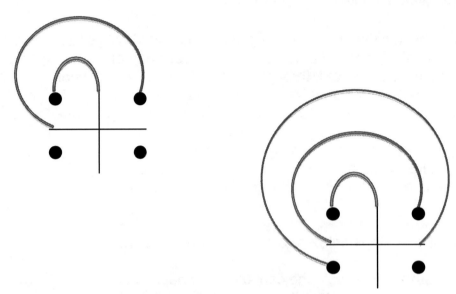

When you finish, you should have a simple labyrinth.

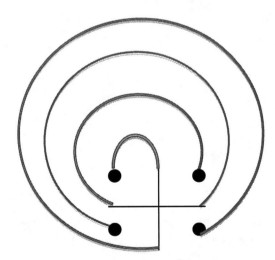

Once you have designed your labyrinth, try it. Use a different colored pen or pencil to trace how you would enter and exit your labyrinth. If you have drawn it correctly, you'll see that there is only one way in and one way out.

You can find directions for creating more intricate labyrinths online. You can also find photos of real labyrinths.

Directions for Playing The Hunger Games Board Game

You'll be playing a board game version of The Hunger Games. You'll need a large piece of construction paper for your game board. Turn your construction paper so it lies horizontally. In the center of the board, draw a large labyrinth. This will be your game board, so make sure it is large enough for game markers.

Divide your labyrinth into sections, creating a pathway; the game pieces will move along the pathway into the center of the labyrinth. You should have at least twenty-five sections; number each section on the path, in order.

On the left side of the page in the space to the left of your labyrinth, draw a cornucopia. If you are unsure what a cornucopia looks like, you may want to check in a dictionary or online.

Prior to playing, cut out the Event Cards and the Skill Cards and separate them into two piles.

Choose a game piece or marker for each player. You may want to create your own "totem" marker.

How to play:

You will need one die.

You will be playing with four or fewer players.

Shuffle the Skill Cards and deal each player three cards. Place the remaining Skill Cards in a pile on the "Cornucopia." Look over your own Skill Cards, but don't show them to other players.

Shuffle the Event Cards and place them face down in a pile on the right side of the labyrinth. Each player will draw an Event Card at each turn.

Roll the die to determine who goes first. The player who rolls the lowest number goes first. Play continues counter-clockwise around the board.

Roll the die and move your marker a matching number of spaces. If you land on an even numbered square, pick up a Skill Card from the Cornucopia. Choose an Event Card, and read it aloud. If you have a Skill Card that will allow you to survive the event, read your Skill Card to the rest of the players and place it face down under the pile of Cornucopia cards. Place your Event Card face down in a discard pile on the right side of the labyrinth.

If you do not have a Skill Card that will allow you to survive the event, you have two choices. You can form an alliance with another player (or players) who will give you a Skill Card so you can survive the event, or you lose a turn. If you lose a turn, keep your Event Card until your next turn. At your next turn, discard your Event Card. That is your turn. You do not roll the die or take a Skill Card.

If there is a question about the use of a Skill Card, explain your reasoning. The majority of the players must agree that the Skill Card will save you from an event.

The next player takes his/her turn by rolling the die and proceeding to the numbered space. Follow the directions on the Event Card.

If the Event Card indicates that other players are affected by the event, they must use a Skill Card. If they do not have a Skill Card, they will lose a turn.

Hints to playing:

Think creatively. You may have a Skill Card that can help you during an event. For example, if a wild animal is attacking you, several Skill Cards can help you avoid losing a turn. Be able to explain to the rest of the players how that skill will help you escape losing a turn.

The Charisma Skill Card allows you to take a Skill Card from any other player. Once you've used your Charisma Card, you must return it to the Cornucopia. You can ask ONE player for a card that will help you. The other player cannot lie and must hand over the Skill Card if he or she has it.

Alliances can be made and broken at any time. You can form and dissolve alliances with one or more players.

Once you have used a Skill Card, it must be discarded.

To Win:

The first player to the center of the labyrinth who can survive the Event Card is the winner. If a player reaches the center and cannot survive the Event Card, the player will remain in the center and continue to play.

Name _____ **Period** _____

Teacher Notes for Playing the Hunger Games Board Game

Students will be creating their own game boards. You may want to allow part of a class period for students to design the game board and totems (markers). Larger game boards could be created on poster board.

There are blank Skill Cards and Event Cards. Students may wish to add new events or skills.

You may want to duplicate the Skill Cards and Event Cards on two different colors of paper or possibly cardstock.

Each group of students should have a list of the game rules.

Each group will need one die.

This is a quick game. If students create more intricate labyrinths, the game will last longer.

Name _____ **Period** _____

Skill Cards

Skill Card You are good with a bow and arrow.	**Skill Card** You are accurate when throwing things.
Skill Card You have charisma! This card allows you to take a Skill Card from any other player.	**Skill Card** You have the ability to sleep safely in a dangerous environment.
Skill Card You have excellent hearing.	**Skill Card** You are healthy.
Skill Card You are able to find shelter.	**Skill Card** You are alert to your surroundings.
Skill Card You can extinguish fires.	**Skill Card** You are good at making booby traps.

Name _____ **Period** _____

Skill Cards

Skill Card You can find water.	**Skill Card** You are skilled at setting snares for small animals.
Skill Card You are able to forage for food and water in a hostile environment.	**Skill Card** You know how to make a fire.
Skill Card You are agile.	**Skill Card** You have physical strength.
Skill Card You are good with explosives.	**Skill Card** You are good at climbing trees.
Skill Card You are skilled in camouflage.	**Skill Card** You are a fast runner.

Name _____ **Period** _____

Skill Cards

Skill Card You can find water.	**Skill Card** You know the edible plants of the forest.
Skill Card You know how to make a safe, dry shelter.	**Skill Card** You know how to make a fire.
Skill Card You can navigate by using the stars.	**Skill Card** You are a healer. You can heal yourself and others.
Skill Card You have a gas mask.	**Skill Card** You know how to make a ladder out of simple things you find around you.
Skill Card You can imitate bird songs.	**Skill Card** You have the ability to walk silently and softly.

Name _____ Period _____

Blank Skill Cards—neatly write out other essential skills on the cards below.

Skill Card	**Skill Card**
Skill Card	**Skill Card**
Skill Card	**Skill Card**
Skill Card	**Skill Card**
Skill Card	**Skill Card**

Name _____ Period _____

Event Cards

Event Card	Event Card
You need water.	Pick a Skill Card from the Cornucopia or any other player.
Event Card You are in a fire. Any other players on the same space on the board with you are in the fire, too. You must each use a Skill Card or lose a turn.	**Event Card** Silver parachute! You've received a gift from your sponsors. Take another turn.
Event Card The stream dries up. You need water.	**Event Card** A wild animal attacks. Any other players on the same space with you are affected. You must each use a Skill Card or lose a turn.
Event Card Sleeping gas. All players on the same space with you are affected.	**Event Card** Tracker jacker attack. Any player behind you on the board is affected.
Event Card Lay a trap for another player. Take a Skill Card from any other player, unless they have a booby trap card.	**Event Card** Explosion causes deafness. What will you do?

Event Cards

Event Card The Careers are chasing you. How can you get away?	**Event Card** It's a cold night. All players must use a Skill Card to survive.
Event Card You haven't eaten in three days. You need food!	**Event Card** Silver parachute! You've received a gift from your sponsors. Take another turn.
Event Card You've found berries. Are they safe to eat?	**Event Card** You have been injured by a fall. Your wounds are getting infected.
Event Card There is a landslide and you're trapped under some rocks.	**Event Card** A Career has jumped out of a copse of trees and is about to attack you.
Event Card Wild boars come charging through the forest at you. Any player *behind* you on the board is affected and will need to use a Skill Card to escape.	**Event Card** The Careers have built a fortress. You must destroy it or get inside of it.

Event Cards

Event Card The Careers are planning another attack. Can you figure out what they are planning?	**Event Card** You have eaten poisoned berries. You need help!
Event Card You haven't eaten in three days. You need food!	**Event Card** A mockingjay gives away your position to the Careers.
Event Card You've fallen into a trap. How can you get out before someone finds you?	**Event Card** You haven't been able to sleep because you are afraid of letting down your guard. You must get sleep!
Event Card You've caught a rabbit, but it isn't safe to eat it raw.	**Event Card** You've decided to climb to the top of a hill to see where the other tributes are. You are getting tired and weak.
Event Card The Careers have raided your camp. Give one Skill Card to the player sitting to your right.	**Event Card** You decide to spy on the Careers at night, but you have no night-vision glasses.

Name _____   Period _____

Event Cards

Event Card You get too close to a mockingjay nest. The birds attack you. Any player sharing the space on the game board is also affected.	**Event Card** You've wandered into an area of the forest you're unfamiliar with. You're lost.
Event Card You haven't eaten in three days. You need food!	**Event Card** A dust storm hits. It's difficult to see and breathe. Any player on an even numbered space is affected by the storm.
Event Card You venture into the flat plains of the arena in search of supplies. You are out in the open and visible to the Careers.	**Event Card** If you are in an alliance, all players in the alliance can draw a Skill Card.
Event Card You have decided to spy on the Careers, and they discover you.	**Event Card** You have captured another tribute. Take all of one other player's Skill Cards.
Event Card The Careers have raided your camp. Give one Skill Card to the player sitting to your left. Any players sharing the space on the board with you must do the same.	**Event Card** You've walked into a minefield. Can you get out without setting off a mine?

Name _____ **Period** _____

Blank Event Cards—neatly write your own events on the cards below.

Event Card	Event Card
Event Card	**Event Card**
Event Card	**Event Card**
Event Card	**Event Card**
Event Card	**Event Card**

Name _____ Period _____

The Hunger Games

Part Three: Chapters Nineteen – Twenty
Note-Taking and Summarizing: Chapters Nineteen-Twenty

Directions: For Chapters 19 – 20, fill in the chart with the necessary information. If you need more room, use an additional sheet of paper.

Main Events of the Chapters	
Characters	
Setting	
Primary Conflict	
Thoughts, Feelings or Predictions	
Thematic Issues Being Raised	

The Hunger Games

Part Three: Chapters Nineteen – Twenty
Comprehension Check

Directions: *To help you understand all aspects of the novel, answer the following questions for Chapters Nineteen – Twenty. Write your answers on a separate piece of paper using complete sentences.*

Update your Character Map from Chapters 15 –16 with any new information about the tributes.

Chapter 19

1. Where does Katniss find Peeta. How did he avoid being found by the other tributes?

2. What is Peeta's condition when Katniss finds him?

3. Why is it surprising that Katniss is squeamish about Peeta's wounds and caring for him?

4. What is Katniss's motivation to find Peeta and keep him alive?

5. What is the relationship between Katniss kissing Peeta and the silver parachute?

Chapter 20

1. What does Katniss expect to find at the feast?

2. How does Katniss make sure she's able to go to the feast?

3. What will happen if Peeta doesn't get medicine?

4. Why is the day Katniss got the goat for Prim a happy memory?

5. Why do you think the sponsors didn't just send medicine for Peeta?

6. Do you agree with Katniss's actions toward Peeta? Why or why not?

The Hunger Games

Part Two: Chapters Nineteen – Twenty
Standards Focus: Inner Thoughts

Part I: As you learned from the Standard Focus activity for Chapters 11 – 12, *The Hunger Games* is written in the first person point of view. This point of view allows the reader to know the protagonist's thoughts and feelings.

At the beginning of Chapter 19, how does the reader know Katniss is talking to herself?

> **The *protagonist* is the main character of the story. The *antagonist* is the rival in the story.**

The typeset of the novel doesn't always tell the reader when Katniss is thinking. Look over the first page of Chapter 19. What are some of Katniss's thoughts? How do you know they are her thoughts? Complete the chart below. Some of the answers have been started for you.

Katniss's thoughts	Proof that they are thoughts
"Whatever doubts I've had about him dissipate because if either of us took the other's life now we'd be pariahs when we returned to District 12."	*Katniss uses the first person pronoun "I." She is also imagining what life would be like back in District 12.*
Peeta has been playing the star-crossed lover role all along.	
"For two tributes to have a shot at winning, our 'romance' must be so popular with the audience that condemning it would jeopardize the success of the Games."	
	She uses the "I" pronoun as she reflects on what she hasn't done.

A character's inner thoughts can also tell the reader what the character is struggling with. Katniss doesn't want to reveal her problems to Peeta or the audience, yet the reader knows what Katniss is thinking and feeling.

1. What are some of the other inner thoughts and problems Katniss struggles with in these two chapters? List some of them on the lines below. _____

_____

_____

_____

2. What doesn't Katniss want Peeta to know about her inner thoughts? _____

_____

_____

3. What doesn't Katniss want the audience watching the Games to know about her inner thoughts? _____

_____

_____

4. As a reader, how does knowing what Katniss is thinking affect the way you feel about her and the situation she's in? _____

_____

_____

5. In these two chapters, what have you learned about Katniss from her inner thoughts? _____

_____

_____

6. Just like the rest of us, Katniss has thoughts that she thinks are true, but they may not be. Are all of Katniss's inner thoughts accurate? Explain your answer.

_____

_____

_____

_____

Name _____ **Period** _____

7. Based on what you know, what kinds of inner thoughts might Peeta be having? What are the thoughts he wants to keep Katniss from knowing? Explain your answer. _____

_____

_____

_____

_____

Part II: Thought Bubbles

Choose one of the inner thoughts Katniss has after she's found Peeta. Draw a cartoon of Katniss with a thought bubble coming from her mind. In the same panel, draw Peeta with his own thought bubble. Draw your cartoon illustrations in the space below.

Part III: Behind the Scenes with Haymitch

Of course, Katniss and Peeta aren't the only characters who have inner thoughts. What might Haymitch's inner thoughts be about the situation Katniss and Peeta are in? Write a diary entry for Haymitch; (a diary is the ultimate place to record inner thoughts – that's why it has a lock and key!). Be sure to include details that explain to the reader exactly what Haymitch is concerned about and why. _____

_____

_____

_____

_____

_____

_____

_____

Name _____   Period _____

The Hunger Games

Part Two: Chapters Nineteen – Twenty
Assessment Preparation: "Showing Not Telling"

Remember "show and tell" from your kindergarten days? If you participated in "show and tell," write a paragraph on a separate sheet of paper, telling about something you brought in to show and why it was important to you.

If you never participated in "show and tell" in school, think back to your younger years. What was a favorite toy or possession of yours? Why was it important? Write a paragraph on a separate sheet of paper, telling about that item and why it was important.

If you stood in front of your kindergarten class sharing a favorite toy and telling about it, you probably didn't need to do much explaining. Once we see an object, most of us understand it. However, when you're writing, especially when you're writing about something more complex than a favorite toy, you'll need much more of an explanation.

You may have heard your English teacher tell you to "show *not* tell" when you're writing. What do you think that means? Write your thoughts in the space below.

_____

_____

_____

Showing rather than telling means that as a writer you are going to *describe* and *explain*. You are going to *narrow your topic* so it is manageable. You are going to include *vivid details* and *sensory language* so your reader will understand exactly what you mean. You might even use *figures of speech* like metaphors and similes. The idea is to *create a clear picture* in the reader's mind through your writing.

Part I: Analyzing "Showing" Writing

Directions: Use the following passage to analyze the elements of "showing." Some of the chart has been filled in for you.

"This, of course, brings on a scowl that makes him grin. That's when I notice how dry his lips are. I test his cheek. Hot as a coal stove. He claims he's been drinking, but the containers still feel full to me. I give him more fever pills and stand over him while he drinks first one, then a second quart of water. Then I tend to his minor wounds, the burns, the stings, which are showing improvement. I steel myself and unwrap the leg." (265)

Name _____ **Period** _____

Words that describe or explain:	The narrowed topic is:	Vivid details include:	Sensory language includes:	Figures of speech:
Scowl, dry lips, test his cheek, I give him more fever pills, he drinks one and then a second quart, I tend to his minor wounds, I steel myself and unwrap…	*Katniss is checking on Peeta after she's been asleep.*			
Why is this passage a good example of "showing" writing?				

"The sun burns off the morning haze almost immediately and I can tell the day will be hotter than usual. The water's cool and pleasant on my bare feet as I head downstream. I'm tempted to call out Peeta's name as I go but decide against it. I will have to find him with my eyes and one good ear or he will have to find me." (250)

Words that describe or explain:	The narrowed topic is:	Vivid details include:	Sensory language includes:	Figures of speech:
Why is this passage a good example of "showing" writing?				

Name _____ Period _____

Part II: Identify "showing" writing. Go back to Chapter 19 or 20. Skim through the chapters looking for a passage that you think is a good example of writing that "shows." Write your passage on the lines below and use the chart to analyze your passage. (*Hint:* Look for a passage of description rather than dialogue.)_____

_____

_____

_____

_____

_____

Words that describe or explain:	The narrowed topic is:	Vivid details include:	Sensory language includes:	Figures of speech:

Why is this passage a good example of "showing" writing?

The Hunger Games

Part Three: Chapters Twenty-One – Twenty-Two
Note-Taking and Summarizing: Chapter Twenty-One – Twenty-Two

Directions: For Chapters 21 – 22, fill in the chart with the necessary information. If you need more room, use an additional sheet of paper.

Main Events of the Chapters	
Characters	
Setting	
Primary Conflict	
Thoughts, Feelings or Predictions	
Thematic Issues Being Raised	

The Hunger Games

Part Three: Chapters Twenty-One – Twenty-Two
Comprehension Check

Directions: *To help you understand all aspects of the novel, answer the following questions for Chapters Twenty-One – Twenty-Two. Write your answers on a separate piece of paper using complete sentences.*

Update your Character Map from Chapters 15 – 16 with any new information about the tributes.

Chapter 21

1. List the events that took place at the feast.

2. Why might a tribute take someone else's backpack?

3. Why doesn't Thresh kill Katniss?

4. Why does Katniss think Cato will chase after Thresh instead of her?

5. What is in the backpack for District 12? Is it helpful?

6. What facts might Katniss use to justify why it was a good idea to go to the feast?

Chapter 22

1. How do Katniss and Peeta manage to receive a silver parachute full of lamb stew?

2. What conclusions can you draw about Thresh's behavior toward Katniss?

3. How does the weather affect the way Katniss and Peeta interact?

4. Explain what Katniss means in the following quote:

   "I wish I could pull the shutters closed, blocking out this moment
   from the prying eyes of Panem. Even if it means losing food.
   Whatever I'm feeling, it's no one's business but mine" (298).

5. Do you agree with Katniss's thoughts about her feelings? Explain your answer.

6. Now that Peeta is feeling better, construct a list of things Peeta and Katniss must do next. Beyond the obvious, win the Games, what else must they do?

The Hunger Games

Part Three: Chapters Twenty-One – Twenty-Two
Standards Focus: Dialogue

Try an experiment. The next time you're sitting at lunch, on the bus, or in the classroom where people are talking, do some eavesdropping.

If you can, write the conversation down. You'll probably find, if you can write fast enough, that conversations often contain words that don't add much to our understanding. You might record a conversation that sounds like this:

> *"Did you hear what Sharon told Mr. Clark?"*
> *"Yeah."*
> *"She has some nerve."*
> *"Yeah."*

The term "eavesdropping" probably came into our language *literally* – that is, someone standing at the eaves "the overhang of a roof" listening in on a conversation.

It's not that our conversations are boring. We all have lively, funny, energetic conversations, but if we were to write down each word, many of our conversations would sound dull and repetitive.

When an author uses conversation or dialogue in writing, the author wants to create interesting, lively conversation that will keep the reader reading. If the author included every "um" or "yeah" in a conversation, you might put the book down and never go back to it.

In general, you'll find that good dialogue in a novel does a several important things:

1. It should help advance the plot. In other words, the dialogue isn't going to be about the weather unless that will provide new information about the plot.

2. It needs to be consistent with the character who is speaking. If a character is from the South, it would be appropriate to have a southern accent. If a character is highly educated, the character might use sophisticated vocabulary.

3. It should sound natural.

4. It allows for a give and take – like a real conversation. One character might talk for a long time, but someone may interrupt or ask questions.

5. It varies in sentence length and phrases. You'll find dialogue doesn't follow the rules of grammar. There may be partial sentences or even just single words in dialogue.

6. It breaks up the exposition. The exposition is the explanation of the novel. Too much exposition, and the novel could get boring.

Name _____ **Period** _____

Part I: Analyzing dialogue

Directions*: Using the six statements of what dialogue should do, review the passage below. Does the passage fulfill the six statements? Use the following table to help you decide. Check the appropriate box and add support for your belief. You may want to go back to the original passage to see what was omitted. The ellipsis shows where the omission takes place. Some of the answers have been started for you.*

> "What'd she mean? About Rue being your ally?"
>
> "I – I – we teamed up. Blew up the supplies. I tried to save her, I did. But he got there first. District One," I say…
>
> "And you killed him?" he demands.
>
> "Yes. I killed him. And buried her in flowers," I say. "And I sang her to sleep"…
>
> "To sleep?" Thresh says gruffly.
>
> "To death. I sang until she died," I say. "Your district… they sent me bread"…
>
> "Just this one time, I let you go. For the little girl. You and me, we're even then. No more owed. You understand?" (287 – 288)

Statement	Yes	No	My reason for believing this is…
It advances the plot.	X		*It tells us that Thresh gives Katniss a chance. He's letting her get away because of what she did for Rue.*
It sounds like the speaker.			
It sounds natural.			
It has give and take.			
It varies in sentence length.			
It breaks up the exposition.			
Anything else you notice about the dialogue? *Thresh sounds like he might not be well educated. He doesn't talk a lot. He uses short, choppy sentences.*			

"Peeta," I say lightly. "You said at the interview you'd had a crush on me forever. When did forever start?"

"Oh, let's see. I guess the first day of school. We were five. You had on a red plaid dress and your hair…it was two braids instead of one. My father pointed you out when we were waiting to line up," Peeta says.

"Your father? Why?" I ask.

"He said, 'See that little girl? I wanted to marry her mother, but she ran off with a coal miner,'" Peeta says.

"What? You're making that up!" I exclaim.

"No, true story," Peeta says. "And I said, 'A coal miner? Why did she want a coal miner if she could've had you?' And he said, 'Because when he sings … even the birds stop to listen.'" (300)

Statement	Yes	No	My reason for believing this is…
It advances the plot.			
It sounds like the speaker.			
It sounds natural.			
It has give and take.			
It varies in sentence length.			
It breaks up the exposition.			
Anything else you notice about the dialogue?			

Part II: Choose another portion of dialogue from the text and analyze it. Use the chart below. Write your sample dialogue here._____

_____

_____

_____

Name _____ Period _____

Statement	Yes	No	My reason for believing this is...
It advances the plot.			
It sounds like the speaker.			
It sounds natural.			
It has give and take.			
It varies in sentence length.			
It breaks up the exposition.			
Anything else you notice about the dialogue?			

Part III: Punctuating Dialogue

What do you notice about the way dialogue is punctuated? How are the quotation marks used?

Directions: *Using the following dialogue, mark the correct punctuation. You may want to make your marks in another color of ink, so it will be easier to see.*

Are you going to eat that last donut? Hugh asked.

I was thinking about it, said Ralphie as he rubbed his stomach. Powdered sugar donuts are my favorite.

Well, I only had one donut today, Hugh said. And yesterday I heard your mom say, Ralphie, you eat too many donuts. So I think it's only fair that you should let me have that last one.

Okay, Ralphie said, you're right. I need to cut down. Go ahead and help yourself. After all, I did eat the other eleven.

Name _____ Period _____

The Hunger Games

Part Three: Chapters Twenty-One – Twenty-Two
Assessment Preparation: The Silver Parachute – Using Well-Chosen Details

In the Assessment Preparation activity for Chapters 19 – 20, you examined "showing not telling" in writing. Review those pages paying attention to the elements a writer should include when writing a piece that "shows." List those ideas on the lines below.

_____   _____

_____   _____

_____   _____

Part I: Compose your own "showing" writing example

1. Go back to the "show and tell" experience you wrote about at the beginning of the Chapter 19 – 20 Assessment Preparation. Revise your writing by using the elements of descriptive writing: a narrowed topic, description/explanation, vivid details, sensory language, and figures of speech.

2. After you have completed your writing, use different colored pencils to underline each of the writing techniques. Create a key that matches the colors and the writing techniques.

Part II: Focus on using well-chosen details

Have you ever had to answer an essay question on a test? Often the teacher will ask for details, details, and more details! The details prove that you know the material. Anyone can write, "The war was terrible." Being able to support that statement with details like facts and examples proves that you know what you're writing about.

In Chapter 14, Katniss receives her first silver parachute.
   "Sitting on my sleeping bag is a small plastic pot attached to a silver parachute….The pot easily fits in the palm of my hand. What can it be? Not food surely. I unscrew the lid and I know by the scent that it's medicine. Cautiously, I probe the surface of the ointment" (188).

The details from this passage help you know what type of container the ointment is in, how big the container is, and what its contents smell like.

Directions: *1. Using a highlighter or colored pencil, underline well-chosen details that prove the gift in the silver parachute could be something real. 2. There are three other incidents of Katniss receiving a silver parachute. Choose one other incident and write the page number in the space below. Then describe what Katniss receives in the parachute and the details that make the parachute and its contents real. Write your answers on the lines on the next page.*

Name _____ Period _____

_____

_____

_____

_____

Part III: Your own silver parachute

Imagine you are sitting in English class and a silver parachute comes floating down to your desk. What is in it? What does it look like?

Directions: *On a separate sheet of paper, use well-chosen details to write a descriptive paragraph about your parachute.*

Part IV: A "silver parachute" conversation

How would your classmates and teacher react to your silver parachute gift?

Directions: *Following the example of the Standards Focus activity for these chapters, write a piece of original dialogue that describes (don't forget the well-chosen details) your class's reactions to your parachute. Include at least five vocabulary words that are listed at the bottom of this activity in your dialogue. You may want to include an illustration with your dialogue. If you teacher allows, duplicate your dialogue for your classmates to read aloud to the rest of the class.*

Part V: Using vocabulary in context

Directions: *On a separate sheet of paper, using the words you did not use in your dialogue, write an original sentence for each word. Include a detailed context clue in the sentence that shows you understand the meaning of the word. You may change the form of the word to fit into your sentence. Underline or highlight your context clue(s). The first one has been done for you.*

1. arduous: The arduous task of mowing the lawn was made even more <u>difficult</u> by the three-foot growth of weeds.

2. asset

3. infusion

4. emanating

5. irreparable

6. ominous

7. staunch

8. vaguely

9. plaintively

10. famished

11. irreverent

12. tirades

13. exorbitant

14. exasperated

Name _____ Period _____

The Hunger Games

Part Three: Chapters Twenty-Three – Twenty-Four
Note-Taking and Summarizing: Chapters Twenty-Three – Twenty-Four

Directions: For Chapters 23 – 24, fill in the chart with the necessary information. If you need more room, use an additional sheet of paper.

Main Events of the Chapters	
Characters	
Setting	
Primary Conflict	
Thoughts, Feelings or Predictions	
Thematic Issues Being Raised	

The Hunger Games

Part Three: Chapters Twenty-Three – Twenty-Four
Comprehension Check

Directions: *To help you understand all aspects of the novel, answer the following questions for Chapters Twenty-Three – Twenty-Four. Write your answers on a separate piece of paper using complete sentences.*

Update your Character Map from Chapters 15 –16 with any new information about the tributes.

Chapter 23

1. What problem does Peeta cause when they go hunting?

2. How does Foxface die?

3. What other ways might Peeta have been useful to Katniss during the hunt?

4. Was Katniss's anger at Peeta for not whistling justified? Explain your answer.

5. What conclusions can you draw about Foxface's behavior in eating the berries?

6. Explain Katniss's statement "No, Peeta, she's your kill not Cato's."

7. What does Foxface's death now mean to Peeta and Katniss?

Chapter 24

1. Why does Katniss save some of the poison berries?

2. What is the significance of the stream drying up?

3. Why does Katniss decide they should eat most of their food and not save it?

4. While Peeta is sleeping, Katniss thinks about Cato. Why does she think she understands him? Explain your answer.

5. How does not knowing where Cato is or what has happened to him increase the tension of this chapter?

6. How is Cato's behavior at the end of the chapter surprising?

The Hunger Games

Part Three: Chapters Twenty-Three – Twenty-Four
Standards Focus: Foreshadowing

Have you ever said, "I'm not surprise that happened" or "I knew that was going to happen" about a classmate or family member? Sometimes we make those predictions about positive events, like someone winning an award or being elected for something. Other times, those predictions might be negative like someone losing their car keys again or forgetting their homework.

We don't make predictions arbitrarily. We don't expect Aunt Frieda to lose her keys unless she's forgetful about other things. We'd be surprised it the smartest student in the class didn't study for the algebra test. Our expectations of how we expect people to act are based on their past behavior.

The same is true in the fictional world. The characters' actions, behaviors, successes and failures are generally consistent. In *The Three Little Pigs*, we'd be suspicious of the wolf if suddenly, at the end of the story, he decided he wanted to befriend the pigs!

Authors use the technique of *foreshadowing* to prepare the reader for something that is going to happen later in the book. Often we don't realize something has been foreshadowed until we finish the book. Then, as we think about what we've read, we may start to see the connections.

In *The Hunger Games,* were there any events that made you think, "I'm not surprised that happened"? Jot those events down. _____

_____

_____

_____

Share your ideas with a classmate.

Foreshadowing takes place when the author gives the reader hints about what's to come later in the book. Why might the writer do this? _____

_____

_____

_____

Name _____   Period _____

Part I: Analyzing Foreshadowing

Directions: *Review the following quotes from Chapter 7 as they relate to Peeta. What are they foreshadowing? Why are they important to the events that occur later in the novel? Some answers have been done for you.*

Foreshadowing	What does this foreshadow?	Why is it important later in the novel?
"You can lift hundred-pound bags of flour." (90)	*That Peeta is strong enough to endure a deadly wound. He's physically strong enough to fight the Careers.*	*He has to fight Cato. He also has to hide himself after he's wounded.*
"He can wrestle," I tell Haymitch. "He came in second in our school competition last year, only after his brother." (90)		
"Peeta, she's right, never underestimate strength in the arena. Very often, physical power tilts the advantage to a player." (91- 92)		
"I hear Peeta's voice in my head. She has no idea. The effect she can have. Obviously meant to demean me. Right? But a tiny part of me wonders if this was a compliment. That he meant I was appealing in some way. It's weird, how much he's noticed me. Like the attention he's paid to my hunting." (93)		
"Then we move on to camouflage. Peeta genuinely seems to enjoy this station, swirling a combination of mud and clay and berry juices around on his pale skin, weaving disguises from vines and leaves." (95)		

"We do pick up some valuable skills, from starting fires, to knife throwing, to making shelter." (96)		
"Despite Hamitch's order to appear mediocre, Peeta excels in hand-to-hand combat." (96)		
"One day, Peeta empties our breadbasket and points out how they have been careful to include types from the districts along with the refined bread of the Capitol." (97)		

What does foreshadowing do to help the reader understand Rue? Analyze the following quotes.

Foreshadowing	What does this foreshadow?	Why is it important later in the novel?
"Rue is a small yellow flower that grows in the Meadow. Rue. Primrose. Neither of them could tip the scale at seventy pounds soaking wet." (99)	*This foreshadows the relationship between Rue and Katniss.*	
"Like me, she's clever with plants, climbs swiftly, and has good aim. She can hit the target every time with a slingshot. But what is a slingshot against a 220-pound male with a sword?" (99)		
"At Rue's suggestion, we lay out all our food to plan ahead....I roll an unfamiliar berry in my fingers. 'You sure this is safe?'" (203)		

Name _____ Period _____

What evidence from the text can you find that supports foreshadowing about Katniss? Using the page numbers and clues in the second and third columns, identify the foreshadowing. Copy the text in the Foreshadowing box.

Foreshadowing	What does this foreshadow?	Why is it important later in the novel?
Page 24	*This is foreshadowing how Katniss says good-bye to Rue.*	*It is important because it explains the meaning of the symbol and why it is so powerful to the people of District 12.*
Page 32	*This is foreshadowing Katniss's mixed feelings about Peeta and her understanding of Thresh.*	
Page 51		*It is important because that is how Katniss keeps Peeta from eating something poisonous. She protects them both by making sure they don't eat something that looks safe but isn't.*
Page 89	*This foreshadows how good an aim Katniss is.*	
Page 90	*This foreshadows the determination and skill Katniss shows in the arena.*	

Page 91	*This foreshadows Peeta's feelings about Katniss and how oblivious she is to them.*	
Page 96		*It's important because they could easily mistake the berries for edible ones.*
Page 101	*This foreshadows Katniss as she blows up the Career's supplies.*	

Part II: *Now that you've analyzed foreshadowing in the novel, evaluate its importance.*

1. How does foreshadowing make the story more believable? Give an example.

_____

_____

_____

2. Which events of foreshadowing did you think were the most important in helping you understand the plot? _____

_____

_____

_____

3. As you review the chart, compare and contrast the foreshadowing information about Peeta and Katniss. What do you think Suzanne Collins thought was important to foreshadow about Katniss? _____

_____

_____

_____

_____

4. What do you think Suzanne Collins thought was important to foreshadow about Peeta? _____

_____

_____

_____

Name _____   Period _____

The Hunger Games

Part Three: Chapters Twenty-Three – Twenty-Four
Standards Focus: The Climax

When you came to the end of Chapter 24, did you close the book or did you continue reading? If you haven't already finished reading the book, at this point in the novel, you may have difficulty putting the book down. There's a good reason for that! If an author has done his or her job in writing a novel, the reader should be so involved in the story, characters, and conflict that the ending of the book is compelling – you have to finish the book.

You've probably seen Freytag's pyramid or a variation of it. It is a plot outline. The peak or highest point of the pyramid represents the *climax*. Sometimes it is also called the *turning point.*

The climax can be described as the most exciting point in the plot, but if you think of climax as a turning point, it might be easier for you to understand the Freytag pyramid. As a turning point, the climax moves from the most exciting point in the plot to *falling action.* That is, after the climax occurs, the primary problem, conflict, and tension of the plot are resolved.

> Gustav Freytag (1816 – 1895) was a German novelist who wrote realistic fiction. He developed a pyramid-shaped diagram for the common structure he noticed in a five-act play. His pyramid is often modified from its original structure.

In most novels, the plot rises and falls as it moves toward the climax. There are small crises, events, or dramas that occur along the way, but the final climax of the story usually happens at or near the end.

For a very simple example, think about the story of the three little pigs. There are small peaks and dips in the plot as one pig after another loses his home to the big, bad wolf. Finally, in the brick house, the pigs are safe … until the wolf comes down the chimney. Once the clever pigs build a fire, they are safe. Where is the climax? It's when the pigs build the fire and the wolf flees. That's the final turning point in the tale. The reader knows the pigs have outsmarted the wolf and the story is over.

Directions: *Using the details about the three little pigs, fill in a plot diagram below. Some of the events have been started for you.*

Notice that the plot continues to move upward even after the first crisis is over. That is because the wolf is still in the story; the initial problem of a hungry wolf in search of a pork dinner has not been resolved. Since the wolf is still in the story, the climax continues to build.

Can you guess what the climax of *The Hunger Games* will be?

Directions*: Using the three little pigs plot diagram as an example, create your own plot diagram. Use the list of statements below to help you create your plot. Choose at least seven statements to include on your diagram.*

> **Hints & suggestions:** You may want to turn your paper horizontally in order to have enough room. If you prefer, you can also create icons and a key rather than writing out each statement on your plot diagram. You may also want to illustrate your plot diagram or color it. (Remember, the final climax of the story has not yet occurred.)

Choose from the following plot events as you create your diagram:

- Prim's name is drawn from the reaping.
- Katniss takes Prim's place.
- Katniss and Peeta arrive at the Capitol.
- Katniss loses her temper and shoots the apple from the pig's mouth.
- In the arena, Katniss runs for a backpack and almost gets stabbed.
- Katniss cannot find water.
- Katniss learns that Peeta has made an alliance with the Careers.
- The forest is on fire.
- The tracker jackers are attacking.
- Katniss blows up the Careers' supplies.
- Rue is shot.
- Two tributes can now win the Games.
- Peeta is close to death.
- Katniss must go to the feast.
- Clove has Katniss pinned down and is going to kill her.
- Thresh saves Katniss.
- Foxface eats the poison berries.
- Katniss and Peeta go to the lake.
- Cato comes running toward them, but something is chasing him.

Part II: Analyze your diagram *Answer the following questions on a separate sheet of paper.*

1. Look over your diagram. Why did you choose the plot elements you chose?

2. In spite of resolutions of small problems (for example, Katniss finding water), the tension in the novel continues to increase. Why is that?

3. How do the Gamemakers contribute to the tension and climax of the story?

4. How does the rising action of the story contribute to your enjoyment of the novel?

The Hunger Games

Part Three: Chapters Twenty-Three – Twenty-Four
Assessment Preparation: Inferring

In the Assessment Preparation for Chapters 15 – 16, you wrote text messages from Katniss. As you learned, we adjust how we write to different audiences.

Today, we have a form of social media that is available to everyone and offers nearly instant information – Twitter. If you're not familiar with Twitter, it's a computer program that allows people to communicate with each other using short pieces of information called "tweets." It's a bit like texting, but it can reach a wider audience and be read on a computer or a phone. People can subscribe to follow someone's tweets, so tweeting is more public than just a text to a friend.

The title of this assessment preparation activity is "Inferring." You may be wondering what inferring and tweeting have to do with each other. As you probably know, inferring or making inferences means drawing conclusions based on what you read, see, hear, or experience. Rather than someone explaining something to you, when you infer, you draw your own conclusions.

For this activity, you'll be drawing inferences based on how different characters see the story as it develops. Instead of quoting directly from the novel, you'll take what you've already read and know about the plot and the characters and develop a twitter conversation.

Part I: Create your own tweets

Directions: *Use the note-taking activity or the comprehension check questions that you completed for the different chapters of the novel to help you review the events of the chapters. You'll be writing a series of ten tweets. You can write from any character's point of view except Katniss's. Your tweets can only be 140 characters, and they are "public" which means anyone can read them. Your teacher may allow you to work with a partner.*

Think about the conflicts, feelings, concerns, and plans the characters have. As you write your tweet from the point of view of a character, infer how that character thinks or feels. What would that character tweet about? You'll have to infer because the only person we really know is Katniss because she's telling the story.

Use the first tweet as an example. A few examples have been started for you. Notice it begins by giving the name of the person (screen name) who is writing the tweet. Can you connect your tweets by having one respond to another as the book progresses?

Name _____ Period _____

Characters who might tweet:

Peeta

Prim

Mrs. Everdeen

Mr. Mellark

Gale

Effie Trinket

Greasy Sae

Mayor Undersee

Haymitch

Cinna

The Avox

President Snow

Caesar Flickerman

Citizens of the Capitol

The Gamemakers

Rue

Cato

Clove

Thresh

Foxface

Examples: Chapters 1 – 2: Mayor Undersee

District 12 is proud of tributes Katniss Everdeen and Peeta Mellark. Katniss surprised us all by taking her little sister's place.

Chapters 3 – 4: Gale in the Seam

Proud? How can we be proud sending her to the arena? I promise to care for her family. I swear I will. Will Haymitch be any help?

Chapters 5 – 6:

_____

_____

Chapters 7 – 9:

_____

_____

Chapter 10:

_____

_____

Chapters 11 – 12:

_____

_____

Chapters 13 – 14:

_____

_____

Chapters 15 – 16:

_____

_____

Name _____ **Period** _____

Chapters 17 – 18:

_____

_____

Chapters 19 – 20:

_____

_____

Chapters 21 – 22:

_____

_____

Chapters 23 – 24:

_____

_____

Part II: Vocabulary
Directions*: Write the meaning and the part of speech of the vocabulary word in the sentences below. Highlight any context clues that help you determine the meaning of the word. The first one has been done for you.*

There are eight parts of speech. You can remember them by using the acronym IVAN CAPP – Interjection, Verb, Adverb, Noun, Conjunction, Adjective, Preposition, and Pronoun

1. Fredricka was savoring her favorite candy bar, eating it bit by bit.

Savoring means – enjoying

Part of speech – verb

2. The judge's noncommittal response to the lawyer's plea made the defendant feel nervous.

Noncommittal means –

Part of speech –

3. The emaciated orphan begged on the corner each morning.

Emaciated means –

Part of speech –

4. The small bit of food sustained the turtle for a long while.

Sustained means –

Part of speech --

5. The surreal colors made the abstract painting hurt my eyes!

Surreal means –

Part of speech –

Part III: Write your own sentences - Using the following vocabulary words, write sentences of your own. Label the part of speech of the vocabulary word as it is used in your sentence.

6. peevishly: _____

_____

_____

7. extricating: _____

_____

_____

8. mesmerized: _____

_____

_____

9. dissonant: _____

_____

_____

10. wielding: _____

_____

_____

The Hunger Games

Part Three: Chapters Twenty-Five – Twenty-Seven
Note-Taking and Summarizing: Chapters Twenty-Five – Twenty-Seven

Directions: For Chapters 25 – 27, fill in the chart with the necessary information. If you need more room, use an additional sheet of paper.

Main Events of the Chapters	
Characters	
Setting	
Primary Conflict	
Thoughts, Feelings or Predictions	
Thematic Issues Being Raised	

Name _____ **Period** _____

The Hunger Games

Part Three: Chapters Twenty-Five – Twenty-Seven
Comprehension Check

Directions: *To help you understand all aspects of the novel, answer the following questions for Chapters Twenty-Five – Twenty-Seven. Write your answers on a separate piece of paper using complete sentences.*

Chapter 25

1. Describe the muttations.

2. Where do the tributes go to escape them?

3. Contrast Katniss and Peeta's reactions to the change in rules. How does each of them react?

4. What do Katniss's actions reveal about her?

5. How do Katniss and Peeta both manage to win the Games?

6. Do you agree with their decision to eat the berries at the same time? Why or why not?

7. Why do you think the Gamemakers believed Peeta and Katniss and didn't think they were bluffing?

Chapter 26

1. How does Katniss react once she's in the hovercraft?

2. What happens to Katniss while she's in the hospital?

3. What is Cinna's purpose in designing the outfit for Katniss that she'll wear for the presentation of the victors?

4. Interpret the Capitol's decision not to allow Katniss to see Peeta until they're on the stage together. Why would they do that?

5. Explain what Katniss means at the end of the chapters when she thinks, "the most dangerous part of the Hunger Games is about to begin"?

Chapter 27

1. What happens at the presentation of the victors?

2. Why is Katniss worried that she is locked in her room?

3. At the interview, what does Katniss learn about Peeta's leg?

4. On the train back to District 12, Katniss changes her clothes, washes her face, and braids her hair. What does she mean by, "I begin transforming back into myself. Katniss Everdeen" (370)?

5. Do you think she can go back to what life was like before the Games?

6. What decision do you think Katniss should make about Peeta?

The Hunger Games

Part Three: Chapters Twenty-Five – Twenty-Seven
Standards Focus: Symbolism

Look around you. What symbols do you see? Perhaps there is a flag, a calendar, or a clock. All of these items are symbols. Jot down some of the symbols you see in your environment and share that list with your classmates.

Choose one of the symbols from your list. What does it symbolize? A flag, for example, can symbolize a state or country. It can also symbolize abstract qualities like freedom, patriotism, or loyalty. Symbols are a kind of shorthand human beings understand. We see a flag and we associate it with many different feelings and ideas.

> A symbol is something that represents itself and also represents or means something else. A flag is a piece of cloth, but it also represents something else.

In literature, symbols do the same thing. An author may intentionally or unintentionally use something as a symbol. The forest in the fairy tale "Little Red Riding Hood" is, first of all, a forest, but if you look at it symbolically, you might decide that it symbolizes confusion, danger, or evil. The wolf is a wolf, but it could also be a symbol of greed, consumerism, or evil. You could read the entire fairy tale in a symbolic way!

Is this what the brothers Grimm had in mind when they wrote the tale? No one knows, but analyzing and discussing symbols in literature reminds us how flexible our language is, and it challenges us to think creatively about what we read and how we understand it.

Remember that symbols usually represent something universal – something all readers can understand. Like the archetypes you studied in the Standards Focus for Chapter 10, symbols are often repeated and understood to mean the same thing in various pieces of literature.

Part I: Analyzing Symbolism

Directions: Choose a fairy tale you are familiar with. Use the chart below to help you isolate the symbols from the tale. What could those items symbolize? An example has been done for you using "Little Red Riding Hood."

Some fairy tales you may want to examine: Three Little Pigs, Hansel and Gretel, The Three Bears, Rapunzel, Snow White, Rumpelstiltskin, The Little Red Hen

You may want to read the fairy tale to refresh your memory.

Name of your fairy tale: "Little Red Riding Hood"

	Name / description	What could it symbolize?
Character(s) in your tale	Little Red	She could symbolize innocence or goodness (she is taking goodies to Grandma)
	Grandmother	She could symbolize age, fragility – probably not wisdom since she's the victim of the wolf.
Setting of the tale	Woods Grandmother's house	Danger Safety
Villain	Wolf	Evil
Hero (if there is one)	The Woodsman	Goodness; righteousness
Is there a struggle for something?	In some versions of the tale, the wolf has eaten the Grandmother and wants to eat Little Red	This could symbolize the struggle between good and evil

Name of your fairy tale: _____

	Name / description	What could it symbolize?
Character(s) in your tale		
Setting of the tale		
Villain		
Hero (if there is one)		
Is there a struggle for something?		

1. How does analyzing a story's symbolism help you understand it on a deeper level? _____

_____

_____

2. How does analyzing a story's symbolism add to the enjoyment of the story?

_____

_____

Part II: Analyzing Symbols in *The Hunger Games*

Places, names, and objects can be symbolic. Usually, our background knowledge will help us determine the meaning of symbols. For example, what do you know about the name Katniss? On page 52, Katniss remembers the story of her father telling her, "As long as you can find yourself, you'll never starve." She is named after a water plant with an edible root. How can Katniss's name be symbolic? Think about how well Katniss can find food. She's an expert hunter and gatherer. Since her name is that of an edible plant, her name symbolizes food, and that is exactly what her skill is: the ability to find food for herself and others.

> Something to think about when you are looking at symbolism – there are many ways to interpret a symbol. Often there is one accepted interpretation of a symbol, but if you can support a different analysis of a symbol with evidence from the text, your interpretation is valid.

1. Have you noticed all the Greek and Roman influences in the Capitol? List some of them below.

_____

_____

2. What do you suppose the residents of the Capitol think those Greek and Roman references symbolize?

_____

_____

3. What do you know about the Roman civilization that may not be as sophisticated as the people of the Capitol think?

_____

_____

_____

4. How are the people of the Capitol similar to the Romans?

_____

_____

_____

5. What are some of the symbols in *The Hunger Games*? List some ideas you have on the lines below. Share your ideas with your classmates.

_____

_____

_____

Name _____ **Period** _____

Directions: Using the chart below, analyze the symbols on your list. Some ideas have been filled in for you. Add your own ideas to the bottom of the chart.

Symbol	Analysis of the Symbol
The name Katniss	*As the name of an edible root, her name can symbolize that she is capable of feeding herself and others.*
The mockingjay	*It symbolizes taking something negative that was created (jabberjay) and combining it with mockingbirds to create a new life form. It's kind of a symbol of rebirth.*
The mockingjay pin	
Cinna	
Prim	
Peeta	
A silver parachute	
Fire	
Water	
TV cameras hidden everywhere	
Tracker jackers	
The muttations	
Effie Trinket	

Name _____   **Period** _____

Part III: Symbolism and irony

Irony refers to the contrast between what appears on the surface and the underlying meaning; it is the difference between what we expect and what reality is. An example of this in *The Hunger Games* is the cornucopia.

1. What is a cornucopia? If you're not sure, check a dictionary. _____

_____

2. The word *cornucopia* is formed from the Latin word for "copious" which means abundant. What do you think of or expect when you hear the word cornucopia?

_____

_____

3. How is the use of the term cornucopia used in an ironic (and opposite) way in *The Hunger Games*? _____

_____

_____

4. In Chapter 20, the tributes are invited to a "feast." What do you think of when you hear the term "feast"? _____

_____

5. What is ironic about the actual feast that Katniss attends? _____

_____

_____

6. Consider the word *"Games"* as in the title of the book. What do you think of when you hear that term? _____

_____

7. How are the Games ironic? _____

_____

_____

8. The Games are seen as a kind of entertainment. What is ironic about the Games as entertainment? _____

_____

_____

9. What does Panem's version of "entertainment" say about the country and its leaders? _____

_____

_____

_____

10. Analyze the irony of Effie Trinket's favorite statement, "May the odds be ever in your favor." _____

_____

_____

11. Symbolism and theme are often intertwined. The author may use symbols to help convey theme. Now that you've examined the symbols of *The Hunger Games*, what themes do you detect in the novel? _____

_____

_____

_____

_____

_____

12. Do you think Suzanne Collins is making a statement about life today through the novel? Explain your answer.

_____

_____

_____

| *Theme* is the message or lesson, presented through the characters and plot, that the writer wants to convey to the reader. |

_____

_____

_____

_____

_____

_____

_____

The Hunger Games

Part Three: Chapters Twenty-Five – Twenty-Seven
Assessment Preparation: Relationships Between Ideas – Subordination, Coordination, and Apposition

In the Assessment Preparation activity for Chapters 17 and 18, you practiced writing powerful sentences when you wrote an interview with Haymitch. If you have that activity, look over how you constructed your longer sentences. Write one of your favorite sentences on the lines below. _____

_____

_____

Here is the sample sentence for that activity: *She was able to blow up supplies, cut down a tracker jacker nest, find food, and survive a fire.*

Analyze the sentence to determine how it was written. What did the writer do to build a longer sentence? _____

_____

One important element in sentence structure is determining the relationship between ideas in the sentence. It's up to you as the writer to make sure the reader knows what that relationship is.

Part I: Coordination
When words, phrases, and clauses contain more than one idea, those ideas can be joined together with coordinating conjunctions. You can remember the coordinating conjunctions by using the acronym FANBOYS.

For, And, Nor, But, Or, Yet, So

"I've never seen these mutts, but they're no natural-born animals." (331)

The coordinating conjunction is: but
It joins: two equal independent clauses.
The relationship between the items joined: both are showing the contrast between what she expects to see (a natural-born animal) and what she currently sees.

> A clause is a group of words that contains a subject and a predicate (verb). A clause can be independent or dependent (subordinate).
> A phrase is a group of words that *might* contain a subject or a predicate but never both. A common phrase is a prepositional phrase that begins with a preposition and ends with a noun or pronoun.

Directions: *Examine the following sentences. Identify the coordinating conjunction; tell what it joins (clauses, phrases, or words). If the conjunction joins words or phrases, list them. Finally, tell what the relationship is between the items joined by the coordinating conjunction.*

1. *"The pure gold surface has been designed to resemble the woven horn that we fill at harvest, so there are little ridges and seams to get a decent hold on."* (331)

The first conjunction is: _____

It joins: _____

The relationship between the items joined: _____

_____

The second conjunction is: _____

It joins:_____

The relationship between the items joined: _____

_____

2. *"Peeta starts up hampered by not only the leg but the knife in his hand."* (332)

The conjunction is: _____

It joins: _____

The relationship between the items joined: _____

_____

3. *"He cries out and reflexively releases Peeta who slams back against him."* (336)

The conjunction is: _____

It joins: _____

The relationship between the items joined: _____

_____

4. *"It's customary for the victor and his or her support team to rise from beneath the stage."* (356) (Hint: In this sentence, "for" is a preposition not a conjunction.)

The first conjunction is: _____

It joins: _____

The relationship between the items joined: _____

_____

The second conjunction is: _____

It joins: _____

The relationship between the items joined: _____

_____

Part II: Subordination

In some sentences, you may want to show the relationship of items in the sentence in a different manner. Using subordination, you can show that events occur at different times or are of different importance.

For example:

> *"As they join together, they raise up again to stand easily on their back legs giving them an eerily human quality."* (332)

The first part of the sentence is a subordinate clause. It can't stand alone and needs the second part of the sentence, the independent clause, to complete the thought.

A subordinate clause will begin with a subordinating conjunction like *because, however, as, since*. You can test to see if a clause is subordinate by reading it out loud. If the clause sounds like a sentence, it's an *independent* clause. For example, if your friend said to you, "As they join together" you wouldn't know what she was talking about. That's a *subordinate* clause.

Directions: *Examine the following sentences. Identify the subordinate clause. Explain the relationship between the clauses in the sentence.*

> Example: *"As they join together, they raise up again to stand easily on their back legs giving them an eerily human quality."* (332)

Subordinate clause: as they join together
Relationship between the clauses: In the first clause, the mutts are gathering together; then they are standing up. They are doing one thing and then the other.

1. *"Before I can get this out, the mutts begin a new assault on the horn."* (334)

Subordinate clause: _____

Relationship between the clauses: _____

_____

2. *"If the stiffness in my limbs is this bad, how can Peeta even move?"* (349)

Subordinate clause: _____

Relationship between clauses: _____

_____

3. *"As I stoop to pick it up, Claudius Templesmith's voice booms into the arena."* (342)

Subordinate clause: _____

Relationship between clauses: _____

_____

4. *"Before I am even aware of my actions, my bow is loaded with the arrow pointed straight at his heart."* (343)

Subordinate clause: _____

Relationship between clauses: _____

Part III: Appositives

Appositives rename a noun or pronoun. An appositive can be restrictive (necessary to understand the sentence) or nonrestrictive (can be removed, and the sentence still makes sense).

Directions: Examine the following. Identify the appositive and tell what it renames.

Example: *"My little sister, Prim, curled up on her side..."* (3)

Appositive: Prim
What does it rename: It gives the name of her little sister.

1. *"Then one of them, a good-sized mutt with silky waves of blond fur, takes a running start and leaps onto the horn."* (333)

Appositive: _____

What does it rename: _____

2. *"All our supplies, our packs, remain down by the lake where we abandoned them when we fled from the mutts."* (338)

Appositive: _____

What does it rename: _____

Subordinate clause: _____

Relationship between clauses: _____

_____

3. *"It's risky business – Peeta may end up losing his leg – but when I weigh this against him losing his life, what alternative do I have?"* (338)

Appositive: _____

What does it rename: _____

Coordinating conjunction: _____

It joins: _____

The relationship between the items joined: _____

_____

4. *"The only indication of the passage of time lies in the heavens, the subtle shift of the moon."* (340)

Appositive: _____

What does it rename: _____

Name _____ Period _____

The Hunger Games

Part Three Activity: Create a Survival Game

What is a reality TV show? _____

_____

How familiar are you with reality TV shows? Are there any you watch regularly? If so, list them. _____

_____

A subgenre of reality TV is the reality TV game show in which the participants are competing to win a prize. This is similar to the Hunger Games. List any competition/ game reality TV shows you're familiar with. _____

_____

Part I: What's on TV?

Directions*: Work with a partner. Using a TV Guide or listing of TV programs, review the offerings, looking for reality TV shows. Highlight titles of the shows and descriptions or create a list.*

1. About how often are these types of shows on each week? _____

2. List two or three titles of shows that you think might be interesting to watch. __

_____

_____

3. What appeals to you about that show? _____

_____

4. List two or three titles of shows that you wouldn't be interested in watching.

_____

_____

5. Why don't those shows appeal to you? _____

_____

6. Why do you think survival and reality TV shows, in general, are so popular?

_____

_____

7. What makes a reality *game* show popular? _____

_____

Name _____   Period _____

Part II: Watch a Reality Game Show

Directions: Watch a reality game show, then complete the viewing sheet below. Be sure to read over the questions before you start, to get an idea of the kinds of questions you will be answering. To get the most out of the activity, watch a show you've never seen. You may find you can give a more objective review if the show is something you're not familiar with. Write your answers on a separate sheet of paper, numbering each answer.

Reality Game/Competition Show Viewing Sheet

1. Name of the TV show:

2. Time and date I watched it:

3. Summary of the episode: (What happened, who were the characters involved, what was at stake)

4. How did the director of the show create drama and tension? For example, did he use dramatic music, special effects, unusual challenges, or emotional events?

5. How did the producer of the show keep the viewer interested when the show was going to go to a commercial break?

6. How is the title of the show important to the events of the program?

7. What kinds of challenges did the contestants face?

8. What was the reward for the winner?

9. After watching the show, how would you rate its entertainment value (use a letter grade, star system, or other measure)? Why?

10. How would you rate its educational value? Why?

11. Would you watch this show again? Why or why not?

12. What kind of viewer would be interested in this program? Why?

13. What suggestions would you make to the producer of the show to make this a better program?

14. What kinds of commercials were shown during this show?

15. Do you think the commercials were appropriate for the audience? Explain your reasoning.

Part III: Design Your Own Survival Show

What if you could design your own survival show? What challenges would you want the contestants to face? What would your setting be? Use the graphic organizer below to help you brainstorm ideas for three different survival shows. Unlike *The Hunger Games*, your game should be safe for the contestants.

	Idea 1	Idea 2	Idea 3
Ideas for the setting of the show			
Challenges the players would face			
Audience this show would appeal to			
Problems you might throw into the show to make it more interesting			
What is at stake? What will the contestants win?			
Possible titles for the show			

Name _____   **Period** _____

Part IV: "Pitch" Your Show

Before a TV show gets on the air, the idea has to be "pitched" to the network. Look over your brainstorming ideas and come up with a show you want to pitch to the network (in this case, your classmates). You'll present the idea for your show, and your classmates will evaluate your presentation.

Some ideas of how to pitch your show:
- Create a PowerPoint presentation
- Design a storyboard using photographs or illustrations
- Act out a scene
- Create a puppet show
- Create a trailer (movie clip)
- Try another idea that you'll discuss with your teacher

Once you have created your visual aids, practice your pitch several times. Whatever format you choose, even if your pitch is a movie clip or PowerPoint, you will want to introduce and conclude your presentation by speaking directly to the audience.

Your teacher may have your classmates vote on the best survivor show idea.

Part V: Peer Evaluation Sheet for Survivor Show Pitch

Directions: You will be completing one peer evaluation sheet for each presentation. Be as objective as possible in your assessment. Most importantly, remember that you are evaluating the idea behind the show rather than the presentation itself.

1. Members of the group: _____

2. Name of the show: _____

3. Idea behind the show: _____

   _____

4. What I liked best about the show idea: _____

   _____

   _____

5. What I think needs to be improved about the show idea: _____

   _____

   _____

   _____

The Hunger Games

Part Three Alternate Activity: Create a Museum Display

In Chapter 11 we learn that the arena and staging areas for the Games will be made into a museum after the Games are over. The museums are popular vacation destinations. What would a museum for the seventy-fourth Hunger Games look like? Your job will be to design a Hunger Games museum display and create artifacts for it.

Part I: Think about a museum you've visited. What are some features that were in the museum? Were there any features of the museum that you particularly enjoyed? List any ideas you have below. _____

_____

_____

If it's been a while since you've been to a museum, you can take a virtual museum tour. Try the National Museum of Natural History. As you take the virtual tour, jot down the items in the museum that you think are interesting.

_____

_____

_____

Part II: Museums are repositories for *artifacts.* Artifacts are items that are used by humans that are interesting to archeologists, historians, scientists, and anyone else interested in or studying human life. Look around your classroom; what artifacts can you find that you think might be interesting to people in the future? Perhaps there are books, posters, pens, computers, or furniture. Would people be interested in those items in 100 years or 1,000 years? _____

_____

What would an archeologist of the future learn about you from the items you use every day? _____

_____

Museums don't just contain artifacts, though. Many museums are interactive and allow visitors to try new things or interact with the displays.

Archeologists excavate trash dumps and old wells that ancient people used for trash. What can be learned about people by what they throw away?

Part III: Begin designing your museum

Your teacher may want you to design a complete museum or just one part of it. Think about what you want your museum to have. Do you want interactive items? Do you want actors who act out a scene? What kinds of artifacts do you want to display?

1. Create a blueprint for your museum. Your blueprint will show how visitors will move through your museum and look at the artifacts. Look at the example on the following page. Remember that people should travel through the museum in a one-way path. Your artifacts should show a pattern. Perhaps you want to show the progression through several days, or maybe just one day. Remember that your museum can cover the reaping and training as well as the actual Games, but it may be easier for you to choose a smaller topic than to try to cover everything.

2. Create your artifacts. This is where your creativity is going to come into play. You'll be creating at least ten artifacts. Try to make your artifacts ten different items. Artifacts can be drawings, photos, diaries, posters, letters, lists, tools, videos, and props – just to name a few. There are many other items that can be artifacts as well. You may also want to have a "living museum" display in which an actor or actors present information or act out an event.

What should your artifacts show? They shouldn't just be a random collection of items. They should work together to explain something about the Games. Use the name of your museum to help you decide what you want your artifacts to show. If your museum is "Foods of the Games" you may want to have recipes, dishes, samples, pictures, ingredients, cooking methods, cooking supplies, and so on. Rather than just randomly placing the artifacts, arrange them purposely so a visitor has a sense that the museum display is trying to communicate something.

Consider creating interactive displays in addition to your artifacts. Could visitors take a quiz at the end of the exhibit? Are there trivia questions you can pose along the way? Can they try out a skill during their visit?

Don't forget to include a caption for each of your artifacts. Your visitors should know what they're looking at.

3. Create a museum display board. Put your blueprint and your artifacts on your display. You may want to draw or string lines from the blueprint of your museum to each artifact.

Part IV: Share your display with your classmates.

Directions: *Answer the following evaluation questions on a separate sheet of paper.*

1. What theme or message did you try to convey in your museum?

2. Do you think you were successful with your museum? Why or why not?

3. What is your favorite artifact? Why?

4. What do you hope your visitors will get out of their visit to your museum?

Name _____   Period _____

Example Foods of the Hunger Games Exhibit floor plan

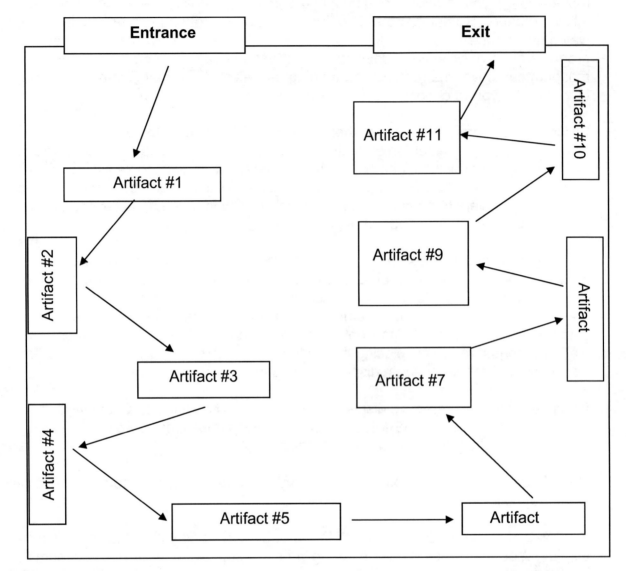

*The arrows indicate the direction visitors to the display will take as they travel through the exhibit.

Below are a few examples of artifacts you can use in your museum. For each of these artifacts, you'll create an actual item (like a recipe or a photograph) and a caption explaining what visitors are viewing.

Artifact 1: A recipe for dandelion salad and dandelion tea.

Artifact 2: A bowl of one of Greasy Sae's stews that she serves in the Hob.

Artifact 3: A place setting that Katniss and her family may have used for meals.

Artifact 4: The cooking pot Katniss used to make meals for her family.

Artifact 5: An actor showing visitors how an animal that Katniss hunted might be skinned and prepared.

Name _____ **Period** _____

The Hunger Games

Movie Connections

The movie adaptation of *The Hunger Games* is expected to be released in March 2012. Depending on when you are using the Literature Guide, decide which of the following activities may be used.

1. Book fans have been vocal about what actors they want to see in the movie. You may be interested in following or reading discussions posted online. After looking online for more information about the movie version of *The Hunger Games*, what other actors and actresses do you think would be best to play the characters from the novel? Give your best reasons for choosing particular actors for their parts, and make an effort to explain fully, as though you were trying to influence an agent.

2. With your classmates, create a list of books that you have read that have also been made into movies you have seen. In small groups, (if possible, with students who have read the same book) create lists that identify items that were better in the movie and those that were better in the book. Include specific examples in your lists. Consider the characters, plot, setting, and themes of the movie/book you are comparing.

3. What do you think are the "must have" elements of *The Hunger Games* that should not be missed in the making of the movie? Write a letter to the director of the movie persuading him to include at least five "must haves" in the movie. Be sure to list your reasons for including those elements.

4. Choose one scene from the book and write a script that could be used in a movie or play adaptation of the book. Before starting on your script, look at how a play is written. Notice how stage directions are given and characters identified. Write your script following that model. Gather classmates as actors who can give a dramatic reading or presentation of your script to the class.

5. Choose a flashback from the novel. Write a script for one of the flashback scenes using the directions from option 4 above. Choose classmates to act out the scene for the class.

6. Use photographs to create a scene from the novel. Using digital photographs, create a storyboard of a scene from the novel. You'll need at least eight to ten photographs. You can use fellow students as actors to stage each scene or you can use puppets, dolls, or clay figures. Stage each scene, photograph it, and then put your storyboard together. Be sure to include captions for each photograph.

7. How will the movie be promoted? Most movies have a tagline or slogan that is used in commercials and on posters. The tagline for *A Bug's Life* was "An epic of miniature proportions." The tagline for *Monsters Inc* was "You won't believe your eye." Create a tagline or slogan for the movie *The Hunger Games.* Design an original movie poster that might be displayed in theaters or on billboards.

Name _____ **Period** _____

*If you have already seen the movie, **The Hunger Games**, choose one of the following activities to demonstrate your understanding of the differences and similarities between the book and the movie. You may write your answer either creatively or in a well-constructed five-paragraph essay format. Write your response on a separate sheet of paper.*

1. Which did you like better, the movie or the book? Write a review of the movie in which you argue which was better. Be sure to include examples from both the movie and the book to support your argument.

2. Was the adaptation of the book into a movie well done? Write a movie review arguing whether or not the screenwriter(s) were truly able to capture the novel in movie form.

3. Read several reviews of the movie. Choose one review and write a response to it in which you either agree or disagree with the reviewer. Be sure to include details and reasons to support your opinion.

4. Did the movie match what you imagined as you read? Choose one character and one setting from the book and write a short comparison/contrast between your imagination and the movie. Explain how the movie did or did not capture what you envisioned as you were reading. Be sure to include specific details to support your opinion.

Name _____ **Period** _____

The Hunger Games

Quiz: Part One: Chapters One – Two

Directions: *Match the character with his or her description. Write the letter of the best answer on the line provided.*

1. _____ Katniss

2. _____ Gale

3. _____ Prim

4. _____ Haymitch

5. _____ Effie Trinket

6. _____ Peeta

a. a great hunting companion
b. This is her first year in the reaping. Her name has only been entered once.
c. She is the Capitol representative for District 12
d. the son of a baker
e. will be representing District 12 in the Hunger Games
f. a former Hunger Games winner from District 12

Directions: *Answer the following questions in complete sentences.*

7. Compared with Madge, why is the reaping dangerous for Gale and Katniss?

_____

_____

_____

_____

_____

8. You learned about a *dystopian society* as part of the pre-reading activities. What evidence can you give that *The Hunger Games* is a dystopian novel? Be specific in explaining your answer. _____

_____

_____

_____

_____

Name _____   **Period** _____

_____

_____

_____

_____

_____

Directions: _Write the correct word on the line in front of its definition._

reaping   adjacent
deterrent   protocol
poaching   dissent
maniacally   plummets
preposterous   radical
haggling   predicament

_____9. extreme

_____10. a discouragement from acting in a particular way

_____11. hunting illegally

_____12. harvesting

_____13. overly enthusiastically

_____14. ridiculous; unbelievable

_____15. problem; troublesome situation

_____16. close to or joining

_____17. the custom or proper way of doing something; etiquette

_____18. protest

_____19. bargaining, usually arguing over a trade or price of an item

_____20. drops dramatically

The Hunger Games

Quiz: Part One: Chapters Three – Four

Directions: Write the letter of the best answer on the line before the example.

_____1. After the reaping, Katniss
a. returns home to pack her clothes.
b. is treated like a hero by District 12.
c. considers running away.
d. is taken to the Justice Center.

_____2. Katniss receives two gifts that surprise her. One of them is
a. cookies from Peeta's father.
b. a bow from Gale.
c. cheese from Prim.
d. a pin from her mother.

_____3. Effie's comment, *"You know your mentor is your lifeline to the world in these Games…Haymitch can well be the difference between your life and your death!"* (46) tells us that
a. if Haymitch is drunk, he can't help Katniss and Peeta.
b. Katniss and Peeta need to find another mentor.
c. Haymitch is going to turn his behavior around and be more responsible.
d. Katniss and Peeta will be on their own in the arena.

_____4. In Chapter 4, Katniss realizes, *"Kind people have a way of working their way inside of me and rooting there."* (49) She realizes this because
a. Haymitch has decided he will help them.
b. She feels a debt to Peeta for being nice to her.
c. She's afraid she won't be able to survive in the arena.
d. Effie Trinket is helping them with their strategies.

_____5. Based on what you've learned so far, what can you infer about Haymitch?
a. He is dedicated to helping Katniss and Peeta survive the Games.
b. He is going to be of no help at all to them.
c. He is really a very kind and thoughtful person.
d. He is willing to help them if they listen to him.

Directions: Using the vocabulary words listed below, fill in the blanks with the words that best complete the sentences.

disastrous	replicate	gnarled
intensity	disgruntled	deteriorate
insurmountable	mentor	deteriorated
gratified	pondering	substantial
sniveling	inexplicable	detest

6. Haymitch is a _____ to Katniss and Peeta.

7. Katniss is worried that her mother's mental state will _____ when Katniss is in the Games.

8. When Katniss is_____Peeta's behavior, she is in deep thought.

9. It is clear that the people of District 12_____the Hunger Games because they don't clap or cheer when Katniss takes Prim's place.

10. Katniss cannot understand why Peeta gave her the burned bread. His behavior was_____ to her.

11. Katniss refuses to cry because she doesn't want the other tributes to think she's a_____coward.

12. The odds of surviving the Games seem_____to Katniss.

13. Katniss is_____that Peeta has offered to clean up Haymitch after he's sick.

14. The death of Katniss's father could have been_____for her family since they nearly starved.

15. The mockingjay can_____the songs of both birds and humans.

16. The winner of the Hunger Games will win a_____ prize and be the richest person in the district.

17. When Peeta and Katniss confront Haymitch, he is surprised by their _____ . He asks, "Did I actually get a pair of fighters this year?"

18. Peeta's mother was_____when she realized he'd burned the bread.

19. Katniss and Gale hunted in the woods. They may have hidden behind a _____ , twisted tree while stalking prey.

20. From the way it's described, it seems like the Seam has_____ over the years and is not very attractive.

Name _____   Period _____

The Hunger Games

Quiz: Part One: Chapters Five – Six

Directions: Write a thoughtful answer to the prompts provided below.

1. Katniss and Peeta's costumes for the Opening Ceremonies are unusual because

_____

_____

2. One of the features of Katniss's apartment in the Training Center is _____

_____

3. Peeta and Katniss choose to talk on the roof because _____

_____

_____

4. The Avox upsets Katniss because _____

_____

_____

_____

5. It is important that Katniss doesn't reveal how she knows the Avox because _____

_____

_____

6. What conclusions can you draw about life in the Capitol? _____

_____

_____

_____

_____

7. Why is it strange that Katniss feels excited by the crowd cheering for her during
   Opening Ceremonies? _____

_____

_____

_____

Name _____ **Period** _____

Directions: *On the line in front of the definition, write the word that most closely matches its definition.*

exclusively   affectations
sustenance   adversaries
barbarism   despicable
mandatory   flamboyant
ironic   vulnerable
tangible

_____9. exposed; open to danger or attack

_____10. flashy; showy

_____11. nourishment

_____12. able to be touched

_____13. enemies

_____14. worthy of being scorned or despised

_____15. only; limited

_____16. uncivilized behavior

_____17. artificial actions; words or habits used for effect

_____18. the opposite of what would be expected

_____19. required

The Hunger Games

Quiz: Part One: Chapters Seven – Nine

Directions: Fill in the blank using the correct vocabulary word listed below.

impulsiveness	ludicrous
amiable	oblivious
surly	sic
banal	potential

1. During the training, Peeta and Katniss must appear _____toward each other.

2. Haymitch thinks Katniss is_____, and he had trouble figuring out how she should act in the interview.

3. Peeta shows _____in camouflage because he has had experience decorating cakes.

4. Katniss is worried that her _____ during the presentation for the Gamemakers will cause her family to be punished.

5. Effie tries to help Katniss walk in high heels, but Katniss feels _____ .

6. Peeta's skills seem _____and ordinary when compared to Katniss's ability to use a bow.

Directions: Match the character with the correct word by writing the letter of your choice on the line in front of the number. Write a one-sentence explanation for your choice.

a.	leniency	d.	unrequited
b.	sever	e.	prestigious
c.	hostile	f.	fixated

_____7. Peeta _____

_____

_____8. Haymitch _____

_____

_____9. A score of eleven or twelve on the performance for the Gamemakers

_____

_____10. Katniss's behavior toward Cinna during the interview _____

_____

_____

_____11. Katniss hopes the red haired Avox will feel this toward her ____

_____

_____

Directions: *Decide if each statement is true or false. Write the word "True" on the line in front of the statement if it is true; write "False" if the statement is false.*

_____12. Katniss *severs* her relationship with Cinna.

_____13. Peeta is *intrigued* by using camouflage.

_____14. The residents of the Capitol are *oblivious* to what life is like in the rest of Panem.

_____15. The red haired Avox has a *sullen* personality.

_____16. In the interview, Katniss's behavior is *irredeemably* dull.

_____17. Caesar Flickerman tries to *demean* the tributes during the interview.

_____18. The Gamemakers have the power to *sic* wild animals on the tributes.

_____19. Peeta *defiantly* requests to be trained separately.

Directions: *On the lines below, write a thoughtful answer the question posed.*

20. Explain the surprise at the end of Part I. How do you think it will affect the rest of the novel? _____

_____

_____

_____

_____

_____

_____

_____

_____

_____

Name _____ Period _____

The Hunger Games

Quiz: Part Two: Chapter Ten

Directions: Write a thoughtful answer to the prompts provided below.

1. Explain Katniss's feelings about Peeta's confession during the interview. _____

_____

_____

2. Why does Haymitch think Peeta's confession helps Katniss? _____

_____

_____

3. Why is Haymitch's advice, *"Stay alive"* different this time than when he first said it on the train? _____

_____

4. When Peeta and Katniss are on the roof, Peeta says, *"I keep wishing I could think of a way to…to show the Capitol they don't own me. That I'm more than just a piece in their Games."* What does Peeta mean by this? _____

_____

_____

_____

5. Why is it important to Katniss when Cinna says that if he could, he'd put his money on Katniss? _____

_____

_____

Directions: Write the letter of the best answer on the line before the example.

6. _____Effie Trinket
    a. hopes for a promotion to a better district at next year's Games.
    b. wishes she had more time to spend with Katniss and Peeta.
    c. gives Peeta and Katniss advice about the Games.
    d. believes Katniss will win the Games.

7. _____Katniss's behavior after the interviews shows that she
    a. knew all along how Peeta felt about her.
    b. trusts Peeta and what he says.
    c. acts impulsively without thinking.
    d. doesn't understand Haymitch's advice.

8. _____The audience of the Games views Katniss and Peeta as
   a. powerful contenders in the Games.
   b. star-crossed lovers who can never be together.
   c. physically weak tributes.
   d. silly and forgettable, but in a tragic situation.

9. _____The arena and catacombs
   a. will become a vacation spot.
   b. are used every year by the tributes.
   c. are the same every year.
   d. are described in detail before the Games begin.

10. _____A district token
   a. should be a secret weapon for the tributes.
   b. must be approved by a review board.
   c. must represent the Capitol is some way.
   d. should represent the tribute.

Directions: *Use each word in a sentence or a series of sentences that includes context clues showing you understand the meaning of the word. Underline the context clues you use. You may change the part of speech of the word to fit into your sentence. The first word has been completed for you.*

Example: assent – Matthew *assented* to his friends when he <u>agreed</u> to save them seats at the concert.

11. breached _____

_____

12. entourages _____

_____

13. aghast _____

_____

14. perceived _____

_____

15. reenactments _____

_____

The Hunger Games

Quiz: Part Two: Chapters Eleven – Twelve

Directions: *Match the vocabulary word with the word that is closest to its definition. Write your choice of words on the line next to the correct definition.*

condenses	dispersed	imprudent
void	lapdogs	dynamic
botched	gall	scarcity
rejuvenating	hoist	

1. _____ rarity

2. _____ pampered pets

3. _____ nerve

4. _____ emptiness

5. _____ energizing; restorative

6. _____ spread around

7. _____ relationship

8. _____ pull; lift

9. _____ not cautious

10. _____ ruined

11. _____ concentrates

Directions: *Write the letter of the correct answer on the line before the prompt.*

12. _____Before making it to the woods, Katniss manages to get
    a. an orange backpack and a sheet of plastic.
    b. a bow and arrow.
    c. a sleeping bag and some rope.
    d. a knife.

13. _____That night, Katniss discovers
    a. another tribute is stalking her.
    b. there are cameras everywhere.
    c. Peeta has joined the Careers.
    d. the Careers have suffered a great loss.

14. _____Katniss also learns
    a. the Avox is in the arena.
    b. the Careers think she is stupid.
    c. the source for water.
    d. Peeta is still in love with her.

15. _____As she struggles to find water, Katniss
   a. calls out to Haymitch for help.
   b. becomes lost in the forest.
   c. wonders why Haymitch won't send her water.
   d. discovers another source of food.

16. _____What does Katniss realize when she falls and is too weak to get up?
   a. She is going to die from dehydration.
   b. She has fallen into mud.
   c. Peeta has betrayed her.
   d. Haymitch will finally send water.

17. _____Katniss puts iodine into the water to
   a. purify it.
   b. cool it off.
   c. make it more nutritious.
   d. remove the dirt.

18. _____Katniss is awaked in the night by
   a. the Career tributes.
   b. another tribute.
   c. a rainstorm.
   d. a fire.

19. _____Katniss doesn't consider making an alliance with other tributes
                because
   a. she doesn't know any of them.
   b. she knows she can survive on her own.
   c. she is following Haymitch's advice.
   d. she has plenty of supplies.

20. _____Choose the list of adjectives that best describe Katniss's
                situation at the end of Chapter 12.
   a. hungry, lonely, sad
   b. confused, heart-broken, disappointed
   c. thirsty, ungrateful, angry
   d. hydrated, endangered, surprised

The Hunger Games

Quiz: Part Two: Chapters Thirteen – Fourteen

Directions: *Use the correct vocabulary word from the word bank below to complete the sentences that follow.*

abate	mayhem
balm	persevere
bravado	precariously
conspiratorially	quell
honing	sated
incompetent	stupor

1. After the tracker jackers attacked the Careers, there was complete _____.

2. As the Careers considered what to do about Katniss at the top of the tree, they talked_____together.

3. The fire in the forest did not_____until after Katniss was burned.

4. Cato showed_____when he tried to climb the tree and follow Katniss.

5. Katniss was afraid to cut the tracker jacker nest down, but she had no choice but to _____ in her efforts to cut through the branch.

6. After a meal of rabbit, Katniss didn't feel_____. She was still hungry.

7. The Gamemakers had the power to_____the fire, but they did not extinguish it.

8. The tracker jackers were in a_____ due to the smoke from the fire, because smoke will calm the wasps down so they don't swarm or sting.

9. Glimmer was_____with the bow and arrow. It was clear she didn't know how to use it.

10. After Katniss's leg was burned, Haymitch sent a_____to make her leg feel better.

11. The tracker jackers were_____in on the Careers and would not leave them alone until they'd stung them.

12. Katniss was_____perched in the top branches of the tree. She was in danger of breaking the branches.

Name _____ **Period** _____

Directions: *Decide if the statement is True or False. On the line before the statement, write "True" if the statement is true. Write "False" if the statement is false.*

13. _____ Katniss receives a gift from her sponsors while she is in the tree.

14. _____ Peeta saves Katniss's life by warning her that she should run away.

15. _____ The tracker jacker venom is deadly.

16. _____ The fire in the forest was caused by a tribute's fire.

17. _____ Peeta joined the Careers because he wanted to help them find Katniss.

18. _____ Cato is known as an excellent tree climber.

19. _____ Katniss's burn is miraculously healed by an ointment.

20. _____ Katniss retrieves the bow and arrows.

The Hunger Games

Quiz: Part Two: Chapters Fifteen – Sixteen

Directions: *Write the letter of the best answer on the line in front of the prompt.*

1. _____Rue is able to help Katniss by
   a. showing her a way through the forest.
   b. giving her leaves to heal her wounds.
   c. telling her the truth about Peeta.
   d. sharing a map of the arena with her.

2. _____The obvious leader of the Careers is
   a. Cato   c. Peeta
   b. Glimmer   d. the boy from District 3

3. _____When Katniss decides to go on the offense, she means
   a. she is going to find a better place to hide.
   b. she won't trust anyone else in the arena.
   c. she wants to make a greater alliance.
   d. she plans to attack the Careers.

4. _____After the tracker jacker stings, Katniss
   a. still feels weak and shaky.   c. continues to have hallucinations.
   b. avoids the trees.   d. is frightened by them.

5. _____Katniss cannot understand
   a. why Rue wants to be her ally.   c. where the Careers are going.
   b. why Peeta saved her life.   d. how to use the new bow and
                                           arrows.

6. _____Katniss and Rue use the mockingjay
   a. as their district token.   c. song as a signal.
   b. as a symbol of their friendship. d. feathers as a signal.

7. _____The Careers leave camp because
   a. they need to hunt.   c. they know where Katniss is.
   b. they see smoke.   d they are looking for water.

8. _____Katniss is confused about the pyramid of supplies because
   a. everyone is guarding it.   c. it isn't guarded.
   b. it is carefully hidden.   d. everyone seems to be afraid of it.

9. _____The Foxface girl
   a. attacks the Careers.   c. hides in the forest with Rue.
   b. is able to steal from the Careers. d. wants to form an alliance with Katniss.

Name _____ **Period** _____

Directions: Choose the correct vocabulary word for the definition given. Write the letter of your choice on the line in front of the word.

10. _____ cautiously
    a. tentatively
    b. noxious

    c. rations
    d. prominent

11. _____ shaken
    a. prominent
    b. wracked

    c. onslaught
    d. copse

12. _____ willing to do favors
    a. prominent
    b. rendezvous

    c. obliging
    d. tentatively

13. _____ harmful; foul smelling
    a. wracked
    b. onslaught

    c. forages
    d. noxious

14. _____ meeting place
    a. forages
    b. noxious

    c. rendezvous
    d. copse

15. _____ searches for food
    a. forages
    b. rations

    c. prominent
    d. tentatively

16. _____ trouble
    a. wracked
    b. noxious

    c. ordeal
    d. onslaught

17. _____ assault
    a. ordeal
    b. onslaught

    c. forages
    d. prominent

18. _____ noticeable; standing out
    a. ordeal
    b. copse

    c. prominent
    d. ration

19. _____ a group of trees or bushes
    a. prominent
    b. rations

    c. forages
    d. copse

20. _____ a portion
    a. ordeal
    b. wracked

    c. ration
    d. copse

Name _____   **Period** _____

The Hunger Games

Quiz: Part Two: Chapters Seventeen – Eighteen

***Directions**: Choose the correct **synonym** for the following words. Write the letter of your choice on the line in front of the vocabulary word.*

1. _____fractured
   a. broken
   b. separated
   c. combined
   d. added

2. _____subsequent
   a. before
   b. next
   c. beside
   d. around

3. _____fragmenting
   a. combining
   b. mixing
   c. splitting apart
   d. fusing

4. _____audible
   a. able to be heard
   b. easy to understand
   c. unbelievable
   d. transform

5. _____lethargy
   a. lack of energy
   b. energetic
   c. wild
   d. sleeping

6. _____inflict
   a. to give something special
   b. to impose something unwanted
   c. to offer as a gift
   d. to tell the truth

***Directions**: Choose the correct **antonym** for the following words. Write the letter of your choice on the line in front of the vocabulary word.*

7. _____doggedly
   a. stubbornly
   b. defeatedly
   c. persistently
   d. unceasingly

8. _____subtly
   a. abruptly
   b. carefully
   c. gradually
   d. seriously

9. _____decadent
   a. rich and luxurious
   b. plain and boring
   c. strong and energetic
   d. serious and thoughtful

10. _____fretful
- a. scornful
- b. irritable
- c. unconcerned
- d. angry

11. _____inadequate
- a. not enough
- b. unheated
- c. preserved
- d. too much

12. _____despondency
- a. hopelessness
- b. joy
- c. generosity
- d. selfishness

Directions: *Write a thoughtful answer to the questions posed below. Use the back of your paper if you need more room to write.*

13. How has Foxface been able to survive? _____

_____

_____

14. Explain how Rue's death was different from any of the other tribute deaths.

_____

_____

_____

15. What will be the impact of the destroyed supply pyramid? _____

_____

16. How does losing her hearing affect Katniss? _____

_____

_____

17. How does Rue's death change Katniss? _____

_____

_____

18. How does the rule change to the Games affect Katniss? _____

_____

19. Why is the silver parachute from District 11 important? _____

_____

20. What role does the mockingjay play in these two chapters? _____

_____

Name _____   Period _____

The Hunger Games

Quiz: Part Three: Chapters Nineteen – Twenty

Directions: Match the solution to the problem. Write the letter of every solution to the problem; there may be more than one. Remember that a solution is something that solves the problem.

Problems

1. _____Katniss doesn't know where Peeta is. She…

2. _____Peeta is injured so Katniss…

3. _____Peeta wants to follow Katniss to the feast, so she …

4. _____The feast brings all the tributes into the arena, and Katniss…

5. _____It is difficult for Peeta to travel, so Katniss…

6. _____Katniss doesn't have medical supplies, so she …

7. _____Katniss doesn't like giving medical help to people who have been injured, but she …

8. _____Peeta has blood poisoning, so Katniss …

9. _____Peeta doesn't want Katniss to go to the feast. She …

Solutions

a. treats Peeta'a tracker jacker stings with the leaves Rue taught her about.

b. has to risk the dangers of the feast to save Peeta.

c. tracks Peeta and tries to imagine where he might be.

d. notices bloodstains along the river and on a rock.

e. drugs Peeta with the sleeping syrup.

f. makes a shelter for them beside the river.

g. thinks about how her mother and Prim treat injured people.

Name _____ **Period** _____

Directions: Write the word that best fits the given definition.

dissipate	pariahs	ruse
evade	peruse	scrupulously
incoherence	potent	tethered
loathe	ratcheting	wheedles

10. _____ turning or cranking

11. _____ carefully

12. _____ hate

13. _____ avoid; hide from

14. _____ outcasts

15. _____ inability to be understood

16. _____ strong; powerful

17. _____ tied to

18. _____ to look over or look through

19. _____ to scatter or spread in different directions

20. _____ persuades

21. _____ a trick

The Hunger Games

Quiz: Part Three: Chapters Twenty-One – Twenty-Two

Directions: Use the vocabulary words in the word bank below to fill in the blank in the following sentences with the word that best completes the sentence.

arduous	famished	plaintively
asset	infusion	staunch
emanating	irreparable	tirades
exasperated	irreverent	vaguely
exorbitant	ominous	

1. A(n) _____ in the arena would include medicine.

2. As the Games go on, the price of gifts to the tributes becomes _____.

3. It seems that Katniss never has enough to eat; she always seems to be

_____.

4. Haymitch is probably_____that Katniss isn't more romantic toward Peeta.

5. Katniss has the_____ task of taking care of Peeta and surviving the feast; she cannot ever let her guard down or stop thinking and planning.

6. When Clove captures Katniss, Katniss wants to die with dignity. She refuses to cry_____and beg for mercy.

7. Because of his fever, Peeta is_____enough heat to keep Katniss warm.

8. Katniss is worried that without medicine Peeta's wound is _____.

9. The lamb stew contains a delicious_____of lamb and plums.

10. The prospect of going to the feast is _____; Katniss is sure there will be a battle.

11. Peeta tries to_____the flow of blood from the cut on Katniss's forehead.

12. Katniss needs to be careful about what she says; she doesn't want to be too

_____toward the Capitol.

13. Katniss thinks about Gale's_____against the Capitol and wonders how Peeta would react to them.

14. Katniss wants to keep her feelings private, so she sometimes answers questions _____. More specific answers would be too personal.

Directions: *Short Answer (2 points each) Write a thoughtful answer to the following prompts, paying special attention to accuracy in your writing.*

15. Contrast the difference between Clove's behavior toward Katniss and Thresh's behavior toward Katniss. _____

_____

_____

_____

_____

_____

_____

16. After Katniss returns from the feast, explain why she and Peeta seem to change roles. _____

_____

_____

_____

_____

_____

_____

17. Explain the importance that Peeta and Katniss now have to each other. _____

_____

_____

_____

_____

_____

_____

The Hunger Games

Quiz: Part Three: Chapters Twenty-Three – Twenty-Four

Directions: *For each of the following statements, write "True" if the statement is true and "False" if the statement is false.*

1. _____Foxface's death was carefully planned.

2. _____Peeta has difficulty walking quietly.

3. _____Katniss is angry that Peeta doesn't return the signal whistle.

4. _____Prior to Foxface's death, she and Cato and were allies.

5. _____The Gamemakers want the tributes to return to the lake.

Directions: *Short Answer: Write a thoughtful answer to the following prompts,*

6. What might the people from Foxface's district say about her abilities in the arena? Explain your answer. _____

_____

_____

_____

7. What skills does Katniss use in continuing to help Peeta and herself continue survive? _____

_____

_____

_____

8. What kind of tribute is Cato? _____

_____

_____

_____

9. What kind of battle can Katniss and Peeta expect to encounter with Cato? ___

_____

_____

_____

_____

Name _____ **Period** _____

Directions: *Choose the best word for each definition. Write its letter on the line.*

10. _____enjoying
    a. savoring
    b. wielding
    c. noncommittal
    d. extricating

11. _____showing annoyance
    a. surreal
    b. extricating
    c. peevishly
    d. sustained

12. _____neutral
    a. sustained
    b. savoring
    c. noncommittal
    d. mesmerized

13. _____dreamlike
    a. mesmerized
    b. peevishly
    c. wielding
    d. surreal

14. _____getting out; removing
    a. emaciated
    b. surreal
    c. dissonant
    d. extricating

15. _____kept going
    a. sustained
    b. savoring
    c. emaciated
    d. noncommittal

16. _____starved; haggard
    a. savoring
    b. surreal
    c. emaciated
    d. wielding

17. _____grouchy
    a. surreal
    b. emaciated
    c. surly
    d. sustained

18. _____transfixed; hypnotized
    a. mesmerized
    b. wielding
    c. dissonant
    d. extricating

19. _____not harmonious
    a. emaciated
    b. savoring
    c. dissonant
    d. surreal

20. _____carrying; brandishing
    a. wielding
    b. sustained
    c. looming
    d. mesmerized

The Hunger Games

Quiz: Part Three: Chapters Twenty-Five – Twenty-Seven

Directions: For each of the following statements, write "True" if the statement is true and "False" if the statement is false.

1. _____Katniss went berserk when she entered the hovercraft and Peeta was taken away.

2. _____The muttations were benign.

3. _____It was difficult for the muttations to find purchase on the Cornucopia.

4. _____Peeta inadvertently swallowed one of the poison berries.

5. _____Katniss used a tourniquet on Peeta's leg.

6. _____Katniss's keen aim with her bow and arrow resulted in Cato letting go of Peeta.

7. _____Peeta and Katniss want to linger in the arena.

Directions: Choose the best answer to complete the statement. Write its letter on the line in front of the prompt.

8. _____Once in the hovercraft, Katniss
    a. behaves callously toward Peeta.
    b. is planning on avenging her time in the arena.
    c. becomes sophisticated.
    d. feverishly tries to reach Peeta.

9. _____A good word to describe the way the Gamemakers behaved toward the tributes is
    a. callously   c. contrived
    b. avenging   d. arbitrary

10. _____The dress Cinna designs for the victor tribute is not
    a. avenging   c. sophisticated
    b. contrived   d. insidious

11. _____Because those in the Capitol were so angry at Katniss's behavior, their response can be described as
    a. garish   c. contrived
    b. disproportionate   d. insidious

12. _____Katniss feels that President Snow is looking at her in this way:
    a. contrived   c. debut
    b. glowering   d. feverishly

13. _____When Katniss and Peeta are standing at the lake ready to eat the berries, they can describe their conflict with the Gamemakers as a

    a. debut
               c. stalemate

    b. segue
               d. disproportionate

14. _____A word that describes Katniss and Peeta returning to District 12 in a new light is:

    a. debut
               c. stalemate

    b. segue
               d. garish

Directions: *Choose the word from the word bank below that best describes the following statements. Write the word on the line in front of the statement. You will not use all the words in the word bank.*

arbitrary	disproportionate	segue
avenging	garish	stalemate
contrived	glowering	
debut	linger	

15. _____The tributes are selected for the Games through the reaping.

16. _____Katniss's story about when she first knew she loved Peeta.

17. _____The bright lights and colors of the Capitol.

18. _____The changes Katniss makes as she moves from the Capitol to District 12 and her old life.

19. _____The amount of time the three-hour film of the Games devotes to Katniss and Peeta rather than the other tributes.

20. _____Katniss fears that President Snow may want to punish her for what she did to embarrass him.

The Hunger Games

Part One Final Test

Part I: Directions: *Decide if each statement is true or false. Write the word "True" on the line in front of the statement if it is true; write "False" if the statement is false.*

1._____Katniss loses her patience with the Gamemakers.

2._____Katniss takes Prim's place in the Reaping.

3._____Katniss and Peeta become friends and hunt together.

4._____Katniss's father is killed in a minor train accident.

5._____Katniss's mother goes into a deep depression and cannot care for her children, so Katniss learns to hunt.

6._____During the interview, Katniss confesses she is in love with Gale.

7._____The Everdeens were on the verge of starvation at one time.

8._____At the reaping, Katniss's name was the first one chosen.

9. _____ Peeta and Katniss must travel to the Capitol for training.

10._____Katniss sees a rabbit and remembers that her father told her there were edible foods in the forest.

11._____Peeta and Katniss teach others new skills to use in the arena.

12._____Katniss becomes a trapper like Gale.

13._____Gale tosses loaves of bread to Prim to share with her family.

14._____Peeta is chosen in the reaping.

15._____Flauvia creates costumes that are on fire for the opening ceremonies.

Part II: Directions: *Match the speaker with the correct quote. Write the name of the correct character on the line before the quote.*

   a. Gale   e. Haymitch
   b. Prim   f. Effie Trinket
   c. Madge   g. Peeta
   d. Cinna

_____16. "May the odds be ever in your favor!"

_____17. "Hey, Catnip"

_____18. "I'm sure the arena will be full of bags of flour for me to chuck at people."

_____19. "When you're asked a question, find me, and answer it as honestly as possible."

_____20. "In public, I want you by each other's side every minute."

Name _____ **Period** _____

Part III: **Directions**: *Write your responses on the lines provided.*

21. Briefly describe the Hunger Games._____

_____

_____

_____

22. Explain how the tessera works._____

_____

_____

23. Explain how the setting of the Capitol provides a contrast to life for Katniss in District Twelve._____

_____

_____

24. How does Suzanne Collins rely on flashback to help the reader understand the world of Panem?_____

_____

_____

25. Discuss some of Katniss's positive and negative qualities._____

_____

_____

_____

_____

The Hunger Games

Part One Vocabulary Test

Part I: Directions - *Match the vocabulary word with the definitions below. Write the correct word on the line in front of its definition.*

sniveling	hostile	gnarled
ironic	preposterous	fixated
sustenance	adjacent	barbarism
despicable	sic	plummets
tangible	haggling	deterrent

_____1. to incite to attack

_____2. a discouragement from acting in a particular way

_____3. drops dramatically

_____4. ridiculous; unbelievable

_____5. worthy of being scorned or despised

_____6. nourishment

_____7. bargaining, usually arguing over a trade or price of an item

_____8. able to be touched

_____9. antagonistic; unfriendly

_____10. whiney or weepy

_____11. close to or joining

_____12. twisted

_____13. the opposite of what would be expected

_____14. uncivilized behavior

_____15. focused

Name _____ **Period** _____

Part II: Directions - *Write the vocabulary word on the line in front of the appropriate name or phrase.*

reaping   adversaries   substantial
gratified   mentor   insurmountable
poaching   amiable
flamboyant   impulsiveness

_____16. Peeta's personality during the interview

_____17. how the odds feel as Katniss and Peeta prepare to go

          into the arena

_____18. Haymitch

_____19. how Katniss felt about Peeta's gift of bread

_____20. The amount of food the tributes have in the Capitol

_____21. how the tributes view one another

_____22. Katniss is worried about this after her performance for

          the Gamemakers

_____23. the process of selecting a boy and a girl from each

          district to be in the Hunger Games

_____24. Katniss and Gale hunt illegally

_____25. Caesar Flickerman and many of the people who live in

          the Capitol

Part III: Directions - *On the line in front of the definition given, write the letter of the best choice of vocabulary word.*

26._____overly enthusiastically
    a. intensity   c. protocol
    b. maniacally   d. detest

27._____the customary or proper way of doing something; etiquette
    a. protocol   c. replicate
    b. pondering   d. surly

28. _____protest
     a. ludicrous   c. dissent
     b. affectations   d. vulnerable

29. _____extreme
     a. radical   c. pondering
     b. disgruntled   d. prestigious

30. _____problem; troublesome situation
     a. banal   c. potential
     b. deteriorate   d. predicament

Part IV: Directions - *Choose the best* **antonym** *for the word. On the line in front of the vocabulary word, write the letter of the best antonym for the vocabulary word.*

31. _____disastrous
     a. unfortunate   c. patient
     b. lucky   d. unclear

32. _____intensity
     a. focus   c. carelessness
     b. boredom   d. frenzied

33. _____replicate
     a. one of a kind   c. several
     b. to create again   d. simple

34. _____disgruntled
     a. hungry   c. happy
     b. empty   d. unhappy

35. _____pondering
     a. concentrating   c. considering
     b. thinking   d. daydreaming

36. _____unrequited
     a. discouraged   c. returned
     b. unnecessary   d. unable to overcome

Part V: Directions - *Choose the best* **synonym** *for the word. On the line in front of the vocabulary word, write the letter of the best synonym for the vocabulary word.*

37. _____inexplicable
     a. unexplained   c. confusing
     b. clear   d. unheard

38. _____deteriorated
   a. sturdy
   b. flimsy
   c. disintegrated
   d. destroyed

39. _____detest
   a. improve
   b. undo
   c. hate
   d. ignore

40. _____vulnerable
   a. exposed
   b. covered
   c. closed
   d. overturned

41. _____sever
   a. strict
   b. unkind
   c. release
   d. cut

42. _____irredeemably
   a. unable to be recovered
   b. unhappy
   c. not in control
   d. unbelievable

Part VI: Directions – *Decide whether the vocabulary word has been used appropriately. On the line in front of each statement, write True if it is used correctly or False if it is not.*

_____ 43. A person with <u>affectations</u> acts in a normal, natural way.

_____ 44. Anyone can take part in an <u>exclusively</u> planned event.

_____ 45. All the students participated in the <u>mandatory</u> meeting after school.

_____ 46. People who are very kind and thoughtful often <u>demean</u> others.

_____ 47. You can easily be <u>oblivious</u> to a wild monkey in English class.

_____ 48. Since we lost the basketball game yesterday, I'm feeling <u>surly</u>. I hate to lose.

_____ 49. I was hoping our math teacher would show some <u>leniency</u> and grade the test on a curve.

_____ 50. The party was <u>banal</u>; everyone agreed it was the best one of the year.

_____ 51. The giant spiders <u>intrigued</u> Reginald; he asked our science teacher many questions about them.

Part VII: Directions - *Use the words in the word bank below to complete the sentences. Be sure your sentences makes sense.*

sullen
potential
ludicrous
prestigious
defiantly

52. The rocket had the _____ to leave the earth's gravitational pull.

53. The student stood_____and refused to clean out her locker.

54. That clown nose looks_____ on you!

55. After a long night of studying for a test she was certain she would fail, Fredricka

felt _____ .

56. I think I deserve the_____award of the top honor roll

student this quarter.

The Hunger Games

Part Two Final Test

Directions: *Match the item or speaker of the quote with the correct quotation by writing the word(s) on the line in front of the quote.*

Cato   Katniss
Caesar Flickerman   Peeta
Claudius Templesmith   Rue
Foxface   silver parachute
Haymitch   tracker jackers

1. _____"Well, best of luck to you, Peeta Mellark, and I think I speak for all of Panem when I say our hearts go with yours."

2. _____ "The most I could say about you after your interview was that you were nice enough, although that in itself was a small miracle. Now I can say you're a heartbreaker…Which do you think will get you more sponsors?"

3. _____ "I'm sure I'll kill just everybody else. I can't go down without a fight. Only I keep wishing I could think of a way to … to show the Capitol they don't own me."

4. _____ My fingertips make small swirling patterns in the cool, slippery earth. *I love mud,* I think.

5. _____ Most people can't tolerate more than a few stings.

6. _____ I unscrew the lid and I know by the scent that it's medicine.

7. _____ His rage is so extreme it might be comical – so people really do tear out their hair and beat the ground with their fists –

8. _____ Slowly, one stem at a time, I decorate her body in the flowers. Covering the ugly wound. Wreathing her face. Weaving her hair with bright colors.

9. _____ There's been a rule change in the Games.

10. _____ She's smarter than the Careers, actually finding a few useful items in the ashes. A metal pot. A knife blade. I'm perplexed by her amusement until I realize that with the Careers' stores eliminated, she might actually stand a chance.

Name _____ **Period** _____

Directions: Write the word or words that best complete the sentences below.

11.   Peeta's confession during the interview that he loves Katniss makes Katniss seem _____

12. The term "star-crossed lovers" means _____

_____

13. At the beginning of the Games, Katniss is able to grab_____ before running to the forest.

14. Katniss forms an alliance with _____

15. The new rule for the Games is _____

_____

Directions: Answer the following questions on the lines provided.

16. What information does Rue share with Katniss about District 11? _____

_____

_____

17. Explain how Rue's death changes Katniss. _____

_____

_____

18. Explain why the ending of Part II is hopeful. _____

_____

_____

19. In Part II of the novel, what qualities does Katniss show that help her gain

sponsors. Explain your answer. _____

_____

_____

_____

20. Predict what you think Katniss is going to do with the new rule of the Games.

_____

_____

_____

Name _____ **Period** _____

Directions: *Decide if the statement is true or false. On the line in front of the statement, write "True" if the statement is true. Write "False" if the statement is false.*

21. _____Katniss has lost hearing in both ears due to the explosion.

22. _____Rue is going to teach a song to the mockingjays so Katniss will know she's okay.

23. _____Cato is a forgiving person.

24. _____Katniss thinks Foxface would be a good ally.

25. _____The fire in the forest is caused by a tribute's cooking fire.

Name _____   Period _____

The Hunger Games

Part Two Vocabulary Test

Directions: *Choose the word that best fits the definition. Write the word on the line in front of its definition.*

aghast	dispersed	lapdogs
assent	entourages	perceived
botched	gall	reenactments
breached	hoist	rejuvenating
condenses	imprudent	void

1. _____concentrates

2. _____energizing; restorative

3. _____agreement

4. _____broken

5. _____not cautious

6. _____pull; lift

7. _____groups of attendants to someone who is famous

8. _____emptiness

9. _____nerve

10. _____believed

11. _____shocked

12. _____reliving or acting out events that happened in the past

13. _____ruined

14. _____pampered pets

15. _____spread around

Directions: *Choose the best words to complete the following sentences. Write your choice of words on the line.*

abate	honing	precariously
balm	incompetent	quell
bravado	mayhem	sated
conspiratorially	onslaught	scarcity
dynamic	persevere	stupor

16. Katniss used a soothing_____on the burn on her leg.

17. Katniss could only_____her thirst by finding water.

18. In District 12, people rarely felt their hunger was completely _____.

19. The Careers were in complete_____when the tracker jackers attacked them. They couldn't get away from the wasps fast enough.

20. Katniss was waiting for a(n)_____from the Careers after she blew up their supplies.

21. After the tracker jacker attack, Katniss felt she was in a(n)_____ . She couldn't move or run away.

22. Katniss and Rue were able to work_____together in order to destroy the Careers supplies.

23. Foxface climbed_____up the pyramid of the Careers' supplies to steal supplies.

24. Katniss had to_____in her search for water. She just couldn't give up.

25. The audience of the Games must have been interested in the love

_____between Katniss and Peeta.

26. There was no_____of wild game for Katniss to hunt in the forest.

27. The special leaves Rue had were able to_____the pain of the wasp stings.

28. The night glasses help Katniss as she is_____in on what's happening in the arena each night.

29. While she was suffering from the tracker jacker stings, Katniss was

_____and unable to do anything to defend herself.

30. Katniss shows great_____in going to the Career camp.

Directions: *Choose the best **synonym** for the following vocabulary words. Write the letter of your choice on the line in front of the word.*

31. _____wracked
    a. shaken
    b. calmed
    c. broken
    d. uncovered

32. _____noxious
    a. boring
    b. harmful
    c. unsure
    d. discomfort

33. _____prominent
    a. shy; withdrawn
    b. confused
    c. noticeable; standing out
    d. in favor of

34. _____tentatively
    a. cautiously
    b. interesting
    c. complicated
    d. surely

35. _____ordeal
    a. agreement
    b. combine
    c. peaceful
    d. trouble

36. _____rations
    a. a portion
    b. division
    c. to switch
    d. not enough

37. _____forages
    a. building a shelter
    b. searches for food
    c. using up resources
    d. bargaining

38. _____obliging
    a. staring at
    b. giving honors
    c. stealing in secret
    d. willing to do favors

39. _____rendezvous
    a. response to a question
    b. ripping carefully
    c. meeting place
    d. small portion

40. _____copse
    a. a dead body
    b. officials of the Games
    c. a secret hiding place
    d. a group of trees or bushes

Directions: *Choose the* **antonym** *of the following vocabulary words. Write the letter of the best choice on the line in front of the word.*

41. _____doggedly
    a. halfheartedly
    b. having a dog
    c. stubbornly
    d. enjoying

42. _____fractured
    a. exploded
    b. disturbed
    c. healed
    d. splintered

43. _____subtly
    a. gradually
    b. suddenly

    c. carefully
    d. slowly

44. _____decadent
    a. ordinary and plain
    b. layered and complicated

    c. rich and luxurious
    d. serious and intense

45. _____fretful
    a. irritable
    b. careful

    c. musical
    d. calm

Directions: *Decide if the statement is true or false. On the line in front of the statement, write "True" if the statement is true. Write "False" if the statement is false.*

46. _____An audible sound cannot be heard.

47. _____If the grocery store shelves are bare, you might think there is an inadequate food supply.

48. _____Some students try to inflict trouble to keep from looking like a gangster.

49. _____If it rains on subsequent weeks, you might be worried about flooding.

50. _____Someone who acts with despondency would be delighted to go to a party.

51. _____After running a marathon, you might feel a form of lethargy.

52. _____Prisms are used for fragmenting light. They create rainbows.

Name _____   **Period** _____

The Hunger Games

Part Three Final Test

Part I: Directions *– Write the name of the character on the line next to his/her quote or description.*

Cato   Katniss
Claudius Templesmith   muttations
Clove   Peeta
Haymitch   Thresh

1. _____ "Shoot me and he goes down with me."

2. _____ "They resemble huge wolves, but what wolf lands and then balances easily on its hind legs?"

3. _____ "We both know they have to have a victor. It can only be one of us. Please take it. For me."

4. _____ "Greetings to the final contestants of the Seventy-fourth Hunger Games. The earlier revision has been revoked. Closer examination of the rule book has disclosed that only one winner may be allowed."

5. _____ "You're in trouble. Word is the Capitol's furious about you showing them up in the arena. The one thing they can't stand is being laughed at and they're the joke of Panem."

6. _____ "As I slowly, thoroughly wash the makeup from my face and put my hair in its braid, I begin transforming back into myself."

7. _____ "Forget it, District Twelve. We're going to kill you. Just like we did your pathetic little ally … what was her name?   The one who hopped around in the trees?"

8. _____ "Just this one time, I let you go. For the little girl. You and me, we're even then. No more owed. You understand?"

Part II: Directions *– Complete the following sentences using words of your own.*

9. Peeta is able to remain alive after Cato wounds him by _____

_____

10. Katniss learns that in order to get food from the sponsors she needs to _____

_____

11. The muttations are part _____ and part

_____

12. Cinna created a dress for Katniss that makes her look like _____

_____

13. Peeta is in danger of dying in the arena because _____

_____

Part III: Directions *– Answer the following questions on the lines provided.*

14. How do the Gamemakers change the rules of the Games in Part Three? ____

_____

_____

15. Name two things the Gamemakers do to manipulate the Games in Part Three.

_____

_____

_____

16. How are the muttations a good example of the horrors of the Games? Explain

your answer. _____

_____

_____

17. How does foreshadowing affect the impact of Katniss and Peeta's decision to

eat the berries? _____

_____

18. Explain Katniss's reasons for agreeing to eat the berries. _____

_____

19. Explain Peeta's reasons for agreeing to eat the berries. _____

_____

20. Explain the new danger that Katniss is in once the Games are over. _____

_____

_____

21. Choose one symbol you noticed in Part 3. Describe the symbol and what it stands for. _____

_____

_____

Part IV: Directions – *Write "True" if the statement is true or "False" if the statement is false.*

22. _____The novel is nicely tied up and the reader is left with no
    unanswered questions.

23. _____Peeta and Katniss are the only ones who do not suffer any
    permanent physical damage as a result of their time in the
    arena.

24. _____Foxface died because she trusted that Peeta knew what he was
    doing.

25. _____When Cato grabs Peeta, Peeta shows an amazing ability to
    think under pressure.

The Hunger Games

Part Three Vocabulary Test

Part I: Directions - *Write the word from the word bank below on the line in front of its correct definition.*

dissipate	potent
evade	ruse
insidious	scrupulously
pariahs	segue
peruse	tethered

1. _____scatter or spread in different directions

2. _____outcasts

3. _____intending to trap; deceitful

4. _____avoid; hide from

5. _____carefully

6. _____a trick

7. _____to look over or look through

8. _____tied to

9. _____strong; powerful

10. _____a transition

Part II: Directions - *Choose the correct word from the word bank to complete the sentence. The words are given in the form you will find them in the novel. You may have to change the word to make it fit the sentence given.*

arduous	irreparable
asset	keen
emanating	ominous
incoherence	vaguely
infusion	wheedles

11. The child tries to_____her mother into buying candy at the store.

12. Because he mumbled, Freddy's_____caused many to misunderstand him.

13. The_____task of building a brick wall around the city took many years for the townspeople to complete.

14. The greatest_____Katniss had in the arena was her survival skills.

15. The_____of cold air at night made it difficult for Katniss to stay warm on the cornucopia the last night in the arena.

16. Heat from the fire was_____ toward the chilled campers.

17. Obviously, the damage to Peeta's leg was_____ since it had to be amputated.

18. The_____clouds on the horizon threatened the day because we worried there would be a tornado.

19. Katniss's normally_____hearing was damaged in the explosion.

20. While she was in the hospital, Katniss was_____aware that someone was yelling.

Part III: Directions - *Choose the correct* **synonym** *or definition for the following words. Write the letter of your choice on the line in front of the word.*

21. _____plaintively
    a. sorrowfully   c. worried
    b. sadly   d. dully

22. _____famished
    a. famous   c. very hungry
    b. employed   d. unsure

23. _____irreverent
    a. unsure   c. unplanned
    b. disrespectful   d. disorderly

24. _____debut
    a. prize winning   c. classical
    b. enduring   d. first appearance

25. _____exorbitant
    a. excessive   c. unequal
    b. exit   d. taxing

26. _____exasperated
    a. overworked   c. frustrated
    b. expected   d. worthless

27. _____disproportionate
    a. unfair
    b. unequal
    c. not final
    d. not included

28. _____noncommittal
    a. controlling
    b. decisive
    c. creative
    d. neutral

29. _____peevishly
    a. showing annoyance
    b. showing understanding
    c. showing humor
    d. showing fear

30. _____surreal
    a. realistic
    b. dreamlike
    c. surprising happenings
    d. carefully planned

Part IV: Directions - *Write "True" to indicate that the vocabulary word is used correctly or "False" if it is used incorrectly. Keep in mind, you are NOT stating whether the statement is true or false, but whether the word is used correctly or not.*

31. _____, _____Katniss was concerned that glowering the arrow from the tourniquet would cause Peeta to bleed to death.

32. _____The tributes were sustained after their time in the arena.

33. _____Many of the tributes were wielding spears during the training.

34. _____Rue was mesmerized by the muttations.

35. _____Katniss emaciated her family by working odd jobs for the people of the Seam.

36. _____Rue taught the mocking jays a dissonant tune.

37. _____Katniss inadvertently called out Peeta's name when the Game rules were changed the first time.

38. _____Katniss and Peeta were often extricating at each other.

39. _____Katniss had no trouble getting purchase on a tree and climbing it.

Name _____ Period _____

Part V: **Directions** - *Choose the correct word for the definition given. Write the letter of your choice on the line in front of the definition. The part of speech may be different in some instances.*

40. _____uncaring
   a. callously   c. stalemate
   b. avenging   d. feverishly

41. _____getting vengeance or revenge
   a. callously   c. garish
   b. avenging   d. arbitrary

42. _____an impasse
   a. benign   c. stalemate
   b. garish   d. contrived

43. _____a bandage placed around a wound the help slow the loss of blood
   a. tourniquet   c. benign
   b. avenging   d. callously

44. _____excitedly; tirelessly
   a. garish   c. stalemate
   b. feverishly   d. arbitrary

45. _____showy; overly flashy or bright
   a. avenging   c. benign
   b. sophisticated   d. garish

46. _____made up
   a. arbitrary   c. tourniquet
   b. callously   d. contrived

47. _____random
   a. arbitrary   c. contrived
   b. stalemate   d. sophisticated

48. _____experienced; mature
   a. garish   c. avenging
   b. contrived   d. sophisticated

49. _____harmless
   a. benign   c. callously
   b. tourniquet   d. arbitrary

Name _____ **Period** _____

Part VI: Directions - *Use the following words in an original sentence that includes context clues to illustrate that you know what the word means. Underline or highlight your context clues. You may change the form of the word to fit your sentence.*

50. staunch: _____

_____

_____

51. tirades: _____

_____

_____

52. berserk: _____

_____

_____

53. savoring: _____

_____

_____

54. linger: _____

_____

_____

55. loathe: _____

_____

_____

56. ratcheting: _____

_____

_____

Name _____   Period _____

The Hunger Games

Final Exam

Part I: Directions - *Write the name of the character in front of the correct description.*

Caesar Flickerman   Katniss
Cato   Peeta
Effie Trinket   President Snow
Gamemakers   Prim
Haymitch   Rue

1. _____Angry at Katniss because she made him look bad in the Games

2. _____Has difficulty with anger. When angry, this character comes completely unglued.

3. _____Excellent with a bow and arrow; doesn't do well with sick people

4. _____Talented at camouflage

5. _____A good example of the fashion tastes of the Capitol

6. _____A kind interview host who makes guests feel comfortable

7. _____Good with animals – loves goats

8. _____Alcoholic

9. _____A tree jumper

10. _____Changes rules of the Games

Part II: Directions – *On the lines provided, write a short answer for each of the following questions.*

11. In Part One of the novel, how is flashback important? _____

_____

_____

12. What is one of the archetypes used in the novel? Explain why it's an archetype and why it is important to the novel. _____

_____

_____

13. Once the rules of the Games change, why is Katniss so concerned about Peeta's survival? _____

_____

14. Why do you think Peeta insists that Katniss must not go to the feast? Explain your answer. _____

_____

_____

15. Hypothesize what might be in the other backpacks that are at the feast. What do you think the other tributes might need to survive? _____

_____

_____

16. What is the primary point of view of the novel? How does this point of view help the story? How does this point of view limit the story? _____

_____

_____

_____

17. Choose one of the four types of conflict (character vs. self, character vs. character, character vs. society, character vs. nature) and a character who experiences that conflict. Analyze how that type of conflict is evident in the novel. Be sure to specify the character and include at least two specific details from the novel to support your answer. _____

_____

_____

_____

_____

_____

18. How does Suzanne Collins use foreshadowing in the novel? Include at least one specific detail to support your answer. _____

_____

_____

19. Identify a symbol used in the novel. Explain why you believe it is a symbol and what it symbolizes. _____

_____

_____

20. What connections were you able to make throughout the novel with the mythical story of Theseus? Use specific details to explain your connections. _____

_____

_____

Part III: Directions - Write "True" or "False" about the following statements.

21. _____ Panem is a democracy.

22. _____ District 12 might be where Appalachia is today.

23. _____ The Gamemakers are concerned about what makes television entertaining.

24. _____ The Hunger Games have some similarities to reality television shows that people watch today.

25. _____ Katniss is an underdog when the Games begin.

26. _____ The mockingjay is a symbol for the Capitol.

27. _____ One function of dialogue in a novel is to reveal its setting.

28. _____ Haymitch ends up being a good mentor to Katniss and Peeta.

29. _____ At the end of the novel, all the loose ends are tied up, and all the reader's questions are answered.

30. _____ *The Hunger Games* is a dystopian novel.

Name _____ **Period** _____

Part IV: Directions – *Choose the best answer to the following prompts. Write the letter of your choice on the line provided.*

31. _____ During the opening ceremonies, Katniss and Peeta

    a. are overshadowed by the tributes from District 1.
    b. have complete confidence in their costumes.
    c. experience stage fright and can't move.
    d. are popular with the crowds.

32. _____ During the period of physical training,

    a. Haymitch recommends that Katniss and Peeta sharpen their current skills.
    b. the District 1 tributes follow Katniss and Peeta around in an attempt to intimidate them.
    c. Katniss and Peeta are together all the time.
    d. Peeta confesses his love for Katniss.

33. _____ Katniss's behavior in front of the Gamemakers shows she

    a. is a skilled trapper.
    b. has a short temper.
    c. is afraid of new challenges.
    d. struggles with respecting adults.

34. _____ The night before the Games, Peeta tells Katniss that he wants

    a. to be her ally in the Games.
    b. revenge on the tributes from District 1.
    c. to die on his own terms.
    d. to marry Katniss.

35. _____ On the first day of the Games, Katniss discovers

    a. a good source for water.
    b. the arena has no trees for her to use for cover.
    c. Peeta has made an alliance with the Careers.
    d. a bow and arrow.

36. _____ Katniss follows Haymitch's advice for survival:

    a. Get away from the Cornucopia and find water.
    b. Make alliances and start attacking.
    c. Hide from the other tributes and find a way out of the arena.
    d. Begin hunting right away and stay close to Peeta.

37. _____ The following event adds to the tension in the arena:

    a. Katniss cannot find food or water in the arena.
    b. the mockingbirds attack Katniss.
    c. Katniss is able to make a bow and arrow out of branches.
    d. The Careers trap Katniss in a tree.

38. _____ Katniss's first silver parachute shows that

    a. her sponsors feel sorry for her and want her to recover.
    b. Haymitch is still drinking and cannot get her good gifts.
    c. her sponsors like her strategy in dealing with the tracker jackers.
    d. Peeta is still the most popular tribute in the arena.

39. _____ After Katniss and Rue become allies, Katniss decides to go on the offensive. This means Katniss is

    a. going to attack the Careers.
    b. planning to spy on the others.
    c. about to shoot them with her bow and arrow.
    d. going to destroy the Careers' food.

40. _____ Katniss shows respect for Rue by

    a. leaving her in peace after she dies.
    b. respecting her wishes to be left alone.
    c. getting revenge on her killer.
    d. singing to her until she dies.

41. _____ In caring for Peeta, Katniss must

    a. show the audience that she loves him.
    b. practice the first aid skills she learned in training.
    c. use the plants she finds in the forest to create a cure.
    d. rely on her hunting skills to save him.

42. _____ The feast promises to

    a. provide the tributes with a way to form new alliances.
    b. restock the tributes' food supplies.
    c. give each tribute something he or she needs.
    d. be an opportunity for Katniss to get revenge.

43. _____ The sponsors didn't send medicine to Peeta because they

    a. wanted him to die.
    b. thought it was better entertainment to send Katniss to the feast.
    c. didn't have the money to provide medicine.
    d. thought Katniss could cure him.

44. _____ You can infer that Clove

    a. is intimidated by Katniss.
    b. wants to help Cato kill Katniss.
    c. has been planning how to kill Katniss.
    d. was quite attached to Rue.

45. _____ Thresh and Katniss are alike because they both

    a. understand what it means to owe someone a favor.
    b. took the place of a loved one in the arena.
    c. experienced great heartache as children.
    d. care about Peeta getting better.

46. _____ The muttations are

    a. mutations created by the Capitol.
    b. scary, but harmless.
    c. only interested in chasing the tributes.
    d. easily defeated.

47. _____ In the end, the Gamemakers reverse their rule-change decision because

    a. they don't think Katniss and Peeta mean what they say.
    b. Katniss and Peeta are too injured to continue.
    c. Peeta has lost so much blood he could die.
    d. they believe Katniss and Peeta will eat the berries.

48. _____ In spite of everything that happened in the arena, Katniss still believes

    a. Peeta was acting.
    b. the Games are worthwhile.
    c. Haymitch was a horrible mentor.
    d. she truly loves Gale.

49. _____ They best symbol for Katniss at the end of the novel is

    a. bread.
    b. the flag of Panem.
    c. flowers.
    d. the forest.

50. _____ One of the ironic events of the novel is

    a. Katniss's skills with the bow and arrow.
    b. The purpose of the feast.
    c. Peeta's wrestling ability.
    d. Gale taking care of Katniss's family.

Name _____ **Period** _____

The Hunger Games

Final Exam: Multiple Choice Version

Part I: Directions - Choose the best response to the prompt and fill in the bubble completely or write the corresponding letter on your answer sheet.

1. Panem
     a. was once North America.
     b. is a democracy.
     c. existed hundreds of years ago.
     d. is a utopian society.

2. The Hunger Games are a
     a. reminder of times when people suffered from a famine.
     b. punishment for an uprising against the government.
     c. celebration of the rebuilding of Panem.
     d. taxation for the Districts that rebelled.

3. Katniss
     a. is chosen in the reaping.
     b. takes Prim's place in the reaping.
     c. had a very small chance of being chosen.
     d. is most concerned that Gale isn't chosen.

4. Peeta
     a. is a friend of Katniss.
     b. lives in the Seam.
     c. volunteers to take someone's place.
     d. saved Katniss's family from starvation.

5. A surprise visitor to Katniss as she waits in the Justice building is
     a. Effie Trinket.
     b. Gale.
     c. Madge.
     d. Haymitch.

6. Haymitch is important to Katniss and Peeta because
     a. he's responsible for their lives in the arena.
     b. he knows how to win the Games.
     c. he's a skilled negotiator.
     d. he's a well respected figure in the Capitol.

7. In a flashback, Katniss remembers
     a. how she learned to survive in the woods.
     b. strategies she can use from past Hunger Games.
     c. happy memories of signing up for the tessera.
     d. how Prim enjoyed hunting with her.

8. Peeta and Katniss
   a. decide to become allies and fight together.
   b. convince Effie to mentor them.
   c. impress Haymitch with their violent response to his drinking.
   d. discuss their fighting strengths and weaknesses.

9. Cinna
   a. is the stylist responsible for Katniss's costumes.
   b. doesn't show much imagination in his work.
   c. has bizarre hair decorations and tattoos.
   d. shows intense interest in Katniss and Peeta's life in District 12.

10. During the opening ceremonies, Katniss and Peeta
    a. are overshadowed by the tributes from District 1.
    b. have complete confidence in their costumes.
    c. experience stage fright and can't move.
    d. are popular with the crowds.

11. Katniss thinks
    a. the food in the Capitol is too rich for her.
    b. she recognizes an Avox.
    c. her room is too plain.
    d. she should drink more wine.

12. Katniss confides in Peeta about
    a. her feelings about the Capitol food.
    b. how she knows the Avox.
    c. her discomfort in the Capitol.
    d. Haymitch's drinking.

13. During the period of physical training,
    a. Haymitch recommends that Katniss and Peeta sharpen their current skills.
    b. the District 1 tributes follow Katniss and Peeta around in an attempt to intimidate them.
    c. Katniss and Peeta are together all the time.
    d. Peeta confesses his love for Katniss.

14. During the private session with the Gamemakers, Katniss
    a. realizes the Gamemakers are not interested in her.
    b. loses the opportunity to show the Gamemakers her skills with the bow and arrow.
    c. forgets to thank the Gamemakers for their time.
    d. keeps her calm even though she's not comfortable with the bow she's chosen.

15. Katniss's behavior in front the of the Gamemakers shows she
    a. is a skilled trapper.
    b. has a short temper.
    c. is afraid of new challenges.
    d. struggles with respecting adults.

16. Katniss feels betrayed by
    a. the score she received from the Gamemakers.
    b. Haymitch's decision to train her how to hunt.
    c. Peeta's request to be coached on his own.
    d. Effie's lack of confidence in her.

17. As they practice for the interview, Haymitch is disappointed in Katniss because she
    a. talks too quietly.
    b. is too shy to speak.
    c. is openly hostile.
    d. doesn't like Haymitch.

18. The most surprising revelation of the interview is
    a. Cinna is an amazing stylist.
    b. Katniss cries about Prim.
    c. Caesar Flickerman tells Katniss about the arena.
    d. Peeta tells Caesar that he loves Katniss.

19. Katniss doesn't understand
    a. Peeta's strategy for the arena.
    b. how Peeta's confession gives her an advantage.
    c. Haymitch's anger toward her.
    d. why she has to change her fighting technique.

20. The night before the Games begin, Peeta tells Katniss that he wants
    a. to be her ally in the Games.
    b. revenge on the tributes from District 1.
    c. to die on his own terms.
    d. to marry Katniss.

21. At the start of the Games, the tributes have the opportunity to
    a. communicate with their mentors.
    b. gather supplies and weapons at the Cornucopia.
    c. make a base camp with the other tributes from their district.
    d. survey the scene before leaving.

22. On the first day of the Games, Katniss discovers
    a. a good source for water.
    b. the arena has no trees for her to use for cover.
    c. Peeta has made an alliance with the Careers.
    d. a bow and arrow.

23. Katniss follows Haymitch's advice for surviving:
    a. Get away from the Cornucopia and find water.
    b. Make alliances and start attacking.
    c. Hide from the other tributes and find a way out of the arena.
    d. Begin hunting right away and stay close to Peeta.

24. As soon as Katniss begins to feel better and healthy, she is awakened at night by
    a. tracker jackers.
    b. Rue.
    c. fire.
    d. rain.

25. The following event adds to the tension in the arena:
    a. Katniss cannot find food or water in the arena.
    b. The mockingbirds attack Katniss.
    c. Katniss is able to make a bow and arrow out of branches.
    d. The Careers trap Katniss in a tree.

26. The appearance of Rue in the trees
    a. eventually saves Katniss.
    b. results in Katniss being discovered.
    c. helps Katniss find water.
    d. surprises the Careers.

27. The tracker jackers are
    a. harmless wasps.
    b. a good source for honey.
    c. muttations.
    d. from District 12.

28. Katniss's first silver parachute shows that
    a. her sponsors feel sorry for her and want her to recover.
    b. Haymitch is still drinking and cannot get her good gifts.
    c. her sponsors like her strategy in dealing with the tracker jackers.
    d. Peeta is still the most popular tribute in the arena.

29. As a result of the tracker jacker event, Katniss
    a. thinks Peeta saved her life.
    b. believes she was attacked by ants.
    c. shows she can avoid injury.
    d. has lost all her supplies.

30. Rue
    a. is a skilled hunter.
    b. has information about the Careers.
    c. lives in a district that is very lenient.
    d. isn't able to teach Katniss anything.

31. After Katniss and Rue become allies, Katniss decides to go on the offensive. This means Katniss is
    a. going to attack the Careers.
    b. planning to spy on the others.
    c. about to shoot them with her bow and arrow.
    d. going to destroy the Careers' food.

32. Katniss discovers something by observing Foxface as she steals supplies. She learns
    a. the supplies are booby trapped.
    b. there is nothing of value in the pile.
    c. Foxface is guarding the supplies.
    d. that she must confront the Careers.

33. Katniss is successful in her plan, but as a result she
    a. has lost her bow and arrows.
    b. cannot find her way back to Rue.
    c. has lost her hearing.
    d. is knocked unconscious.

34. Rue is
    a. captured by the Careers.
    b. killed by a boy from District 1.
    c. lost in the forest.
    d. poisoned by the berries she eats.

35. Katniss shows respect for Rue by
    a. leaving her in peace after she dies.
    b. respecting her wishes to be left alone.
    c. getting revenge on her killer.
    d. singing to her until she dies.

36. After Rue's death, you can infer that Katniss
    a. has a renewed energy for revenge.
    b. is depressed.
    c. hates the Capitol even more.
    d. hopes she'll be captured by the Careers.

37. The rules of the Games have changed. The Gamemakers tell the tributes
    a. there will be extra food and supplies for them.
    b. they are releasing mutts into the arena.
    c. two tributes from the same district can win.
    d. they must return to the lake to battle.

38. In caring for Peeta, Katniss must
    a. show the audience that she loves him.
    b. practice the first aid skills she learned in training.
    c. use the plants she finds in the forest to create a cure.
    d. rely on her hunting skills to save him.

39. The feast promises to
    a. provide the tributes with a way to form new alliances.
    b. restock the tributes' food supplies.
    c. give each tribute something he or she needs.
    d. be an opportunity for Katniss to get revenge.

40. The sponsors don't send medicine to Peeta because they
    a. want him to die.
    b. think it is better entertainment to send Katniss to the feast.
    c. don't have the money to provide medicine.
    d. think Katniss can cure him.

41. You can infer that Clove
    a. is intimidated by Katniss.
    b. wants to help Cato kill Katniss.
    c. has been planning how to kill Katniss.
    d. was attached to Rue.

42. Thresh and Katniss are alike because they both
    a. understand what it means to owe someone a favor.
    b. took the place of a loved one in the arena.
    c. experienced great heartache as children.
    d. care about Peeta getting better.

43. Katniss returns to Peeta with the medicine, and
    a. they realize they need to leave the cave.
    b. Peeta begins to heal and take care of Katniss.
    c. Cato begins hunting them.
    d. they stop talking to each other.

44. Peeta tells Katniss that he
    a. has been pretending to love her.
    b. loved her ever since they were chosen at the reaping.
    c. wants to learn to hunt.
    d. has loved Katniss since he heard her sing.

45. Peeta and Katniss leave the cave because they
    a. need to find a safer camp.
    b. are going to attack Cato.
    c. need food.
    d. want to find Foxface.

46. Foxface
    a. attacks Peeta while Katniss hunts.
    b. steals their food.
    c. is in alliance with Cato.
    d. has been hunting them.

47. When Katniss and Peeta return to the lake, they discover
    a. Cato is ready for them.
    b. the Cornucopia still has supplies in it.
    c. something is chasing Cato.
    d. they are too weak to fight.

48. The muttations are
    a. mutations created by the Capitol.
    b. scary, but harmless.
    c. only interested in chasing the tributes.
    d. easily defeated.

49. Cato threatens to kill Peeta, but
    a. the mutts grab Cato.
    b. Katniss shoots Cato in the hand.
    c. Peeta wrestles away from him.
    d. Cato decides to let him go.

50. The Gamemakers change the rules again.
    a. The tributes must now defeat all the mutts.
    b. Katniss and Peeta must now leave the arena.
    c. There can now be only one winner.
    d. Now, they cannot leave without bringing back the mutts.

51. In the end, the Gamemakers reverse their rule change decision because
    a. they don't think Katniss and Peeta mean what they say.
    b. Katniss and Peeta are too injured to continue.
    c. Peeta has lost so much blood he could die.
    d. they believe Katniss and Peeta will eat the berries.

52. Once back in the Capitol, Katniss learns that
    a. President Snow is angry with her.
    b. Haymitch had been lying to them all along.
    c. Cinna created a strange, new outfit for Katniss.
    d. the audience wanted Peeta to win.

53. In spite of everything that happened in the arena, Katniss still believes
    a. Peeta was acting.
    b. the Games are worthwhile.
    c. Haymitch was a horrible mentor.
    d. she truly loves Gale.

54. They best symbol for Katniss at the end of the novel is
    a. bread.
    b. the flag of Panem.
    c. flowers.
    d. the forest.

55. One of the ironic events of the novel is
    a. Katniss's skills with the bow and arrow.
    b. The purpose of the feast.
    c. Peeta's wrestling ability.
    d. Gale taking care of Katniss's family.

Name _____   **Period** _____

The Hunger Games

Vocabulary Final Test

Directions: Write the correct word on the line in front of its best definition.

adjacent   maniacally   protocol
deterrent   plummets   reaping
dissent   poaching
haggling   preposterous

1. _____ harvesting

2. _____ drops dramatically

3. _____ protest

4. _____ close to or joining

5. _____ ridiculous; unbelievable

6. _____ bargaining, usually arguing over a trade or price of an item

7. _____ overly enthusiastically

8. _____ the customary or proper way of doing something; etiquette

9. _____ hunting illegally

10. _____ a discouragement from acting in a particular way

abate   incompetent   scarcity
conspiratorially   predicament   stupor
dynamic   quell
imprudent   radical

11. _____ extreme

12. _____ problem, troublesome situation

13. _____ not cautious

14. _____ relationship

15. _____ rarity

16. _____ to put an end to; to extinguish

17. _____ diminish; lessen

18. _____ daze; unclear mental state

19. _____ not capable of doing something; lacking ability

20. _____ plotting together

Name _____ **Period** _____

Directions: Write "True" in the blank if the vocabulary word is used correctly in the sentence. Write "False" if it is used incorrectly.

21. _____ The destruction from the tornado was <u>disastrous</u> for the small town.

22. _____ Clyde focused on his algebra homework with great <u>intensity</u>.

23. _____ The task of washing the dishes seemed <u>insurmountable</u> after the banquet.

24. _____ Shawna was <u>gratified</u> when she received an F on her English paper.

25. _____ The <u>sniveling</u> audience was laughing at the comedian's show.

26. _____ The quarterback was hoping to <u>replicate</u> the pass he'd made for the touchdown.

27. _____ The <u>disgruntled</u> student danced around the classroom with joy when the project was announced.

28. _____ Your <u>mentor</u> might be a guidance counselor.

29. _____ The scientist was <u>pondering</u> over the failed experiment as she tried to figure out what went wrong.

30. _____ Fred's anger over the lack of homework was <u>inexplicable</u>.

31. _____ We measured the <u>gnarled</u>, straight rails of the fence.

32. _____ The new house <u>deteriorated</u> because it was able to withstand the tornado and flood.

33. _____ The thieves got away with a <u>substantial</u> amount of cash from the bank robbery. They walked away with only $5.00.

34. _____ I refuse to eat lima beans because I <u>detest</u> them.

35. _____ The unarmed tributes felt <u>vulnerable</u> in the arena.

36. _____ The <u>affectations</u> of the movie star made her difficult to understand.

37. _____ I wore a <u>flamboyant</u> coat that was a plain gray.

38. _____ The starving children lacked <u>sustenance</u>; consequently they were malnourished.

39. _____ We visited the <u>despicable</u> historical monument in Washington D.C.

40. _____ The soft yarn of the sweater was <u>tangible</u>.

Directions: *Choose the best vocabulary word to complete the sentence. Write your choice of words on the line.*

adversaries	exclusively
amiable	ironic
barbarism	mandatory
debut	oblivious
demean	surly

41. We tried to be_____toward the new neighbors and welcome them to the neighborhood.

42. The gift of a free TV was offered_____to members of the club.

43. The invaders acted with_____as they destroyed the priceless pieces of artwork in the museum.

44. We thought it was_____that the world-renowned chef couldn't boil water.

45. The two rival football teams had been_____for many years.

46. Before school starts, we have to attend a_____ orientation; if we miss it, we do not get to start school until we make it up.

47. His cruel comments were designed to_____the helpless child.

48. Because we were having so much fun, we were_____to the fact that it was long past our curfew.

49. We felt_____after we'd only had three hours of sleep. None of us was very happy that we had to get up.

50. We went to the_____of the movie on the first day it opened.

Directions: *Choose an **antonym** for the vocabulary word. Write the entire word of your choice on the line in front of the vocabulary word.*

51. _____banal
    a. boring   c. happy
    b. exciting   d. sad

52. _____void
    a. clear   c. full
    b. simple   d. shiny

53. _____impulsiveness
    a. intentionally   c. ashamed
    b. rash   d. fulfilled

54. _____sullen
   a. irritated
   b. saved
   c. forceful
   d. happy

55. _____bravado
   a. cowardice
   b. cold
   c. slippery
   d. hostile

56. _____fractured
   a. split
   b. silly
   c. whole
   d. burned

57. _____famished
   a. empty
   b. hateful
   c. full
   d. extreme

58. _____exorbitant
   a. reasonable
   b. extreme
   c. dirty
   d. spongy

59. _____emaciated
   a. healthy
   b. uneducated
   c. withered
   d. lost

60. _____hostile
   a. kidnapped
   b. friendly
   c. saddened
   d. practiced

Directions: Choose a **synonym** or definition for the vocabulary word. Write the entire word(s) of your choice on the line in front of the vocabulary word.

61. _____sever
   a. cut
   b. strict
   c. unhappy
   d. complete

62. _____fixated
   a. repaired
   b. focused
   c. controlled
   d. volume

63. _____leniency
   a. upright
   b. silent
   c. controlled
   d. mercy

64. _____sic
   a. to incite to attack
   b. to give up
   c. to uncover
   d. to create

65. _____irredeemably
    a. easy to control
    b. without cause
    c. unable to be recovered
    d. incompletely

66. _____potential
    a. unearth
    b. possible capacity
    c. energetic
    d. surprised

67. _____defiantly
    a. rebelliously
    b. seriously
    c. unconscious
    d. sloppily

68. _____ludicrous
    a. wealthy
    b. certainly
    c. laughable
    d. delicious

69. _____intrigued
    a. stately
    b. itchy
    c. fascinated
    d. painted

70. _____prestigious
    a. fancy
    b. written
    c. enclosed
    d. respected

71. _____benign
    a. harmless
    b. musical
    c. adventurous
    d. frail

Directions: *Choose the best word from the word bank to complete the sentence. Write your choice of words on the line.*

aghast	entourages	reenactments
assent	feverishly	rejuvenating
avenging	gall	stalemate
botched	hoist	tentatively
breached	lapdogs	tourniquet
condenses	perceived	unrequited
dispersed	precariously	

72. The water_____in the clouds and forms rain drops.

73. Bradley had the_____to complain to the crabby manager of the store.

74. The teacher's pets were like little_____.

75. The latest edition of the newspaper was freely_____
to everyone in the neighborhood.

76. We had to_____the dresser out of the truck and carry it into
the house.

77. Mother gave the children her_____which allowed them to
watch the scary movie.

78. The dam was_____by the flood waters, and soon the entire
town was flooded.

79. Florence was_____when she saw the poor grade on her book
report; she was shocked since she'd worked so hard on it.

80. No one_____the danger in allowing the genie to escape
from the bottle.

81. Sadly, on Valentine's Day, Bob's love for Maylee was _____.

82. The_____followed the king around on his tour of the town.

83. The Civil War_____were well attended at the battlefield in
Gettysburg.

84. Because it was ruined, Cliff's_____Halloween costume
looked more silly than scary.

85. A swim in the pool on a hot day is _____ .

86. The dishes were stacked_____and in were danger of
crashing down off of the table.

87. The doctor_____examined the rabid dog.

88. The rebels were bent on in_____the death of their leader after
the battle.

89. When neither one could win the argument, the two students decided they had
reached a_____ .

90. Because the bleeding was so severe, the medic used a_____
to try to save the soldier.

91. The student council worked_____to finish the
decorations for the dance.

Directions: *Choose the correct word to complete the analogy. Write the word that best completes the analogy on the line.*

92. sweet smelling : aromatic :: noxious : _____
    a. foul smelling
    b. sated
    c. balm
    d. ordeal

93. cry : mourn :: persevere : _____
    a. quit
    b. persist
    c. whimper
    d. rejoice

94. hot : cold :: sated : _____
    a. starving
    b. famished
    c. unhappy
    d. hungry

95. clown : silly :: balm : _____
    a. irritating
    b. soothing
    c. burn
    d. freeze

96. tight : loose :: honing : _____
    a. sharing
    b. accepting
    c. dulling
    d. flattering

97. happy : party :: mayhem : _____
    a. calmness
    b. simplicity
    c. riot
    d. sadness

98. generosity : giving :: onslaught : _____
    a. attack
    b. shredding
    c. confusion
    d. forgetful

99. silent : noisy :: calm : _____
    a. wracked
    b. injured
    c. quiet
    d. juicy

100. building : skyscraper :: noticeable : _____
    a. eligible
    b. uncomfortable
    c. clean
    d. prominent

101. cupcake : cake :: trouble : _____
    a. decorations
    b. superstitions
    c. forgiving
    d. ordeal

Directions: *Choose the correct definition for the vocabulary word. Write the letter of your choice of definitions on the line in front of the vocabulary word.*

102. _____rations
    a. a decision
    b. set point
    c. a portion
    d. simplicity

103. _____forages
    a. forest
    b. searches for food
    c. confuse
    d. undisclosed

104. _____obliging
    a. willing to do favors
    b. to stare with intent
    c. unsure of how to act
    d. surprised

105. _____rendezvous
    a. respond
    b. complaints
    c. force
    d. meeting place

106. _____copse
    a. close by
    b. a dead body
    c. complete
    d. a group of trees or bushes

107. _____doggedly
    a. like a dog
    b. stubbornly
    c. overly
    d. taxing

108. _____subsequent
    a. before
    b. during
    c. next
    d. over

109. _____fragmenting
    a. mending
    b. splitting apart
    c. partial
    d. combined

110. _____subtly
    a. gradually
    b. softly
    c. uneasily
    d. quality

111. _____decadent
    a. evil
    b. damaged
    c. luxurious
    d. fulfilled

112. _____fretful
    a. musical
    b. distressed
    c. teasing
    d. balanced

113. _____audible

    a. without a sound   c. unstable
    b. tasting carefully   d. able to be heard

114. _____inadequate

    a. too full   c. expensive
    b. not enough   d. underfed

115. _____inflict

    a. impose something unwanted   c. understand difficult concepts
    b. help someone   d. disguise

116. _____despondency

    a. currency   c. repellant
    b. responsive   d. hopelessness

117. _____lethargy

    a. deadly   c. unarmed
    b. sluggishness   d. unimpressed

118. _____dissipate

    a. to review   c. to scatter
    b. to sell   d. to contain

119. _____pariahs

    a. deadly   c. fish
    b. outcasts   d. forecast

120. _____loathe

    a. chafe   c. hate
    b. tantrum   d. bully

121. _____arbitrary

    a. divide   c. expertly
    b. amplify   d. random

Directions: *Choose the correct vocabulary word based on the definition. Write the letter of your choice on the line in front of the definition.*

122. _____avoid; hide from

    a. plaintively   c. vaguely
    b. irreparable   d. evade

123. _____carefully

    a. famished   c. scrupulously

    b. irreverent   d. exorbitant

124. _____a trick

    a. ruse   c. surly

    b. noncommittal   d. mesmerized

125. _____to look over or look through

    a. peruse   c. segue

    b. wielding   d. linger

126. _____tied to

    a. tethered   c. incoherent

    b. potent   d. infusion

127. _____strong; powerful

    a. doggedly   c. potent

    b. emanating   d. arduous

128. _____turning or cranking

    a. wheedles   c. extricating

    b. ratcheting   d. tethered

129. _____persuades

    a. scrupulously   c. infusion

    b. ruse   d. wheedles

130. _____inability to be understood

    a. incoherence   c. audible

    b. fretful   d. lethargy

131. _____very difficult

    a. famished   c. extricating

    b. exorbitant   d. arduous

132. _____something useful or desirable

    a. glowering   c. stalemate

    b. asset   d. garish

133. _____mixture

    a. asset   c. infusion

    b. purchase   d. potent

134. _____radiating outward
- a. avenging
- b. irreparable
- c. emanating
- d. wheedles

135. _____unable to be repaired
- a. callously
- b. irreparable
- c. vaguely
- d. peruse

136. _____foreboding; threatening
- a. ominous
- b. evade
- c. potent
- d. ratcheting

137. _____stop
- a. pariahs
- b. loathe
- c. staunch
- d. tethered

138. _____not specifically
- a. vaguely
- b. scrupulously
- c. emanating
- d. infusion

139. _____mournfully
- a. ominous
- b. plaintively
- c. savoring
- d. peevishly

140. _____disrespectful
- a. surreal
- b. extricating
- c. irreverent
- d. irreparable

141. _____tantrums
- a. tirades
- b. exorbitant
- c. emaciated
- d. ratcheting

142. _____sharp
- a. purchase
- b. keen
- c. noncommittal
- d. surreal

143. _____frustrated
- a. evade
- b. ruse
- c. exasperated
- d. peruse

144. _____enjoying
- a. tether
- b. potent
- c. savoring
- d. wheedles

145. _____neutral
    a. incoherence
    b. arduous
    c. asset
    d. noncommittal

146. _____showing annoyance
    a. peevishly
    b. potent
    c. incoherence
    d. avenging

147. _____dreamlike
    a. noncommittal
    b. surreal
    c. peevishly
    d. savoring

Directions: *Use the following words in a sentence. Include context clues that show you understand the meaning of the word. Underline or highlight your context clues.*

148. extricating _____

_____

149. sustained _____

_____

150. mesmerized _____

_____

151. dissonant _____

_____

152. wielding _____

_____

153. inadvertently _____

_____

154. glowering _____

_____

155. purchase _____

_____

156. callously _____

_____

157. garish _____

_____

158. contrived _____

_____

159. sophisticated _____

_____

160. berserk _____

_____

161. disproportionate _____

_____

162. linger _____

_____

163. insidious _____

_____

164. segue _____

_____

Name _____   Period _____

The Hunger Games

Multiple Choice Vocabulary Test

Directions: *Choose the correct definition for the vocabulary word.   Write the letter of your choice on the line in front of the word, or follow your teacher's directions.*

1. _____forages
   a. forest
   b. searches for food

   c. confuse
   d. undisclosed

2. _____obliging
   a. willing to do favors
   b. to stare with intent

   c. unsure of how to act
   d. surprised

3. _____rendezvous
   a. respond
   b. complaints

   c. force
   d. meeting place

4. _____doggedly
   a. like a dog
   b. stubbornly

   c. overly
   d. taxing

5. _____subsequent
   a. before
   b. during

   c. next
   d. over

6. _____subtly
   a. gradually
   b. softly

   c. uneasily
   d. quality

7. _____audible
   a. without a sound
   b. tasting carefully

   c. unstable
   d. able to be heard

8. _____inadequate
   a. too full
   b. not enough

   c. expensive
   d. underfed

9. _____inflict
   a. to impose something unwanted
   b. to help someone

   c. to understand difficult concepts
   d. to disguise

10. _____despondency
    a. currency
    b. responsive

    c. repellant
    d. depression

Name _____ **Period** _____

11. _____lethargy
    a. deadly
    b. sluggishness
    c. unarmed
    d. lethal

12. _____dissipate
    a. to review
    b. to sell
    c. to scatter
    d. to contain

13. _____pariahs
    a. deadly
    b. outcasts
    c. fish
    d. forecast

14. _____loathe
    a. chafe
    b. tantrum
    c. hate
    d. bully

15. _____arbitrary
    a. divide
    b. amplify
    c. expertly
    d. random

Directions: Choose the best **antonym** for the vocabulary word. Write the letter of the best answer on the line before the word.

16. _____banal
    a. boring
    b. exciting
    c. happy
    d. sad

17. _____void
    a. clear
    b. simple
    c. full
    d. shiny

18. _____impulsiveness
    a. intention
    b. haste
    c. shame
    d. fulfilled

19. _____sullen
    a. irritated
    b. saved
    c. forceful
    d. happy

20. _____bravado
    a. cowardice
    b. cold
    c. slippery
    d. hostile

21. _____fractured
    a. split
    b. silly
    c. whole
    d. burned

22. _____famished
    a. empty
    b. hateful
    c. sated
    d. extreme

23. _____exorbitant
    a. reasonable
    b. extreme
    c. dirty
    d. spongy

24. _____emaciated
    a. healthy
    b. uneducated
    c. forgotten
    d. withered

25. _____hostile
    a. kidnapped
    b. friendly
    c. sad
    d. practiced

Directions: Choose the best **synonym** for the vocabulary word. Write the letter of the best answer on the line before the word.

26. _____sever
    a. cut
    b. strict
    c. unhappy
    d. complete

27. _____fixated
    a. repaired
    b. focused
    c. controlled
    d. volume

28. _____leniency
    a. upright
    b. silent
    c. controlled
    d. mercy

29. _____irredeemably
    a. easy to control
    b. without cause
    c. unable to be recovered
    d. incompletely

30. _____potential
    a. unearth
    b. possible capacity
    c. energetic
    d. surprised

31. _____defiantly
    a. resistantly
    b. seriously
    c. unconsciously
    d. sloppily

32. _____ludicrous
    a. wealthy
    b. certainly
    c. laughable
    d. delicious

33. _____intrigued
   a. stately
   b. itchy
   c. fascinated
   d. painted

34. _____prestigious
   a. fancy
   b. written
   c. enclosed
   d. respected

35. _____benign
   a. harmless
   b. musical
   c. adventurous
   d. frail

Directions: *Choose the correct word or words to complete the analogy. Write the letter of your choice on the line.*

36. sweet smelling : aromatic :: noxious : _____
   a. foul smelling
   b. sated
   c. balm
   d. ordeal

37. cry : mourn :: persevere : _____
   a. quit
   b. persist
   c. whimper
   d. rejoice

38. hot : cold :: hungry : _____
   a. starving
   b. famished
   c. unhappy
   d. sated

39. clown : silly :: balm : _____
   a. irritating
   b. soothing
   c. burn
   d. freeze

40. generosity : giving :: onslaught : _____
   a. attack
   b. shredding
   c. confusion
   d. forgetful

Directions: *Choose the correct vocabulary word based on the definition. Write the letter of your choice of answers on the line provided.*

41. _____avoid; hide from
   a. plaintively
   b. irreparable
   c. vaguely
   d. evade

42. _____carefully
   a. famished
   b. irreverent
   c. scrupulously
   d. exorbitant

43. _____to look over or look through
    a. peruse
    b. wielding
    c. segue
    d. linger

44. _____tied to
    a. tethered
    b. potent
    c. incoherent
    d. infusion

45. _____strong; powerful
    a. doggedly
    b. emanating
    c. potent
    d. arduous

46. _____unable to be understood
    a. incoherence
    b. fretful
    c. audible
    d. lethargy

47. _____very difficult
    a. famished
    b. exorbitant
    c. extricating
    d. arduous

48. _____something useful or desirable
    a. glowering
    b. asset
    c. stalemate
    d. garish

49. _____mixture
    a. asset
    b. purchase
    c. infusion
    d. potent

50. _____radiating outward
    a. avenging
    b. irreparable
    c. emanating
    d. wheedles

The Hunger Games Teacher Guide
Sample Agenda

The following agenda is based on a 45 – 50 minute class period. This agenda assumes students have time to read together as a class. It will need to be modified if you intend to have students read at home or complete a combination of reading in class and at home.

Week One

Day One: Introduce *Author Biography – Suzanne Collins,* pp. 9-11 having students complete corresponding questions. Discuss question responses as a class. Introduce the *Pre-Reading Activity,* The Myth of Theseus, pp. 12-14. Have students complete the comprehension questions for homework.

Day Two: Review the comprehension questions from last night's homework. Read and complete the pre-reading activity, *Genre,* pp. 15-17 including the corresponding questions. Go over *Historical Context: Roman Influences* as a class. Have students read and complete the pre-reading activity, …*Propaganda* pp. 18-19 and corresponding questions for homework. At this time, you may want to introduce *Pre-Reading Ideas and Activities* pp. 7-8. You may wish to have students work on one or more of these projects before reading or while they are reading the novel.

Day Three: Go over *Elements of Fiction*, p. 23. Provide students with *Allusions, Unique Terminology,* p. 22 and the *Vocabulary List* either with or without definitions, pp. 24-26 or pp. 250-254. Encourage students to use the lists as reference while reading. Introduce and explain the *Note-Taking and Summarizing* chart example, p. 29. It may be helpful to duplicate the charts for overhead or whiteboard projections. Begin reading Chapter One. Pause during reading to complete items in the Note-Taking and Summarizing chart as a class. Finish reading Chapter One. Encourage students to return to the text to complete the questions. When students have completed the questions, you may review the answers together as a class or allow students to discuss questions in small groups. If students discuss the questions in small groups, allow time as a whole class to clarify any questions the groups may have.

Day Four: Review events of Chapter One. Introduce *Standards Focus: The Cast of Characters*, p. 32 and begin completing as a class. Instruct students to continue to complete the Note-Taking chart, p. 30 as they read Chapter Two. When students have finished Chapter Two, they should complete the *Comprehension Check* questions, p. 31. If time allows, review the Comprehension Check questions.

Day Five: Have students complete *Assessment Preparation: Verb Tenses and Moods,* pp. 33-35 . You may want to allow extra time for students to complete the news report activity, p 34. or you may wish to assign it for homework.

Week Two

Day One: Give *Quiz: Chapters 1 – 2,* pp. 157-158. Begin reading Chapters 3 – 4. Use *Note-Taking and Summarizing* charts, pp. 35-36 and complete *Comprehension Check* questions, p. 37.

Day Two: Review chapters and *Comprehension Check* questions. Complete *Standards Focus: In Media Res*, pp. 38-39.

Day Three: Complete *Assessment Preparation: Coordinate and Cumulative Adjectives,* pp. 40-41. You may wish to have students to work with partners for the vocabulary activity.

Day Four: Give *Quiz: Chapters 3 – 4,* pp. 159-160. Begin reading Chapters 5 – 6; begin *Note-Taking and Summarizing* charts, pp. 42-43 and *Comprehension Check* questions, p. 43.

Day Five: Review *Comprehension Check* questions either as a whole class or in small groups. Complete *Standards Focus: Building a Fictional World,* pp. 45.

Week Three

Day One: Complete *Assessment Preparation: Etymology,* pp. 46-48. Be sure to have dictionaries available for student use.

Day Two: Give *Quiz: Chapters 5 – 6,* pp. 161-162. Begin reading Chapter 7 – 9. Begin the *Note-Taking and Summarizing* charts, p. 49 and *Comprehension Check* questions, p. 50.

Day Three: Finish reading Chapters 7 – 9; complete the *Note-Taking and Summarizing* chart and *Comprehension Check* questions. If there is time, allow students to review comprehension questions for Chapters 7 – 9 either as a whole class or in small groups.

Day Four: Complete *Standards Focus Activity: Character Analysis – Close Up on Katniss and Peeta,* pp. 51-53.

Day Five: Complete *Assessment Preparation: Author's Purpose – Greek Themes,* pp. 54-55. You may want students to complete the writing activity for homework.

Week Four

Day One: Give *Quiz: Chapters 7 – 9,* pp. 163-164. Begin *Part One Activity: What's In Your Backpack,* pp. 56-57. Provide students with reference materials or Internet access for research. You may want to extend this activity over two days or have students complete as a homework assignment. Students may want to share their research with the class.

Day Two: Give Part One Test, pp. 183-184 and Part One Vocabulary Test, pp. 185-189. Begin reading Chapter 10. Begin the *Note-Taking and Summarizing* chart, p. 58 and *Comprehension Check* questions, p. 59.

Day Three: Complete *Standards Focus: Star-crossed Lovers and Other Archetypes of Literature*, pp. 60-62.

Day Four: Complete *Assessment Preparation: Writing with Purpose/ Concise Word Choice,* pp. 63-65. You may want to allow students to work with a partner on the haiku activity. That could also be completed for homework.

Day Five: Give *Quiz: Chapter 10,* pp. 165-166. Begin reading Chapters 11 – 12. Begin the *Note-Taking and Summarizing* chart, p. 66 and *Comprehension Check* questions, p. 67.

Week Five

Day One: Allow students to review comprehension questions either as a whole class or in small groups. Complete *Standards Focus Activity: Point of View – The World According to Katniss*, pp. 68-69.

Day Two: Complete *Assessment Preparation: Reflective Writing*, pp. 70-71. You may want to allow for additional class time for students to record or share video diaries. The vocabulary activity can be assigned for homework.

Day Three: Give *Quiz: Chapters 11 – 12*, pp. 167-168. Begin reading Chapters 13 – 14. Begin the *Note-Taking and Summarizing* chart, p. 72 and *Comprehension Check* questions, p. 73.

Day Four: Allow students to review comprehension questions either as a whole class or in small groups. Complete *Standards Focus Activity: Conflict in the Arena*, pp. 74-76. You may want to allow extra class time for students to complete the "Behind the Scenes with Haymitch" activity, p. 76. This could also be assigned for homework.

Day Five: Complete *Assessment Preparation: Using Vocabulary Words*, pp. 77-78.

Week Six

Day One: Give *Quiz: Chapters 13 – 14*, pp. 169-170. Begin reading Chapters 15 – 16. Begin the *Note-Taking and Summarizing* chart, p. 79 and *Comprehension Check* questions, p. 80.

Day Two: Allow students to review comprehension questions either as a whole class or in small groups. Complete *Standards Focus Activity: Character Map*, pp. 81-83.

Day Three: Complete *Assessment Preparation: Who Is the Audience?*, pp. 84-85.

Day Four: Give *Quiz: Chapters 15 – 16*, pp. 171-172. Begin reading Chapters 17 – 18. Begin the *Note-Taking and Summarizing* chart, p. 86 and *Comprehension Check* questions, p. 87. If there is time, allow students to review comprehension questions either as a whole class or in small groups.

Day Five: Complete *Standards Focus Activity: Map of the Setting/ Visualization*, pp. 88-89.

Week Seven

Day One: Complete *Assessment Preparation: Writing Powerful Sentences*, pp. 90-92. You may want to allow for additional class time to complete the "Behind the Scenes with Haymitch" and vocabulary activities. These can also be completed as homework.

Day Two: Give *Quiz: Chapters 17 – 18*, pp. 173-174. Begin *Part Two Activity: Exploring the Labyrinth*, pp. 93-106. You may want to allow two class periods for this. Create the labyrinth and game board today, and play the game tomorrow.

Day Three: Play the board game. Administer *Part Two Test*, pp. 190-192.

Day Four: Administer *Part Two Vocabulary Test*, pp. 193-196. Begin reading Chapters 19 – 20. Begin the *Note-Taking and Summarizing* chart, p. 107 and *Comprehension Check* questions, p. 108. If there is time, allow students to review comprehension questions either as a whole class or in small groups.

Day Five: Complete *Standards Focus Activity: Inner thoughts,* pp. 109-111. Students may need additional time to complete the "Thought Bubbles" and the "Behind the Scenes with Haymitch" activities. They can also be completed for homework.

Week Eight
Day One: Give Quiz: Chapters 19-20, pp. 175-176. Complete *Assessment Preparation: "Showing Not Telling,"* pp. 112-114.
Day Two: Begin reading Chapters 21 – 22. Begin the *Note-Taking and Summarizing* charts, p. 115 and *Comprehension Check* questions, p. 116. If there is time, allow students to review comprehension questions either as a whole class or in small groups.
Day Three: Complete *Standards Focus Activity: Dialogue,* pp. 117-120.
Day Four: Complete *Assessment Preparation: The Silver Parachute – Using Well-Chosen Details,* pp. 121-122. You may want to allow additional class time for students to present their "Silver Parachute" conversations to the class.
Day Five: Give *Quiz: Chapters 21 – 22,* pp. 177-178. Begin reading Chapters 23 – 24. Begin the *Note-Taking and Summarizing* charts, p. 123 and *Comprehension Check* questions, p. 124.

Week Nine
Day One: Allow students to review comprehension questions for Chapters 23 – 24 either as a whole class or in small groups. Complete *Standards Focus Activity: Foreshadowing,* pp. 125-129. You may also wish to have students do the activity, *Standards Focus: The Climax,* pp. 130-131, or choose one or the other.
Day Two: Complete *Assessment Preparation: Inferring,* pp. 132-135. Students may need additional time to complete the vocabulary activity. It could also be completed for homework.
Day Three: Give *Quiz: Chapters 23 – 24*, pp. 179-180. Begin reading Chapters 25 – 27. Begin the *Note-Taking and Summarizing* charts, p. 136 and *Comprehension Check* questions, p. 137.
Day Four: Allow students to review comprehension questions for Chapters 25 – 27 either as a whole class or in small groups. Complete *Standards Focus Activity: Symbolism,* pp. 138-143.
Day Five: Complete *Assessment Preparation: Relationships Between Ideas – Subordination, Coordination, and Apposition,* pp. 144-147.

Week Ten
Day One: Give *Quiz: Chapters 25 – 27* pp. 181-182. Begin *Part Three Activity: Create a Survival Game,* pp. 148-151. This activity will take more than one class period. You may want to allot a portion of the next few classes for students to work on their "pitches" while they review the novel. As an alternative, you may wish to have students begin *Part Three Activity: Create a Museum Display,* pp. 152-154. You may also wish to give students a choice of Part Three Activity.
Day Two: Administer *Part Three Test,* pp. 197-199 and *Part Three Vocabulary Test* pp. 200-204.

Day Three: Review novel for Final Exam. Include an extensive vocabulary review if you are planning to use the Vocabulary Test.

Day Four: Give either version of the *Final Exam,* pp. 205-210, or pp. 211-217. Alternative Assessments for tests can be found in *Post-Reading Ideas and Alternative Assessment*, pp. 255-257 as well as *Essay and Writing Ideas*, pp. 258-259. The vocabulary test should be given on a separate day.

Day Five +: Administer *Vocabulary Final Test*, pp. 236-248, or *Multiple Choice Vocabulary Test* pp. 231-235. If you intend to continue the study of the novel, use *Post-Reading Ideas and Alternative Assessment,* pp. 255 or *Essay and Writing Ideas,* pp. 258-259.

Notes to the Teacher

1. Page numbers in this Guide refer to the Scholastic paperback version of the novel. ISBN – 13: 978-0-439-02352-8

2. There are two Standards Focus activities included for Chapters 23-24. You may choose which one to use or use them both.

3. There are many opportunities for assessment throughout the Guide. Included in this Guide are a Final Test and Final Vocabulary Test for each Part of the novel (Parts I, II, and III.) In addition, there are two versions of the Final Exam, located on pp. 205-210 and pp. 211-217 You will need to choose whether to administer the *Final Exam* or *Final Exam Multiple Choice Version*, depending upon your and your students' needs. Also included are two versions of Final Vocabulary Exams. One includes all 165 vocabulary words from the novel; the second is a shortened version of the same exam, with only fifty challenging, high-frequency vocabulary words. You should use one or the other of these, but not both.

4. You may want to have Suzanne Collins's other series *Gregor the Overlander* or the second and third books in *The Hunger Games* series on display in the classroom.

5. You may want students to keep reading notes, comprehension activities, standards focus and assessment preparation activities as well as assessments in a folder with brads or a small three-ring binder. This will make it easier for students to study for the novel exam and for you to assess student performance both during and after the novel study. Students are sometimes told to refer to previous work so it is recommended that they keep everything.

6. It may be helpful to duplicate graphic organizers and *Note-Taking and Summarizing charts* to use on an overhead transparency. The *Note-Taking and Summarizing* chart can be used as a large wall display. Students can add notes and questions to the wall display using sticky notes.

7. You may want to begin class by having small groups share their answers from the *Note-Taking and Summarizing* chart. A speaker for each group may share with the entire class.

8. Once students reach Part Two of the novel, you may want to create a wall display of the tributes, what students know about them, and what happens to them. You can use the character map from the Standards Focus activity for Chapters 15 – 16 as a blueprint for your wall display. Encourage students to record page numbers on the chart for easy reference.

9. Some activities, such as the video diary, news report, haikus, and "I Am" poems may be suitable for sharing either through your classroom web page or as a wall display.

10. Depending on the reading level of your class, students may move at a faster or slower pace. Adjust the agenda to meet your students' needs.

11. Audio recordings of the novel are available from audible.com.

12. Many pre-reading activities can be used for writing assignments.

13. Research activities can be found in both pre-reading and post-reading activities.

14. Notes for Part Three Activity: Create a Survival Game
    - Students will need a TV Guide listing of programs. A weekly TV guide from the newspaper will suffice.
    - This is recommended as a group activity, but you may choose to have students work independently instead.
    - If students will be viewing a reality TV show, you may want to inform parents of the assignment or require one particular show that you know will be appropriate for the age of your students.

The Hunger Games

Summary of the Novel

Part I: The Tributes

Chapter 1: Katniss Everdeen is a sixteen-year-old girl who lives in District 12 in the country Panem. Today, like every day, Katniss will sneak into the meadow with her friend Gale. The two of them hunt for food for their families and to trade at the black market they call the Hob. Hunger, starvation, and poverty are common in the poor coal-mining district; by hunting illegally, Katniss is able to keep her mother and sister alive. They also stop by the Mayor's house to sell strawberries. Today they see Madge, the Mayor's daughter, who opens the door. She is preparing for the reaping. She and Katniss are in the same grade at school.

It is the day of the reaping. The district will choose one boy and one girl between the ages of twelve and eighteen to participate in the Hunger Games: a fight to the death among the tributes from all twelve districts. The Games commemorate the government's repression of an attempted overthrow. All the people are required to meet in the town square for the reaping – a drawing. Each child's name is entered into the drawing each year, and if the family is starving, the child's name can be entered twice or more in return for extra food rations. This is the first year Prim, Katniss's little sister, is in the reaping. Katniss has made sure to protect Prim, and her name has only been entered once. The "festivities" begin with the reading of the history of the Games. The only living winner of the Games from District 12 is Haymitch Abernathy who arrives at the reaping drunk. Effie Trinket, the escort from the Capitol for District 12, is going to draw the names. The first slip is pulled from the bowl – Prim's name is called.

Chapter 2: Katniss immediately volunteers to take Prim's place in the Games. The reaction of the crowd is silence and, as a sign of thanks and goodbye, they make a gesture by placing their three fingers to their lips and then holding them out to Katniss. Katniss, knowing the reaping will be televised, is concerned that she look strong and doesn't cry. The boy tribute is selected – Peeta Mellark. Katniss knows him from school and as the son of the baker. After Katniss's father died, the family was starving. Katniss happened to wander to the back of the bakery to look for food in the trash; Peeta gave her two loaves of bread that he had burned. The bread saved Katniss's family from starvation. Katniss feels conflicted because she feels a debt of gratitude toward Peeta, but in the Games, she may have to kill him.

Chapter 3: Katniss is taken to the Justice Building to say goodbye to her family before being taken to the Capitol. She says goodbye to her mother and Prim. Peeta's father visits next. He gives Katniss cookies and promises to look after Prim and make sure she's eating. Madge comes by and gives Katniss a pin she'd been wearing. It's a bird in a circle. Madge makes Katniss promise to wear it into the arena. Gale visits and the two of them discuss strategies for the Games. He, too, promises to look after her family.

Katniss and Peeta will be traveling to the Capitol on a high-speed train. Katniss recalls that the Capitol is located in what was once called the Rockies, and District 12 is in what was once called Appalachia. The tribute train is plush and as Katniss explores it she remembers the pin Madge gave her. It is a likeness of a mockingjay. The bird is a cross between the genetically engineered jabberjay and the mockingbird. The jabberjay is what they call a muttation. The jabberjay was used during the rebellion to spy on the rebels and report back to the Capitol, but when the rebels realized what the birds did, they gave the birds false information. The jabberjays were left in the wild to die, but they bred with the mockingbird to create a bird that can imitate human melodies and bird whistles.

Effie, Katniss, and Peeta meet in the dining car for dinner. Haymitch is napping. The food is sumptuous and plentiful. They then go to watch the reapings in the other districts on TV. As they watch the replay of District 12, Haymitch is featured – drunk. Effie informs Peeta and Katniss that as a former winner of the Games, he is responsible for them and can get them special gifts and help in the arena. But as a drunk, he is useless. A drunken Haymitch then enters the room, vomits, and passes out.

Chapter 4: Katniss and Peeta help Haymitch back to his room. Peeta offers to clean him up and get him to bed. Katniss returns to her room and suspects that Peeta's kindness is a ploy to gain the upper hand. A flashback tells how, after Peeta's kindness, Katniss managed to hunt and forage enough food to ensure her family's survival. The next morning at breakfast, Katniss and Peeta stand up to Haymitch and confront him about his drinking. Peeta smashes his glass and Haymitch punches him; Katniss slams her knife on the table between Haymitch's hand and his bottle of alcohol. Encouraged that they might show spunk, Haymitch promises to help them if they don't interfere with his drinking and they do exactly what he says. As the train pulls into the Capitol, Peeta waves at the crowd. Katniss suspects he is planning to win a sponsor through his outgoing personality.

Chapter 5: It is the day of the opening ceremonies. Katniss is being prepared to meet her stylist who is in charge of how she looks for the opening ceremonies and the Games. Cinna, her stylist, lacks the odd affectations of the others at the Capitol. He and Portia, Peeta's stylist, have planned Katniss and Peeta's costumes for the opening ceremonies. Katniss is afraid it will be something horrible like past costumes, but they are dressed in a costume that is "on fire." Peeta and Katniss hold hands as they ride in a chariot through the streets; their costumes are spectacular and the crowd and television cameras love them. They return from the parade and Cinna and Portia put out the fire. Peeta compliments Katniss on how good she looks in flames. Katniss, suspicious that Peeta is saying this to weaken her defenses, decides she can play this game as well and kisses him on the bruise Haymitch had given him on the train.

Chapter 6: They are in the training center. Katniss experiences the luxury of her apartment – such a contrast to her life in District 12. Katniss, Peeta, Haymitch, Effie, Cinna, and Portia meet for dinner. During dinner, Katniss thinks she recognizes one of the servers. The girl is an Avox – someone who's committed a crime and whose tongue has been cut out. In an awkward moment when the adults assure Katniss she doesn't know the girl, Peeta comes to the rescue by telling Katniss she looks like a girl they both know from District 12. It wouldn't be right for Katniss to know a criminal. They watch a televised replay of the parade. Haymitch comments that Peeta and Katniss holding hands is a touch of rebellion. Katniss and Peeta are sent to bed so the adults can talk about their strategies.

Peeta and Katniss leave and Peeta asks Katniss about the Avox. They go up to the roof to talk where their voices can't be heard. Katniss tells Peeta that she had once seen the girl in the woods. She and a boy were obviously running away when suddenly a hovercraft came and captured them. The boy was killed and the girl disappeared into the hovercraft. Katniss didn't know where they were going. Beyond District 12 is wilderness and the smoldering remains of District 13. Katniss returns to her room where she sees the Avox girl again cleaning her room. Katniss feels guilty she didn't try to help her when she had the chance.

Chapter 7: Training begins. At the end of the training, each of the tributes will be given a numerical rating by the Gamemakers. Haymitch asks Peeta and Katniss if they want to be trained together or separately. They decide to train together. As they begin the training, Haymitch tells them they need to be together every time they're in public so they appear to be friends. During the training, Peeta and Katniss work on new skills – making snares, fires – anything they hope will help them in the arena.

On the second day of training, they notice they are being followed by Rue, the tribute from District 11 who reminds Katniss of Prim. On the last day of training, the tributes will go in front of the Gamemakers. District 12 goes last; that means Katniss will be the last to go. When it is finally her turn, she realizes that the Gamemakers are bored and have had too much to drink. They are not paying attention to her, in spite of the fact that she's making an impressive show with the bow and arrow. Finally, in frustration that the Gamemakers are more interested in the roasted pig than her, she shoots an arrow that pierces the apple in the pig's mouth. With that, Katniss leaves.

Chapter 8: Afraid that her rash actions will cause her family to be punished or to be imprisoned, Katniss locks herself in her room and cries. Finally, she comes out for dinner and confesses what happened, to Haymitch, Effie, Peeta, Cinna, and Portia.

When the ratings come out, Katniss has scored eleven points out of a possible twelve. This could increase her chances of getting sponsorship. The next morning, Katniss goes down to breakfast to learn that Peeta has asked to be coached separately.

Chapter 9: While Katniss is upset by Peeta's decision, she decides it's better that way. Effie and Haymitch work with her to prepare for the televised interview. Effie helps with her presentation, and Haymitch tries to coach her for the interview. Haymitch accuses her of being sullen, and Katniss can't figure out what her persona should be for the interview.

That night, Katniss breaks down. She has a dish-breaking temper tantrum in her room. When the Avox comes in to ready her room for bed, it is the same redheaded girl Katniss saw in the woods. Katniss apologizes and the girl obviously forgives Katniss for her actions.

The next day, Cinna coaches Katniss on her interview. He encourages her to pretend she's talking to him during the interview. The interview is frightening for Katniss, but

Caesar Flickerman interviews the tributes and does his best to make them feel at ease. Cinna's idea works for Katniss and she does a good job on the interview. When it is Peeta'a turn for the interview, Caesar asks him if he has a girlfriend. He confesses that he has a crush on Katniss.

Part II "The Games"

Chapter 10: Katniss is furious about Peeta's story of unrequited love for her. Later, she confronts him and tells her she thinks it makes her look weak. Haymitch tells her it's her only hope for him to get her sponsors. Katniss recognizes that this is true.

That night, unable to sleep, Katniss goes up to the roof. She finds Peeta there. He talks about how he wants to maintain his identity in spite of the brutality of the Games. They end their conversation with harsh words to each other.

The next morning, Katniss goes to the arena with Cinna who helps her prepare. She wears the mockingjay pin and has a tracker inserted under the skin of her arm. At the close of the chapter, as Katniss is going into the arena she hears the announcer's voice proclaim that the seventy-fourth Hunger Games have begun.

Chapter 11: In the arena, Katniss has exactly one minute to survey her surroundings. She sees the Cornucopia that is full of supplies and for a moment she decides to disregard Haymitch's advice to run away. She thinks she'll run in and get weapons, but she's distracted by Peeta, and when the starting gong goes off, she's lost time. She runs to the woods, but not before she witnesses a tribute's death and is chased by a knife-wielding girl. Katniss has managed to pick up a backpack and piece of plastic on her way.

As she runs through the woods, she is in search of water. As the night falls, she sees on the sky those tributes who died that day: eleven had lost their lives that day. That night she sleeps in a tree. During the night, she witnesses another tribute building a fire nearby. The tribute is soon discovered by a pack of tributes who have formed an alliance. Katniss listens from her hiding place as the pack of tributes argue about whether or not the girl is dead. Katniss recognizes one of the voices as Peeta's.

Chapter 12: Katniss cannot believe that Peeta has aligned himself with Career Tributes. As she continues her search for water, she contemplates Peeta's strategy. She is also aware that she is being televised. She travels through the woods desperately searching for water. She is becoming weaker and weaker. She comes to a cluster of berry bushes, but the berries aren't familiar to her. Rather than risking being poisoned, Katniss leaves the berries and continues her search for water. She is hoping Haymitch will send her water. When he doesn't, she figures she must be close it, but she collapses into the mud unable to go any further. She realizes there must be water nearby and finds a pond. She spends the rest of the day drinking water and eating – which makes her feel better and better. She beds down for the night, but is awaked a few hours later by a stampede and the smell of smoke. A fire is heading her way.

Chapter 13: Katniss races ahead of the fire – a fire deliberately set by the Gamemakers to force the tributes to fight. Then fireballs come crashing toward her, making it impossible for her to rest. One hits her calf, and she's burned. She finds a pool of water and soaks her burned calf and hands. As she rests, she hears the pack of Careers and Peeta coming through the forest. Katniss finds a tree and climbs it. Unable to follow her up the tree, they leave her until morning. As darkness falls, Katniss sees another tribute in the next tree. It's Rue. She points to something in Katniss's tree that is above her head.

Chapter 14: Rue has pointed to a nest of tracker jacker wasps that are muttations of wasps with a poisonous sting and tracking ability. Katniss begins to cut through the branch during the anthem so the Careers won't hear her. The wasps are still groggy from the smoke of the fire, but they are beginning to rouse in the nest. She leaves the rest of the cutting for dawn and inches back down the tree to find she's received a gift from a sponsor: ointment for her burns. It heals her burns nearly instantly.

The next morning, Katniss is able to cut the rest of the branch, sending the nest down on the Careers. Two are killed by the stingers and the rest run away. Katniss gets down from the tree, but not without being stung three times herself. She realizes she should go back and retrieve the bow and arrow from one of the dead Careers. When she returns to the body, she begins hallucinating. Peeta arrives at the tree. Rather than kill her, he saves her from Cato by telling her to run away.

Chapter 15: Katniss awakens from the tracker jacker induced hallucinations. She begins to travel upstream and hunts with the bow and arrow. She encounters Rue and forms an alliance with her. She learns from Rue that Peeta is no longer with the Career Tributes and is on his own. The Careers are at the lake with all the provisions and tools. Katniss formulates an idea that will put her on the offensive.

Chapter 16: Katniss sneaks down to the Career camp to figure out how to destroy their food source. Rue has set a fire in the forest to draw the tributes away from the camp. As Katniss watches the camp, she sees the fox-faced girl sneak carefully into the camp to steal supplies. Katniss realizes the supplies are booby trapped with explosives. Using her arrows, she shoots down a bag of apples that triggers an explosion of the supply pile.

Chapter 17: The explosion knocks Katniss over and deafens her. Unable to run away from the camp, Katniss crawls into the underbrush and hides. She sees the Careers come back to the camp to survey the damage. Cato is furious – all of their supplies are destroyed. Katniss can see this from her hiding place, but cannot hear. She spends the night in the underbrush while the Careers go on a night hunt in the forest. As day breaks, Katniss returns to the forest to meet up with Rue. The hearing in her right ear has returned, but she still cannot hear with her left ear. She goes to the rendezvous place to find Rue, but she isn't there. Katniss begins searching for her when she hears Rue calling to her. Rue has been trapped in a net and the boy from District 1 has speared her.

Chapter 18: Katniss shoots the boy from District 1 and pulls Rue from the net. It is too late, though. As Rue is dying, she asks Katniss to sing to her. Katniss sings a lullaby while Rue dies and then, in an act of defiance, Katniss decorates Rue's body with wild flowers before the hovercraft takes it away. She is distraught and despondent over

Rue's death. She receives a silver parachute gift of bread from District 11 – the district Rue was from. The following day, Katniss is still despondent. She travels around the forest aimlessly, thinking about her family, Rue, and the boy she killed. That evening after the anthem, there is a trumpet blast. This means a communication from outside the arena. The announcement is that the rules of the Games have been changed: two tributes, if they come from the same district, can now win the Games.

Part III: The Victor

Chapter 19: Katniss begins looking for Peeta. She knows he's injured, and she begins searching for him along the river. She finds him completely camouflaged in the mud of the stream. He is seriously injured, and Katniss gets him cleaned up and tries to treat his wounds. Peeta, in spite of his fever, pain, and injuries, reminds Katniss that they are supposed to be in love and she should kiss him. Katniss manages to find a rock enclosure that offers minimal hiding for them. She finally kisses Peeta and is rewarded with a silver parachute of hot broth. She realizes that in order for them to receive anything better, she must play the game of being in love with Peeta.

Chapter 20: There are six tributes left. Katniss and Peeta, Cato and Clove (both from District 2), Tresh, and Foxface. Katniss and Peeta spend time in the cave, with Katniss continuing to care for Peeta. When she checks his wound, she notices red streaks which indicate blood poisoning. Peeta asks Katniss to tell him a story of the happiest day of her life. She tells him the story of the day she got a goat for Prim. Later that night after the anthem plays, the trumpets blare again with the announcement that there will be a feast. At the feast will be a backpack for each district that will include something they critically need. Katniss knows their backpack will include medicine for Peeta, but Peeta doesn't want her to go. He threatens to follow her. When Katniss goes out to the stream, she receives a silver parachute that contains a sleeping syrup. She mixes it with berries and feeds it to Peeta. Before he falls asleep, he realizes what she has done.

Chapter 21: Katniss arrives at the Cornucopia before dawn. When dawn breaks, a table comes up through the ground with four backpacks on it. The one for District 12 is so small, it would fit on Katniss's wrist. Foxface is the first to get her backpack, then Katniss runs to the table to get her backpack when she's struck in the forehead by a knife. Clove tackles her and pins her to the ground. She promises to give the audience a good show as she plans how she's going to kill Katniss, and she taunts Katniss about killing Rue. Suddenly, Clove is yanked away by Thresh who kills her, and after she explains what she did for Rue when she died, he declares that he will let Katniss go. Thresh warns that they are now even. As Katniss runs back to the woods, she sees that Thresh has taken both his backpack and the one for District 2. He's run in the opposite direction. Katniss returns to the cave, wounded, but opens the tiny backpack to find a syringe of medicine that she gives to Peeta.

Chapter 22: Katniss and Peeta are in the cave. Peeta has made a remarkable recovery due to the medicine. Now it is Peeta who's caring for Katniss's wounded forehead. The two of them spend the day resting and talking. They are hungry and the rain continues to make it impossible for Katniss to go hunting. Katniss knows that in order to get food from Haymitch they must play up their romance for the audience. The next day, it continues to rain. With no chance of hunting, they are counting on Haymitch for food. Peeta seems earnest as he confesses his feelings for Katniss – that he has loved her since the first day of school and heard her sing. She reciprocates his feelings enough to earn them a silver parachute full of food – including her favorite lamb stew.

Chapter 23: The two rejoice over the much-needed food. They eat a small portion so they don't get sick, and return to talking. They talk about what will happen if they win the Games. They will live in a luxury home and be neighbors with Haymitch. Neither of them thinks Haymitch is very fond of them, but Katniss believes that Haymitch sends the silver parachutes as messages of how to act or what to do. That night as the anthem plays, Peeta sees that Thresh has died. Katniss is upset, but tries not to show it. The rain stops and the next day they leave the cave to hunt. Peeta is loud as they walk through the woods and eventually suggests that he stay and gather roots while Katniss hunts. They agree to use a whistle to signal back and forth to each other that everything is okay. When Katniss doesn't hear Peeta's whistle in awhile, she rushes back to find he's gathering berries in the woods. Katniss also notices some of their food is missing and that Peeta has gathered a poisonous berry called nightlock. The cannon goes off and the hovercraft comes in to gather the body of Foxface who stole their food and ate the poisonous berries.

Chapter 24: Katniss puts the poisonous berries in a leather pouch as a weapon they may be able to use against Cato. They eat their food and return to the cave for the night. The next morning, they discover the stream has been drained and the only water is at the lake. The Gamemakers want them to return to the lake for the final battle. When Katniss and Peeta arrive at the lake, there is no sign of Cato. Katniss teaches the mockingjays Rue's song, but suddenly Cato bursts through the trees toward them. Katniss shoots an arrow, but it falls away. He is wearing body armor, but instead of attacking them, Cato runs right past Katniss and Peeta. Katniss sees what he is running from – muttations.

Chapter 25: The three of them run to the Cornucopia and climb up on it. The muttations look like giant wolves, but Katniss recognizes something about them – they resemble the dead tributes. Katniss manages to keep them at bay with her bow and arrow, but Peeta is caught, and his leg is badly wounded before Katniss pulls him to safety. Cato grabs Peeta who is forced to stand with him at the edge of the Cornucopia. Peeta gives Katniss a sign to shoot Cato's hand, which she does. He releases Peeta and falls into the pack of mutts. Since this seems to be the last battle of the Games, Katniss and Peeta know that Cato's death will be long and agonizing. Through the cold, long night they listen to Cato suffer. As dawn arrives, Katniss ends Cato's life with her last arrow. They climb off the Cornucopia and head for the lake as the hovercraft arrives. They wait for the announcement that they're the winners, but instead there is an announcement that there can only be one winner. After arguing about who should or shouldn't die, Peeta's reasons are his love for Katniss, and Katniss knows she would never be able to stop thinking about the arena. They decide they'll eat the poison berries on the count of three. Just as they are about to eat the berries, Claudius Templesmith stops them and they are both declared winners of the Games.

Chapter 26: The hovercraft appears and takes them away from the arena. Peeta has lost a lot of blood and falls unconscious into the hovercraft. A team of doctors quickly begins to work on him. Katniss panics and tries to get to him, but a glass door separates them. Katniss is then drugged and awakens later in a hospital bed. She alternates between consciousness and sleep for several days before she is well enough to get out of bed. All her scars have been removed, and she is ready to be presented to the public as the victor. She wants to see Peeta, but the Gamemakers want their reunion to occur on live TV. Cinna dresses Katniss in a dress that makes her look like a young girl. Katniss suspects that there is a reason for that. As she waits to be presented to the audience, Haymitch tells her that the Capitol is angry with Katniss and Peeta for showing them up in the arena. He tells her the only excuse she and Peeta can have for their actions is that they are madly in love. Katniss struggles with her feelings toward Peeta and wonders about his feelings toward her. Were they real or were they just due to the circumstances they were forced into? As Katniss prepares to enter the ceremony, she realizes that the most dangerous part of the Hunger Games is about to begin.

Chapter 27: On the stage, Katniss sees Peeta again and runs to him. After an enthusiastic crowd greets them, they watch the highlights of the Hunger Games. President Snow crowns them, but his eyes show his anger at Katniss. After the victory banquet, Katniss tries to get time alone with Peeta, but she is locked in her bedroom. The next day, Caesar Flickerman interviews them. Katniss learns that Peeta's leg was amputated and replaced by an artificial leg. Katniss and Peeta again profess their love though Katniss does so with the belief that it is all an act.

They get on the train to return to District 12. On the way, Katniss washes off her makeup, rebraids her hair, and changes her clothes. She is struggling to understand who she is now that the Games are over. When the train stops for fuel, she and Peeta walk along the tracks together. Haymitch tells them to keep up the act until the cameras are gone. Peeta is confused. Katniss had thought all along that Haymitch had been giving Peeta the same advice he'd given to her – to pretend they love each other. Katniss tells Peeta that she's not sure how she feels. Peeta retreats to the train clearly upset and hurt. The next day they arrive at District 12. Peeta holds her hand as they prepare for the cameras waiting for them, but this time he is doing it only for the camera.

The Hunger Games
Vocabulary with Definitions

Chapter 1
reaping (3) – harvesting
deterrent (4) – a discouragement to act in a particular way
poaching (5) – hunting illegally
maniacally (7) – overly enthusiastically
preposterous (9) – ridiculous; unbelievable
haggling (10) – bargaining, usually arguing over a trade or price of an item
adjacent (17) – close to or joining

Chapter 2
protocol (22) – the customary or proper way of doing something; etiquette
dissent (24) – protest
plummets (24) – drops dramatically
radical (26) – extreme
predicament (27) – problem; troublesome situation

Chapter 3
disastrous (35) – extremely unfortunate
intensity (35) – concentration; focus
insurmountable (36) – unable to overcome
gratified (40) – satisfied
sniveling (41) – whiney or weepy
replicate (43) – duplicate; to create again
disgruntled (46) – unhappy; dissatisfied

Chapter 4
mentor (48) – a supporter, guide, or trusted advisor
pondering (49) – thinking deeply
inexplicable (51) – unable to be explained
gnarled (53) – twisted
deteriorated (54) – disintegrated, fell apart
substantial (55) – very large
detest (56) – hate

Chapter 5
vulnerable (62) – exposed; open to danger or attack
affectations (63) – artificial actions; words or habits used for effect
flamboyant (64) – flashy; showy
sustenance (65) – nourishment
despicable (65) – worthy of being scorned or despised
tangible (71) – able to be touched

Chapter 6
exclusively (73) – only; limited
barbarism (74) – uncivilized behavior
ironic (74) – the opposite of what would be expected
adversaries (79) – enemies
mandatory (81) – required

Chapter 7
amiable (92) – friendly
demean (93) – to put down or degrade
oblivious (93) – unaware
surly (99) – grumpy
sever (101) – cut
fixated (101) – focused

Chapter 8
impulsiveness (103) – acting without thinking; hastiness
leniency (104) – mercy
sic (104) – to incite to attack
irredeemably (104) – unable to be recovered
potential (104) – possible capacity
defiantly (106) – resistantly; rebelliously

Chapter 9
ludicrous (114) – ridiculous; laughable
banal (115) – boring and ordinary
intrigued (116) – fascinated
sullen (116) – in a bad mood; irritated
hostile (116) – antagonistic; unfriendly
prestigious (124) – honored; respected
unrequited (130) – not returned; not reciprocated

Chapter 10
assent (133) – agreement
breached (134) – broken
entourages (134) – groups of attendants to someone who is famous
aghast (134) – shocked
perceived (135) – believed
reenactments (145) – reliving or acting out events that happened in the past

Chapter 11
condenses (150) – concentrates
void (151) – emptiness
botched (151) – ruined
rejuvenating (152) – energizing; restorative
dispersed (152) – spread around

Chapter 12
lapdogs (161) – pampered pets
gall (162) – nerve
hoist (163) – pull; lift
imprudent (164) – not cautious
dynamic (165) – relationship
scarcity (167) – rarity

Chapter 13
quell (173) – put an end to; extinguish
abate (176) – diminish; lessen
stupor (180) – a daze; unclear mental state
incompetent (182) – not capable of doing something; lacking ability
conspiratorially (183) – plotting together
bravado (183) – pretentious display of courage

Chapter 14
precariously (187) – dangerously
persevere (187) – to persist; not give up
sated (187) – satisfied; full
balm (188) – a soothing ointment
honing (190) – sharpening; focusing
mayhem (190) – chaos; disorder

Chapter 15
onslaught (195) – assault
wracked (195) – shaken; damaged
noxious (197) – harmful; foul smelling
prominent (198) – noticeable; standing out
tentatively (200) – cautiously

Chapter 16
ordeal (210) – trouble; severe occurrence
rations (211) – a portion or fixed amount
forages (211) – searches for food
obliging (211) – willing to do favors
rendezvous (213) – meeting place
copse (214) – a group of trees or bushes

Chapter 17
doggedly (223) – persistently; stubbornly
subsequent (225) – next
fractured (227) – broken
fragmenting (227) – splitting apart; breaking up
subtly (228) – difficult to notice; gradually
vulnerable (229) – able to be easily hurt
decadent (230) – rich and luxurious

Chapter 18
fretful (234) – distressed; irritable
audible (235) – able to be heard
inadequate (236) – not enough
inflict (236) – to impose something unwanted
despondency (238) – depression; hopelessness
lethargy (240) – lack of energy; sluggishness

Chapter 19
dissipate (247) – scatter or spread in different directions
pariahs (247) – outcasts
loathe (247) – hate
evade (248) – avoid; hide from
scrupulously (249) – carefully
ruse (250) – a trick
peruse (252) – to look over or look through

Chapter 20
tethered (263) – tied to
potent (266) – strong; powerful
ratcheting (266) – turning or cranking
wheedles (268) – persuades
incoherence (276) – inability to be understood

Chapter 21
arduous (278) – very difficult
asset (279) – something useful or desirable
infusion (279) – mixture; concoction
emanating (281) – radiating outward
irreparable (281) – unable to be repaired
ominous (282) – foreboding; threatening
staunch (289) – stop

Chapter 22
vaguely (290) – not specifically
plaintively (294) – mournfully; sorrowfully
famished (294) – very hungry
irreverent (296) – disrespectful
tirades (296) – tantrums
exorbitant (299) – excessive
exasperated (302) – frustrated

Chapter 23
savoring (303) – enjoying
surly (306) – crabby and grouchy
noncommittal (308) – neutral
peevishly (308) – showing annoyance
surreal (318) – dreamlike; unreal
extricating (312) – getting out; removing
emaciated (318) – starved; haggard

Chapter 24
sustained (322) – kept going
oblige (323) – to happily act in a certain manner
mesmerized (329) – transfixed; hypnotized
dissonant (329) – not harmonious
wielding (329) – carrying; brandishing

Chapter 25
inadvertently (332) – accidentally
glowering (333) – glaring; staring in a menacing way
purchase (333) – grasp; footing
callously (334) – without caring; insensitivity
avenging (334) – getting vengeance or revenge
stalemate (336) – impasse; deadlock
tourniquet (338) – a bandage placed around a wound the help slow the loss of blood

Chapter 26
feverishly (347) – excitedly; tirelessly
garish (354) – showy; overly flashy or bright
contrived (355) – made up; artificial
arbitrary (355) – random
sophisticated (355) – educated; mature; experienced
benign (355) – harmless

Chapter 27
keen (360) – sharp
debut (360) – first appearance
berserk (361) – crazy
disproportionate (362) – unequal
linger (362) – remain
insidious (365) – intending to trap; deceitful
segue (368) – transition

The Hunger Games
Post-Reading Activities and Alternative Assessment

After completing the novel, students may be interested in reading the second and third books in the series (*Catching Fire* and *Mockingjay*). Some other dystopian genre books students may be interested in:

- *1984* by George Orwell
- *The Giver* by Lois Lowry
- *The Maze Runner* by James Dashner
- *The Other Side of the Island* by Allegra Goodman
- *Among the Hidden (series)* by Margaret Peterson Haddix
- *Uglies* by Scott Westerfeld
- *Unwind* by Neal Shusterman
- *This Side of Paradise* by Steven L. Layne
- *The Silenced* by James DeVita
- *Surviving Antarctica: Reality TV 2083* by Andrea White
- *City of Ember* by Jean DuPrau

Suzanne Collins's other series, *Gregor the Overlander*, is an excellent fantasy series. While written for a slightly younger audience, many fans of *The Hunger Games* will enjoy this series as well.

Cross-Curricular Activities
Many of these activities are suitable for small groups.

Social Studies
1. Panem is a fictional country based on North America. Challenge students to use clues from the novel to determine where the districts are located.

2. Map making. Using the information from the novel about the location of the districts, have students create a map of Panem.

3. Just because something is on TV doesn't necessarily mean it is true. Have students discuss how those who write or report news can shape how the events are viewed. Using the *Assessment Preparation Chapters 1 – 2* news writing activity, have students try writing the same news report from different points of view.

4. What if the Gamemakers were to go on trial? Create a mock trial in which the Gamemakers are held responsible for what they've done.

5. Games are an important part of our society today and have been important to civilizations throughout the ages. Have students choose a country and then research games the children there play. Or choose a time period and find out what games were played during that time.

6. What were the gladiator games like that the Romans enjoyed? Research what the games were and how they were similar and different from the Hunger Games.

7. The ancient people who lived in Central American played a Mesoamerican ballgame. Have students research the game and why it might have been important to the civilization.

8. What are our rights to privacy? Katniss is keenly aware that she's being filmed while she's in the arena. She and Peeta are also aware they're not able to speak freely while they're in the Capitol. Have students find out what rights to privacy citizens have today. Additionally, have them discuss what rights they'd be willing to give away and why (for example, airport screening, school locker searches, etc.)

9. Propaganda. Using the pre-reading propaganda article, have students write propaganda ads for the Hunger Games.

Art

1. Costume design. Using descriptions of the costumes Katniss and Peeta wear, have students choose a costume and draw it.

2. Illustrate a scene. This can be an extension of the *Standards Focus* activity: Chapters 17 – 18. Have students choose a scene from the novel to illustrate.

3. An alternative to illustrating one scene is to create a cartoon strip or graphic novel page. Students may benefit from reviewing some graphic novel examples (*Bone* by Jeff Smith or *Artemis Fowl* by Eoin Colfer) and discussing how graphic novels differ from traditional novels.

4. What do the muttations look like? Using descriptions in the novel, have students create an illustration of one.

5. Create an illustration of one of the buildings or streets in the Capitol. Alternately, create an illustration of Katniss's room in the Capitol.

6. Using descriptions of characters, draw a Capitol resident.

7. Imagine the merchandising opportunities after the Games. Have students design a product that might come about as a result of the Games.

8. Imagine Katniss kept a scrapbook of the important things that happened to her in the arena. What would she put in it? Create her scrapbook.

Drama/ Technology

1. Have students choose a scene to use for a readers' theater enactment. Allow students to work in groups.

2. Using the *Assessment Preparation* activity: Chapters 1 – 2, create a series of news reports that cover the Games. You may want to divide students into news teams that report on different days. Set up your classroom like a TV news desk. Film the news report to share.

3. Dress up! Allow students to dress up like a person from the Capitol. Review descriptions of the citizens of the Capitol, and then allow students to dress up in costumes of their own creation. Take pictures and perhaps give awards. Encourage students to create their own Roman influenced names.

4. Create and film a movie trailer for the movie version of *The Hunger Games*.

Science

1. As an extension of the activity for Part I, ask students to consider what it would it take to survive in the wild. Have students research what basic needs human beings would need to take care of to ensure survival in a setting similar to the arena.

2. At one point in the novel, Katniss discusses eating pine tree bark and dandelions. Have students research edible plants. Could someone survive on that kind of diet?

3. In the arena, Katniss puts iodine in water she plans to drink. Have students find out what iodine does in drinking water and what might happen if she didn't use it.

4. Modern mutations. How do scientists use mutations or hybrids today? Research what is really meant by the term mutations. Are the mutts in *The Hunger Games* mutations or something else?

5. The ethics of science. The science behind the Games is more focused on entertainment than improving life. Set up a debate in which students debate the roles and responsibilities of science.

Music

1. Discuss the importance of music in creating a theme for TV and movies. Have students create a playlist for the televised Games. Students should provide a list of songs, when they would be played, and why they chose those particular songs.

2. Katniss sings to Rue as she is dying. Have students write a melody to accompany the song. Students could record and share their songs with classmates.

3. What does the mockingjay sound like? Students can create the call/response between Katniss and the mockingjays.

Language Arts

1. Create a District 12 cookbook. Using the description of a meal that Katniss may have eaten at home, write a recipe for the meal. Consult real recipes as a pattern.

2. Imagine a restaurant in the Capitol. Using descriptions of meals Katniss had in the Capitol, create a menu for the restaurant. Name the restaurant and describe the dishes a patron may want to order.

3. Create a "How to Survive" guide for the Games. One option is to write it from the standpoint of Haymitch. Another option is to write it from one of the tributes. What kind of advice would they give about staying alive?

4. Profiles/resumes. Have students create profiles for the different characters and tributes. They can create a resume with picture or they can create a profile sheet that describes the character. Although Facebook pages already exist for characters in the novel, this assignment could also be adapted for a Facebook page.

The Hunger Games

Essay/Writing Ideas

Several of the Standards Focus and Assessment Preparation activities can be expanded into writing assignments.

Essay Ideas

1. How is *The Hunger Games* a good example of the dystopian genre? Explain what elements of the novel make it dystopian.

2. What was your opinion of the novel? Use specific details from the novel that support your opinion.

3. There are two more books in the trilogy. Are you interested in reading them? Explain why you would or wouldn't want to read them.

4. If you haven't read the other books in the series, what do you predict will happen in those books? Support what you think, based on details from the novel.

5. If you have read the other books in the series, how do the events in the first book prepare you for the second (and even third) book? What characters from the first book have increasing importance?

6. In the Standards Focus activity for Chapters 25 – 27, you answered a question that asked what commentary about society you thought Suzanne Collins might be trying to communicate to readers through the novel. Do you agree with her view of society? Explain your answer by using details both from life and from the novel.

7. Could something like the Games ever happen or is this too far-fetched an idea? Explain how realistic the novel is by using details from the story.

8. What does the word "dehumanization" mean? How does the novel illustrate what happens to a society that dehumanizes its citizens?

9. Choose a character other than Katniss and discuss his or her motives and personality traits. What makes the character "tick"? Did Suzanne Collins create a believable character?

10. "All of the tributes are victims." Respond to that statement by agreeing or disagreeing. Explain your response by using evidence from the novel.

11. What is the responsibility of science to society? In the Games, scientists created mutations to entertain. Should scientists use technology and new ideas to improve life or should they be able to create entertainment like life video games and interesting new food products?

12. Return to the reaping scenes with Haymitch. Prior to his drunken fall off the stage, he nearly accuses the Capitol of something. Now that you've finished the novel and understand his character better, do you think he's making a political statement or is he just ranting? Explain your answer by using details from the novel.

13. People talk about "important books" or books everyone should read. Do you think *The Hunger Games* is one of those books? If so, explain your reasoning. If not, explain why not and then propose a book you do think everyone should read and include your reasoning.

Writing Ideas

1. *The Hunger Games* has been a great success among both adult and young adult readers. Write a review in which you support its popularity or question it.

2. Imagine you were chosen to be in the Games. What would your talent be? Explain how your talent might help you in the arena.

3. Katniss is alone in the arena and has to rely on her own skills to survive. Describe a time when you've had to rely on your own skills to get through a situation.

4. The meals that Katniss has are vividly described. Choose a memorable meal and describe it in detail. Can you make your reader's mouth water?

5. Choose a minor character from another district. Write a narrative about what that character's skill is as he or she prepares to go into the arena.

6. Write a dialogue between Cato and Clove after they learn that both of them can survive the Games. What strategy do they have when they go to the feast? How do their feelings toward each other change?

7. The citizens of the Capitol seem shallow and materialistic. Write a "day in the life" chronology of a Capitol citizen. Contrast that with a "day in the life" of Katniss or someone else in District 12.

8. As you learned in the pre-reading activities, the idea for the novel came from Suzanne Collins's childhood interest in the myth of Theseus. Try your hand at writing a myth.

9. Suzanne Collins had to create a believable fictional world as the backdrop of the novel. In the genre pre-reading activity, you began developing ideas to create your own fictional world. Either go back to your original ideas or revise them. Write a description of what the cities and towns look like and how technology is used in your fictional world.

10. In the Standards Focus activities for Chapters 25 – 27, you examined symbolism. Create a new symbol for the novel and describe what it represents.

11. "May the odds be ever in your favor." Do you agree with Effie Trinket's favorite phrase? How much of life is do you believe is based on "odds" and how much is under your control?

12. Haymitch is such an interesting character that the reader knows little about. Speculate on what Haymitch's experience in the Games must have been like. Support your ideas by using details about Haymitch from the novel.

13. Write a letter to Suzanne Collins telling her what you thought of the novel. Mail it!

14. In the Assessment Preparation for Chapters 13 – 14, you wrote an "I Am" poem for one of the characters. Write another "I Am" poem for another minor tribute from Games, or from your own point of view as if you were going to be in the Games.

Project Rubric A

Category	Score of 5	Score of 4	Score of 3	Score of 2	Score of 1	Score
Required Elements	Includes all of the required elements as stated in the directions.	Includes all but one or two of the required elements as stated in the directions.	Missing 3 or 4 of the required elements as stated in the directions.	Missing 5 or 6 of the required elements as stated in the directions.	Project does not follow the directions.	
Graphics, Pictures	All pictures, drawings, or graphics are appropriate and add to the enjoyment of the project.	Some pictures, drawings, or graphics are included, are appropriate, and add to the enjoyment of the project.	A few pictures, drawings, or graphics are included and are appropriate to the project.	A few pictures, drawings, or graphics are included, but may not be appropriate to the project, or may be distracting.	Pictures or drawings are not used and/or are inappropriate or distracting to the project.	
Creativity	Exceptionally clever and unique; design and presentation enhance the project.	Clever at times; thoughtfully and uniquely presented.	A few original or clever touches enhance the project.	Little evidence of uniqueness, individuality, and/or effort.	No evidence of creativity or effort. Project is not unique.	
Neatness, Appeal	Exceptionally neat and attractive; typed or very neatly hand-written, appropriate use of color, particularly neat in design and layout.	Neat and attractive; typed or neatly handwritten, good use of color, good design and layout.	Generally neat and attractive; handwritten, some use of color, some problems in design and layout.	Distractingly messy or disorganized; handwritten; little use of color; several problems in design and layout.	Work shows no pride or effort. Project is incomplete, illegible, or particularly messy and unattractive.	
Grammar, Spelling, Mechanics	Little to no problems with grammar, spelling, and mechanics. Project was clearly proofread.	A few problems with grammar, spelling, or mechanics. Errors are minor and do not distract from the project.	Several errors in grammar, spelling, or mechanics. Errors can be slightly distracting at times.	Several problems with grammar, spelling, or mechanics. Errors are distracting.	Many problems with grammar, spelling, or mechanics. Mistakes clearly show project was not proofread.	

Comments:

Final Score: _____ out of 25

Project Rubric B

Category	Score of 5	Score of 4	Score of 3	Score of 2	Score of 1	Score
Required Elements	Includes all of the required elements as stated in the directions.	Includes all but one or two of the required elements as stated in the directions.	Missing 3 or 4 of the required elements as stated in the directions.	Missing 5 or 6 of the required elements as stated in the directions.	Project does not follow the directions.	
Creativity	Exceptionally clever and unique; design and presentation enhance the project.	Clever at times; thoughtfully and uniquely presented.	A few original or clever touches enhance the project.	Little evidence of uniqueness, individuality, and/or effort.	No evidence of creativity or effort. Project is not unique.	
Neatness, Appeal	Exceptionally neat and attractive; typed or very neatly hand-written, appropriate use of color, particularly neat in design and layout.	Neat and attractive; typed or neatly handwritten, good use of color, good design and layout.	Generally neat and attractive; handwritten, some use of color, some problems in design and layout.	Distractingly messy or disorganized; handwritten; little use of color; several problems in design and layout.	Work shows no pride or effort. Project is incomplete, illegible, or particularly messy and unattractive.	
Grammar, Spelling, Mechanics	Little to no problems with grammar, spelling, and mechanics. Project was clearly proofread.	A few problems with grammar, spelling, or mechanics. Errors are minor and do not distract from the project.	Several errors in grammar, spelling, or mechanics. Errors can be slightly distracting at times.	Several problems with grammar, spelling, or mechanics. Errors are distracting.	Many problems with grammar, spelling, or mechanics. Mistakes clearly show project was not proofread.	
Citation of Sources	All graphics, pictures, and written work are original, or if they have been obtained from an outside source, have been properly cited.	All graphics, pictures, and written work that are not original or have been obtained from an outside source have been cited, with a few problems.	All graphics, pictures, and written work that are not original or have been obtained from an outside source have been cited, with several problems.	Some attempt has been made to give credit for unoriginal graphics, pictures, and written work.	No attempt has been made to give credit for unoriginal graphics, pictures, and written work.	

Comments:

Final Score: _____ out of 25

Response to Literature Rubric

Adapted from the **California Writing Assessment Rubric**
California Department of Education, Standards and Assessment Division

Score of 4
☐ Clearly addresses all parts of the writing task.
☐ Provides a meaningful thesis and thoughtfully supports the thesis and main ideas with facts, details, and/or explanations.
☐ Maintains a consistent tone and focus and a clear sense of purpose and audience.
☐ Illustrates control in organization, including effective use of transitions.
☐ Provides a variety of sentence types and uses precise, descriptive language.
☐ Contains few, if any, errors in the conventions of the English language (grammar, punctuation, capitalization, spelling). These errors do not interfere with the reader's understanding of the writing.
☐ Demonstrates a *clear* understanding of the ambiguities, nuances, and complexities of the text.
☐ Develops interpretations that demonstrate a thoughtful, comprehensive, insightful grasp of the text, and supports these judgments with specific references to various texts.
☐ Draws well-supported inferences about the effects of a literary work on its audience.
☐ Provides *specific* textual examples and/or personal knowledge and details to support the interpretations and inferences.

Score of 3
☐ Addresses all parts of the writing task.
☐ Provides a thesis and supports the thesis and main ideas with mostly relevant facts, details, and/or explanations.
☐ Maintains a generally consistent tone and focus and a general sense of purpose and audience.
☐ Illustrates control in organization, including *some* use of transitions.
☐ Includes a variety of sentence types and *some* descriptive language.
☐ Contains some errors in the conventions of the English language. These errors do not interfere with the reader's understanding of the writing.
☐ Develops interpretations that demonstrate a comprehensive grasp of the text and supports these interpretations with references to various texts.
☐ Draws supported inferences about the effects of a literary work on its audience.
☐ Supports judgments with some specific references to various texts and/or personal knowledge.
☐ Provides textual examples and details to support the interpretations.

Score of 2

- ☐ Addresses *only parts* of the writing task.
- ☐ *Suggests* a central idea with *limited* facts, details, and/or explanation.
- ☐ Demonstrates *little* understanding of purpose and audience.
- ☐ Maintains an *inconsistent* point of view, focus, and/or organizational structure which may include *ineffective or awkward* transitions that do not unify important ideas.
- ☐ Contains *several errors* in the conventions of the English language. These errors may interfere with the reader's understanding of the writing.
- ☐ Develops interpretations that demonstrate a limited grasp of the text.
- ☐ Includes interpretations that *lack* accuracy or coherence as related to ideas, premises, or images from the literary work.
- ☐ Draws *few* inferences about the effects of a literary work on its audience.
- ☐ Supports judgments with *few, if any*, references to various text and/or personal knowledge.

Score of 1

- ☐ Addresses *only one* part of the writing task.
- ☐ *Lacks* a thesis or central idea but may contain *marginally related* facts, details, and/or explanations.
- ☐ Demonstrates *no* understanding of purpose and audience.
- ☐ *Lacks* a clear point of view, focus, organizational structure, and transitions that unify important ideas.
- ☐ Includes *no* sentence variety; sentences are simple.
- ☐ Contains *serious errors* in the conventions of the English language. These errors interfere with the reader's understanding of the writing.
- ☐ Develops interpretations that demonstrate *little* grasp of the text.
- ☐ *Lacks* an interpretation or *may* be a simple retelling of the text.
- ☐ *Lacks* inferences about the effects of a literary work on its audience.
- ☐ *Fails* to support judgments with references to various text and/or personal knowledge.
- ☐ *Lacks* textual examples and details.

The Hunger Games

Answer Key

Note: Answers may not be given in complete sentences, as most student answers should be. Many answers will vary, but sample student answers are given for each example.

Author Biography
Page 11: Comprehension Check: Exploring Expository Writing
Answers may vary. Sample student answers

1. As a child, she was interested in myths. She used the myths as a basis for her writing.
2. She was flipping through channels and watching two different shows which helped her come up with the idea for the novel.
3. People no longer think of what they see as actual people. They think of what is on TV as entertainment. The hardships people experience on TV aren't real to many people.
4. I think that people are desensitized because everything seems like a reality TV show. It's staged for entertainment and not realistic.
5. She might think that war hurts all people, not just those who are in the war. She probably remembers how scary it was to think of her dad who was in the war. Even though she was safe at home, it is frightening to think of loved ones who are in harm's way and you can't do anything to protect them.
6. She is someone who isn't afraid to voice her opinion. For example, she states that she thinks people don't realize that war is real and the people involved are real. On TV, the events that happen to people are real and not just a show. She feels strongly that people's problems need to be taken seriously. She's also aware of how to write for children, and she can probably tell a good story. If you write TV scripts, you have to be able to write a story.
7. I think writing for TV, especially for children's television, is probably a bit easier. There is a limited amount of time for the show, the show has to end happily, and TV is immediate. When writing a novel, I think it would be harder because the writer would need to develop the characters, setting, and theme more.
8. I would ask her who her favorite writers are. I would also want to ask her how she decided on the names of the characters. I would want to ask her what she worried about and what she thought about when she was my age.

Page 14: Comprehension Check: The Myth of Theseus
Answers may vary. Sample student answers

1. A story passed down through the generations to help explain a natural phenomenon, such as evil in the world. Myths often include gods and goddesses and heroes who perform amazing feats.
2. He buried a sword and sandals under a boulder. Theseus could take these to Aegeus to prove he was his son.
3. Perephites, Sinis, Sciron, the giant sow, Cercyon, Procrustes
4. He had several enemies that wanted to fight. Some of them simply wanted to kill him. Some wanted to trick him. First, Periphetes tried to club him, then Sinis tried to rip him apart with the pine tree trick, then he killed the giant sow, then came across Sciron, who ended up falling into the sea. Then he met Cercyon, whom he defeated, then Procrustes, who "made" people fit into his bed.
5. He has to show physical and mental superiority in order to defeat his adversaries. He was obviously witty, strong, and courageous.
6. He wants to help others in spite of the dangers to himself. He chooses the difficult route in order to end the misery of people. For example, he volunteers to go to Crete to stop the injustices that were going on.
7. He is vindictive to ask for a tribute of children.
8. Children would be helpless against the Minotaur. They wouldn't have a chance to survive the labyrinth. Plus, taking someone's child is the ultimate punishment.
9. He is a hero, and as a hero, he's never going to be happy if he isn't helping others and making the world a better place. He also enjoyed the challenges of battle since he continually chose challenges over the easy way.
10. I like the part about Procrustes. I think it's the strangest way to kill someone.

Page 17: Comprehension Check: Fantasy, Sci-Fi, and Dystopia
Answers may vary. Sample student answers are given for numbers 4-10.
1. It's a further classification of fiction.
2. Fantasy could never happen. It includes things like talking animals, wizards, and fairies. Science fiction is based on science that perhaps someday might happen – like flying cars or computers that clean our houses.
3. A book that depicts a society that represses individuals. The government doesn't take care of the rights of citizens.
4. fairies, ogres, Greek gods and goddesses, sorting hats, magic rings, talking spiders
5. clothing that cleans itself, light sabers, robots that are servants, hover crafts.
6. Since the word means "no place" and "a world that is well," the word probably means that he thought there was no such place as a perfect world. He may have thought it was an impossible dream.
7. Perhaps allow for more personal freedoms and improve educational opportunities for the members of my society.
8. I don't think my world would work because not everyone follows the rules. I think that's why it's hard to have a perfect society. There will always be people who don't agree or want to do things a different way.
9. I don't think so for the same reasons my own perfect world wouldn't exist. People won't want to follow the rules; they'll want to do things their own way.
10. I prefer fantasy because I like imagining things that could never really happen like magic and talking animals and wizards.

Page 19: Comprehension Check: Who's In Control? A Look at Propaganda
Answers may vary. Sample student answers are given.
1. Propaganda is the intentional spread of true or false information to the public with the goal of influencing public opinion and behavior.
2. They used it to influence public opinion about the Jews. They made it permissible to discriminate against Jews.
3. Propaganda doesn't use all the facts. It relies on emotional arguments. The goal of propaganda is to influence the public rather than to influence one person or a small group of people.

4. Propaganda relies on an emotional response from people. An emotional response to an issue is often more powerful than a logical or factual response.
5. It doesn't include facts. It's emotional since there is a child in the picture. It has a memorable slogan. It is red, white, and blue – the colors of the flag, so it has a patriotic feel to it.
6. It might be easier and faster to use propaganda rather than creating a persuasive argument. A propaganda poster will be easier to read and understand than an argument or essay.
7. Green initiatives such as not using plastic water bottles, biking to work or school, reusing items. Exercising and eating a balanced diet.
8. If there aren't many facts or if the argument is based on emotion, it might be propaganda.

Page 30: Note-Taking and Summarizing
Answers will vary. For a good example of what students might write on the Note-Taking and Summarizing pages for each chapter, simply refer to the Summary of the Novel, pp. 242-244.

Page 31: Comprehension Check: Chapters 1-2
Chapter 1
1. She's going hunting.
2. It is a coal-mining town that is very poor. People are often hungry or starving. It is a gray, depressed place.
3. A girl and boy from each district in Panem will be chosen to compete in the Hunger Games.
4. As punishment for an uprising against the government, each district sends one girl and one boy, ages 12 – 18, to the Capitol where they participate in a battle to the death.
5. It is a way for poor families to get more rations by putting the children's names into the drawing more often, so it punishes the poor people for being poor. It increases the chances that the poor will continue to suffer by either starving or losing their children to the reaping.
6. Katniss knows that her family and Gale's would starve if they didn't provide food for them. Katniss is aware that Gale is handsome and girls like him, she's also by confused by his comment that he'd want to have children. Katniss pushes away the thought that her jealously comes from anything other than a need for a good hunting partner.

7. She will panic because she has done everything she can to protect Prim, but she can't protect her from the reaping.

8. The government is cruel and vindictive. I know this because it allows its citizens to starve or gamble away their children through the tesserae. It controls the country through the fear of the Hunger Games, which it makes everyone watch or participate in.

9. It's a geological term that means a layer of material – such as coal. It's an appropriate name because the people who live there are miners.

Chapter 2

1. She runs up onto the stage and takes her place.

2. She thinks it will make her look weak.

3. The reaping is televised all around Panem. Others will be making judgments about Katniss based on her behavior after her name is called.

4. They don't clap or cheer. They also use a district gesture of thanks and farewell. The people are on her side, and they are unhappy with the reaping. It may also mean that Katniss is better known in the town than she realizes.

5. He gave her bread when her family was starving.

6. In spite of the fact that his mother would probably beat him, he burned the bread and gave it to Katniss. He is a kind person since he tries to reassure Katniss with a handshake. Perhaps he likes Katniss or maybe he pities her because of what happened to her father.

7. When she saw Peeta in the schoolyard, she also saw a dandelion. She knew when she saw a dandelion that she'd be able to survive because she could go into the woods and hunt and gather.

8. Katniss feels like she's in debt to Peeta and she never thanked him for the bread. She may have to kill him in the arena. How can she kill the person who helped her family survive?

Page 32: Chapters 1 – 2 Standards Focus: The Cast of Characters

Character Name	Character Description
Father	Killed in a mining accident when Katniss was eleven.
Mother	Seriously depressed after the death of her husband, she was unable to care for her children.
Katniss	Sixteen-year-old girl who lives in Seam of District 12. She hunts for her family. Her best friend is Gale.
Prim	Twelve-year-old sister of Katniss. She is the one person Katniss knows she loves.

Gale	Eighteen-year-old hunting partner and friend of Katniss. His nickname for her is "Catnip."

Peeta Mellark	The boy tribute from District 12. His family members are bakers. Katniss remembers him because he gave her bread when her family is starving.

Haymitch Abernathy	The only living winner of the Hunger Games from District 12. He is an alcoholic and shows up drunk to the reaping.
Effie Trinket	The Capitol representative for District 12. She is overly happy and chipper.

Madge Undersee	Friend to Katniss. She gives Katniss a pin of a mockingjay.

District 12	A mining area. The part where Katniss lives is called the Seam. The area is very poor. It is not uncommon for people to starve to death here.
The Capitol	The central government; put down the rebellion and started the Hunger Games; responsible for creating muttations and keeping the people in the districts hungry

Pages 33-35 : Chapters 1 – 2: Assessment Preparation: Verb Tenses & Moods

Answers may vary. Sample student answers are given

1. present tense
2. The sentences are written like the action of the story is taking place right now. "Gale and I divide our spoils" they are doing it right now.
3. By writing in the present tense, the book feels like it's happening right in front of me. It sounds different because she's not telling something that she's already lived through. I didn't really notice the tense because I've read other books that are written in the present tense.
4. First person because she uses the pronoun "I"
5. When books are written in the past tense, the reader knows the action has already taken place and the main character survived. If it's written in the first person point of view, we're not as sure.
1. Indicative. It makes a statement.
2. Indicative. It states an opinion.
3. Subjunctive: "if there were no ears…" She is indicating that it's something that might happen – something he might say.
4. Imperative. He's making a command.
5. Indicative. It is a statement.
6. Subjunctive. She is making a wish or desire that they will have favorable odds.
7. Imperative. He's giving a command.
8. Indicative. It's a statement of what is happening.
9. Subjunctive. She is wishing she'll still be alive on her birthday. They are on the verge of starvation.
10. Imperative. The mother is giving a command to Peeta.

Part III: Vocabulary

Answers will vary. Sample student answer:

Today events for the District 12 *reaping* took an interesting turn. District 12's ever *radical* former winner, Haymitch Abernathy, showed an interesting display as he *plummeted* from the stage in a drunken stupor. But Haymitch's *preposterous* behavior didn't upstage the drama surrounding the choice of the girl tribute. Katniss Everdeen found herself in a *predicament* when her little sister Prim was chosen first. Katniss volunteered to take her place. The drama of the arena wasn't a *deterrent* to her taking her sister's place. At first, Effie Trinket wanted to check the *protocol* of the switch, but there was no other *dissent* or *haggling* over who the tribute would be. You may have thought the crowd would be *maniacally* cheering over the drama, but the crowd was surprisingly silent. In *adjacent*

districts, no other drama surrounding the annual reaping.

In other news, the Capitol would like to remind citizens that *poaching* on restricted land is punishable by death.

Page 37: Comprehension Check: Chapters 3-4

Chapter 3

1. Her mom, Prim, Gale, Peeta's father, and Madge.
2. She'll go into a depression and stop taking care of Prim.
3. Peeta's father brings her cookies; Madge brings her a pin of a mockingjay to wear in the arena.
4. The television cameras will be filming everything. She doesn't want to appear weak to the other tributes.
5. Effie has no idea what their life is like in the Seam. She doesn't realize that people are starving and manners aren't the most important part of a meal that they might not even get. Katniss responds by eating with her hands and wiping them on the tablecloth.
6. A mentor is a guide or sponsor. It is an experienced person who helps a new person along the way. A mentor in the arena helps get the tributes sponsors and gifts.
7. A sponsor might provide food or shelter. The sponsor could also give the tribute weapons.
8. If he's drunk all the time, he won't be able to help them in the arena. He doesn't seem to really care about them or the Games.

Chapter 4

1. Katniss thinks that Peeta is being kind, and that will make her feel obligated to him. She doesn't want to feel that way, so she decides to stay away from him as much as possible.
2. When she saw them in the schoolyard, she remembered they were edible. Then she and Prim collected them and began looking for more things to collect. Katniss eventually began going into the woods and learning how to hunt.
3. They confront him about his drinking. Peeta knocks a glass from his hand and Katniss stabs her knife into the table near his hand.
4. He is always drunk, so for him to agree to help them, he's going to have to get sober. He could be their lifeline in the arena. By having a mentor who actually helps them, Katniss and Peeta have some hope.
5. I don't think Peeta is that calculating. I don't think he's intentionally planning how he's going to kill Katniss. I think he's just trying to get a sponsor in any way he knows how.

6. Based on what kind of food they're served on the train, I can infer that food is going to be wonderful in the Capitol. Also, based on what Katniss sees out the window, the Capitol is beautiful and new as compared with District 12, which is described as run down and desolate.

Pages 38-39: Chapters 3-4 Standards Focus: In Media Res
Answers may vary. Sample student answers are given.

I'd probably start with when I went to the bus stop because that's where the interesting part of the story happens.

It might be boring; it would take a long time to get to the good parts. There might be information that you don't need.

The reader gets interested right away, something is happening, the reader doesn't have to wait for the action.

It starts with the reaping.

When Prim's name is drawn and Katniss takes her place.

Past	Present	Future (predictions)
Peeta gave Katniss bread	Katniss feels in debt to Peeta	Katniss will want to make that up to Peeta in some way
Katniss learned to hunt to save her family from starvation	Katniss and Gale are great hunters	Katniss will use her hunting skills to survive
Katniss loves Prim more than anyone in the world	Katniss takes her place at the reaping	Katniss will make sacrifices for those she loves
Haymitch won the Hunger Games	He is Peeta and Katniss's mentor.	He will be too drunk to help them very much.
Peeta might have burned the bread on purpose	He is kind to Katniss and offers to help Haymitch	Peeta will do things for others because he's a kind person
The Capitol genetically engineered the jabberjay	It bred with the mockingbird and became the mockingjay	The mockingjay pin that Katniss received will be important.
Katniss's mother has a book of edible plants	Katniss and Prim learned which plants were safe to eat	Katniss might need this knowledge about plants in the arena.
Katniss finds the katniss plant that grows in water – it's edible	Katniss can find this plant and her family won't be hungry	Katniss might need this information to survive.
There was never enough food – Katniss was always hungry	Katniss has plenty to eat on the train as they go to the Capitol	In the Capitol, Katniss will have great food

Answers may vary. Sample student answer: In Harry Potter, the inciting incident is Harry's birthday when he gets the invitation to Hogwarts.

Pages 40-41: Chapter 3 – 4 Assessment Preparation – Coordinate And Cumulative Adjectives
1. It's cumulative because you can't switch the adjectives without changing the meaning.
2. It's coordinate because it can be small and circular pin, plus the adjectives can be in any order.
3. This is cumulative because the meaning of the braid changes if the words are switched.
4. This is coordinate because each adjectives describe the liquid independently.
Answers may vary. Sample student answers:
1. The disastrous, deadly storm destroyed several homes.
2. The gnarled, old tree was home to several generations of squirrels.

3. Three disgruntled students complained about the lunch menu.
4. Jacob worried about Mary's insurmountable pile of homework.
5. (coordinate) Students were concerned about the strange, inexplicable noise coming from the teacher's desk. (cumulative) Several inexplicable coincidences led Holman to believe his locker was haunted.

Answers may vary. Sample student answers:
1. daydreaming
2. happy
3. solid
4. minute; tiny
5. to love
1. concentration; focus
2. thankful
3. duplicate; to create again
4. a supporter, guide, or trusted advisor

Page 43: Chapters 5 - 6 Comprehension Check

Answers may vary. Sample answers are given.

Chapter 5

1. It's to prepare the tributes for the opening ceremonies.
2. She's hoping she won't be naked or wearing something horrible like the tributes in the past.
3. It can win favor with the crowd. It can help them be memorable.
4. Cinna isn't as flamboyant as the others. He doesn't have strange hair or make up. Katniss thinks he's attractive. He doesn't talk in the Capitol-affected speech. He seems to understand Katniss and how she feels about the Capitol.
5. They love them.
6. She thinks that Peeta compliments her because he's planning to kill her. She's suspicious of his intentions. She kisses him because she wants to use the same strategy on him.
7. I think Peeta is sincere because he's done nothing so far in the book to indicate he's anything but sincere and kind.

Chapter 6

1. Their conversation is private because there is noise that blocks their conversation. They have privacy.
2. Her apartment there is larger than her whole home in District 12. There is a shower, a programmable closet, magnifying windows, and menu of whatever she wants to eat. It's more luxurious than anything she's ever known.
3. She's not very sensitive because she's constantly insulting the people from District 12. She's ignorant because she thinks coal turns into pearls. However, she does want Katniss and Peeta to do well.
4. A criminal whose tongue has been cut out. People cannot speak to them unless they're giving an order.
5. She and Gale saw her and a boy in the woods. They were obviously running away, and before Katniss or Gale could help, a hovercraft came along and captured them. The boy was killed. Katniss feels sure that the girl saw them and called for help.
6. He may have just been being helpful. He might be being nice to Katniss. He saw she needed help, and he helped her. Perhaps he's trying to gain the upper hand by making Katniss grateful to him. Delly would be someone they should not have interaction with.
7. She feels guilty that she didn't try to help her when she saw her in the woods. She wonders if the girl remembers her. She wishes she could apologize.

Pages 44-45: Chapters 5 –6 Standards Focus: Building a Fictional World

Answers may vary. Sample student answers are given.

The earth rotates, earth follows an orbit, seasons change, and water runs downhill.

It came from a place once called North America. It was a Capitol surrounded by thirteen districts.	We are familiar with North America. The United States started with thirteen colonies.	We are already familiar with North America. We know the country. It is important because I am familiar with it.
During the "Dark Days," the districts rebelled and District 13 was destroyed.	It could be similar to the Civil War when the South rebelled – or the Revolutionary War.	We know that everyone isn't happy with the way the government runs the country.
As a result of the rebellion, the districts must participate in the Hunger Games.	We have games like the Olympics, but nothing like the Hunger Games. I'm also familiar with the story of the Minotaur which is similar to the tributes being sent to battle.	I know that when a country loses a battle the loser is often punished.
The Hunger Games are treated like a celebration.	We have games like the Super Bowl and the Olympics that are big celebrations. Everyone watches it on TV and talks about it. We also have many national holidays.	It shows the reader that the Capitol doesn't value the life of the tributes because it is just a party to them.
People in District 12 are very poor and starving, but people in the Capitol are rich.	There are places where people are poor and there are places where people are rich.	We realize there is a big difference between District 12 and the rest of Panem.

District 12 is a mining area.	There are places in our country in which there are mines.	The people who work in the mines are poor and not taken care of. The government doesn't protect them from dangerous working conditions.
Children can receive tesserae which allow them to get food in exchange for entering their names another time in the reaping.	We have social services that provide food for poor families.	It helps explain how desperate the people are. They're so hungry, they're willing to put the names of their children in the reaping.
Everything that happens with the Games is televised.	We have reality TV shows that are very popular. We also have "survival" TV shows where people complete to be the winner.	Just like our world, people watch TV. TV is entertainment, and people enjoy watching shows about real people.
High speed trains can travel at 250 miles per hour.	We have airplanes and high speed rails.	In Panem, technology has advanced.
Certain places, like the woods, are restricted with electrified fences.	I know places that are fenced so people can't get in. Often the fences are electrified.	The government certainly wants people to stay in a particular area. They want to control where people go and what they do.
People from the Capitol have a strange way of talking; they wear bright makeup and wigs.	Some fashions are odd. Singers like Lady GaGa wear outrageous makeup and costumes.	The people in the Capitol can worry about fashion since they don't have to worry about survival.

Answers may vary. Sample student answer: I do think this world could exist because we already have reality TV that people love watching. I also think our technology is close to being similar to the technology of the book. I'm not sure the people in the future would put up with a government that would sacrifice their children.

Pages 46-48: Chapters 5 – 6 Assessment Preparation: Etymology

Word	Where it came from	What it originally meant
Vulnerable	Latin	Able to wound
Flamboyant	French	Flame
Sustenance	French & Latin	Means of living
Despicable	Latin	To look down on
Tangible	Latin	Capable of being touched
Barbarism	Greek	To do as a foreigner does
Exclusive(ly)	Latin	As to exclude
Ironic	Latin	insincere
Adversary (ies)	Latin	opponent
Mandatory	Latin	mandate
Affectation(s)	Latin	Striving after

Affix	Meaning	Vocabulary Word	Root or other information about the word	Definition
in-	not	insurmountable	insurmountable – the root means "to rise above"	unable to overcome

		inexplicable	inexplicable – the root "explicate" means to "unfold"	unable to explain
dis -	not, apart	dissent	dissent—the root word is means to feel or think	protest
		disaster	disaster – the root means "star" – people thought bad things happened because of the stars	extremely unfortunate
		disgruntled	disgruntle – gruntle means to grumble	unhappy, dissatisfied
-ment	act of, state of, result	predicament	predicate – to declare publicly	difficult situation
-ous	full of, having	preposterous	preposterous –with the hind end coming first	ridiculous
		disastrous (see dis-)		
-ity	state of, quality	intensity	intense – stretch out	concentration
-able/ -ible	able, capable	insurmountable, Inexplicable (see in-)		
		vulnerable	vulnerable – wound	exposed
		despicable	despicable – to look down on	worthy of being scorned
		tangible	tangible – may be touched	able to be touched
-ance	action, process, state	sustenance	sustain – to endure or hold up	nourishment
-ism	system, manner, condition, characteristic	barbarism	barbarian – what is not Greek, foreigner	uncivilized
-ic	nature of, like	ironic	irony – dissembler	unexpected

Part III: *Answers may vary. Sample student answers are given.*

I was surprised by the words barbarism and flamboyant. The word barbarism surprised me because the root referred to things that were not Greek. I thought that showed that the Greeks thought their civilization was superior to all others. I also thought flamboyant was interesting. The root means "flame," and I also learned that it refers to a type of showy architecture.

It can help me understand where the word came from and how people felt about the word. For example, disaster is based on people believing

that the planets determined what happened to a person.

Page 50: Chapters 7 – 9: Comprehension Check
Answers may vary. Sample answers are given.
Chapter 7
1. It is three days; the tributes all practice together. On the third day they perform for the Gamemakers.
2. He tells them to try to learn a new skill during training and to stay together all the time while they're in public.

3. He means that Katniss isn't aware that people admire and recognize her confidence and skill. He may also mean that she has an effect on him; Peeta, too, is drawn to Katniss.

4. He decorates the cakes at the bakery.

5. They are tired and have been drinking. They aren't paying attention to her.

6. I think she shouldn't have taken a chance by shooting at the pig. She could have missed. But she certainly got their attention when she made the shot.

Chapter 8

1. If her score is high enough, she'll get sponsors. Sponsors can make the difference between life and death in the arena.

2. At first he seems concerned, but then he thinks it's funny.

3. She receives the highest score – an eleven. She was sure her score would be lower.

4. The televised interview.

5. Katniss has spent more time with Gale. They've shared time together while they've hunted. She feels close to Gale. Katniss is just pretending to be close with Peeta. She is only acting a certain way with him because Haymitch has told her to do so.

6. They both are relationships for survival.

7. He may be feeling too much stress between

himself and Katniss. He may be hurt by Katniss's behavior toward him.

Chapter 9

1. She has trouble walking in high heels, she doesn't have good posture, and she doesn't smile enough.

2. She doesn't present herself well. She won't answer questions, and she's hostile and sullen.

3. She eats dinner in her room and breaks dishes.

4. She takes Cinna's advice and imagines she's talking to him. It does work, and the interview goes well.

5. Even though she's very uncomfortable, she ends up acting silly and giggly – unlike how she is in real life.

6. That he has a crush on Katniss and has liked her for as long as he can remember.

7. He has done kind things for Katniss like offer to clean up Haymitch, he's covered for her when she said she knew the Avox, he tries to be nice to her.

8. He is trying to win the Games as well. He wants to get sponsors, and he needs a strategy to do this since he isn't particularly skilled like Katniss is. He knows how popular Katniss is, and he may be trying to gain popularity by saying he likes her.

Page 51-53: Chapter 7 – 9 Standards Focus – Character Analysis: Close Up on Katniss and Peeta

Answers may vary. Sample answers are given.

Harry Potter

He has magical powers plus something interesting is always happening to him. He seems like a real person.

Chapter & Page	Event or description	What does that tell us about Katniss?
Chapter 1, p. 7	Katniss killed a lynx because he scared off game. "he wasn't bad company. But I got a decent price for his pelt."	Even though it sounds like she liked the lynx, she was practical enough to kill the lynx, and practical enough to sell the pelt. She isn't sentimental about animals. She's not a fan of pets.
Chapter 1, p. 8	"But to be honest, I'm not the forgiving type."	She's not going to give her mother a second chance. She's pretty cynical for a young person.
Chapter 1, p. 14	"But what good is yelling about the Capitol in the middle of the wood? It doesn't change anything. It doesn't make things fair."	Katniss doesn't think anything she does or thinks will change the way things are. She doesn't want to get involved in the politics of life. She's more worried about surviving.

Chapter 2, p. 32	"I feel like I owe him something, and I hate owing people."	Katniss doesn't like to be indebted to others. She likes her independence.
Chapter 4 p. 49	"A kind Peeta Mellark is far more dangerous to me than an unkind one. Kind people have a way of working their way inside me."	Katniss is afraid that Peeta's kindness to her will make it impossible for her to kill him when they are in the arena.
Chapter 3, p. 35	"There's no me to keep you both alive. It doesn't matter what happens. Whenever you see on the screen. You have to promise me you'll fight through it!"	She is determined that her mother not fall into a depression like she did when Katniss's father died.
Chapter 4, p. 51	"The woods became our savior, and each day I went a bit father into its arms. It was slow-going at first, but I was determined to feed us."	She's determined to keep her family alive.
Chapter 5, p. 72	*"Peeta is planning how to kill you…He is luring you in to make you easy prey."*	Katniss is suspicious of Peeta.
Chapter 6 p. 85	"That I'm ashamed I never tried to help her in the woods. That I let the Capitol kill the boy and mutilate her without lifting a finger."	Katniss feels guilty for not helping someone in need.
Chapter 7, p. 102	"I pull an arrow from my quiver and send it straight at the Gamemaker's table…Everyone stares at me in disbelief."	She is impulsive. When she's angry, she doesn't think about what she's doing.
Chapter 9 p. 124	"I can feel my pulse pounding in my temples. It's a relief to get to my chair, because between the heels and my legs shaking, I'm afraid I'll trip."	She's nervous.

Positive qualities	Negative Qualities
She looks out for her family	She is suspicious
She wants to help others	She doesn't like to accept things from others
She is determined	She doesn't like to talk in front of crowds
She is practical	She's impulsive and acts without thinking
She is resourceful	
She is brave	

Positive Qualities & Evidence	Negative Qualities & Evidence
He is generous – he gives Katniss bread when her family is starving	He has a temper – he smashes the glass out of Haymitch's hand
He is observant – he watches and understands what Katniss's family is going through	He shows his emotions – he's been crying before they get on the train to the Capitol
He is friendly – he waves to the crowds when the train pulls into the Capitol	
He is funny – he's able to make jokes at the interview	

Answers may vary. Sample student answer: Peeta is a dynamic character because he has both good and bad qualities. I can imagine him as a real person.

Effie Trinket		Cinna	
Positive qualities	Negative qualities	Positive qualities	Negative qualities
She really likes the Hunger Games	She doesn't think of the tributes as real people	He seems to really care about Katniss	
She understand what stage presence is	She is silly and superficial	He does a good job on her costumes	
		He isn't as fake as the other stylists	

Answers may vary. Sample answers are given:
I think both of them are static characters because the reader doesn't really know enough about them. We don't know what their motives are and why they act the way they do.
If every character in the novel were dynamic, the novel would be long and probably confusing.
The author would have to provide the reader with lots of information about each character in order to make the character dynamic – especially if the character is going to change throughout the course of the plot.

Pages 54-55: Chapters 7 – 9: Assessment Preparation – Author's Purpose – Greek Themes
Answers may vary. Sample answers are given.

Romans were interested in entertainment – they had the gladiator games. Romans were also great builders.
Venia, Portia, Cinna, Flavius, Octavia, Panem, Caesar Flickman
They were educated and revered as being the best civilization. They might like the advances in civilization the Romans and Greeks had. They might like their culture.
For the people who live in wealthy districts, the Hunger Games are a form of entertainment. They make them seem like a party with the Opening Ceremonies and all the TV coverage. The winners of the Games are given a special house and food.
She may want the reader to know that the people of Panem looked up to the Roman culture. It fits in better with the Games since they're based on the story of the Minotaur.

	Meaning of the name	Does this name seem to fit the character? Why or why not?
Euphemia (Effie)	Melodious talk	It fits her because she talks a lot and her is described as cheerful
Flavius	Golden or yellow haired	Yes, he's described as having orange corkscrews
Venus (Venia)	Goddess of love	It's hard to say since she's just described as someone with aqua hair and gold tatoos
Caesar	Ruler of the Roman empire	It does fit him; he's like the ruler of the interviews – he's been doing it forever
Octavia	Female version of Octavius which means eighth	Not really – it says she's plump
Portia	Roman family name meaning pig	Not really – there are no clues that she's like a pig

a- means "not" and vox means "voice"
The avox doesn't have a voice since they cut out their tongue. Also, since they are being punished, they are simply called Avox. They have no name. They really don't matter.

	Denotation	Connotation
Chariot	A carriage drawn by horses	I think of something fast and sleek – used by gladiators. The word feels positive to me.
Tribute	A gift given in gratitude	It sounds like it should be a positive word. It's something given to someone you esteem.
sponsor	Someone who's responsible for the well-being of another	It should have a positive meaning. The sponsor is going to be responsible for the tribute's survival.
arena	Center stage with seats all around it.	It sounds like it's a positive thing. A stage or the center of a theater is a good thing.
game	A competitive activity using skills.	If you like playing games, this will have positive connotations.

They would want people to view the Games in a positive light. They chose words that sound positive. Tribute could be replaced with sacrifice, tax, slave; sponsor could be replaced with odds maker; arena could be replaced with slaughterhouse; game could be replaced with penalty, punishment, battle, fight

Pages 56-57 What's in Your Backpack?
Student projects will vary widely.

Page 59: Chapter 10: Comprehension Check
Answers may vary. Sample student answers
1. She thinks it makes her look weak.
2. It makes her desirable, and sponsors will want to support her.
3. Get out as fast as possible, get away from others, find water, and stay alive.
4. Peeta wants to show the Capitol that he isn't a piece of property. He wants to maintain his identity and not become just a part of the Games. He's planning his death. Katniss wants to survive. She isn't planning her death; she's planning on surviving.
5. I had a big presentation to make at school. I was anxious because I didn't know if I was ready. My experience was similar to Katniss's because I kept thinking about how it was going to go. I was playing the events that could happen over and over in my mind. My experience was different because I wasn't going into a life or death situation. I knew I would make it through the end of the day.
6. It is a device that it inserted under the skin to keep track of the tributes in the arena.
7. They're treated as historical sites where people can tour, visit, and even participate in reenactments. The Capitol regards the Games as an historic event. They have completely dehumanized the event.
8. The mockingjay pin.
9. She claims she didn't know it had a poisoned spike, but whether she knew it or not, it doesn't sound like a fair item to bring into the arena. I can infer that she may have been trying to cheat.
10. I was waiting for the school play to start. I had a big part, and I was very nervous. I was sure I would forget my lines and forget what to do.

Pages 60-62: Chapter 10: Standards Focus: Star-crossed Lovers and Other Archetypes of Literature
Answers may vary. Sample answers

Villain:

1. From *The Hunger Games*: Haymitch because he and Katniss have conflicts. They cannot get along or agree.	
2. Other character/s: Voldemort	From: *Harry Potter*

Hero:

1. From *The Hunger Games*: Katniss because the story is told from her point of view. Also, she is better suited to go into the arena because she can use her survival skills.	
2. Other character/s: Harry Potter	From: Harry Potter

Scapegoat:

1. From *The Hunger Games*: The tributes because they are being sacrificed for past sins of their districts.	
2. Other character/s: Jews during the Holocaust	From: Number the Stars

1. They have to get the witch's broomstick.
2. She has to travel through a scary forest, fight adversaries, and confront the witch.
3. She'll survive the Games.
4. She may encounter tributes who are stronger than she is, she may encounter a strange environment, she may have different challenges waiting for her.
5. White: purity, cleanliness, youth, innocence
Black: power, death, forcefulness
Blue: royalty, peacefulness
Purple: royalty, power
Green: life, nature
6. Fire: destroying, cleansing, purging; water: life, purifying

Pages 63-65: Chapter 10 Assessment Preparation: Writing with Purpose/ Concise Word Choice
Answers may vary. Sample answers

Purpose:
Inform
Request something and explain a problem
Explain and describe what you've read
Thanking someone for a gift
Inform, possibly explain
Inform, explain, give directions
Inform, share facts

The reader needs to understand the world of Panem and how it works and what the Games are in order to understand the novel.

Part I
1. The words "balance," "crashes," "ugly," "urn," and "fake" are specific words.
I picture Peeta falling violently into a big, ugly pot.
I've seen big pots of fake plants in the lobby of a hotel. We have a big urn on our front porch that is filled with plants in the summer.
2. The word "on" rather than the word "to." We know what it means when someone or something "turns on you."
I picture a dog ready to attack.

I've seen TV shows where a dog attacks someone. This is what I imagined Haymitch would do. He has a short temper and gets angry easily.
3. The phrase "eat that stuff up" which means the people in the Capitol can't get enough of something. They swallow the story whole. The reader pictures a greedy audience gobbling up something as if it were a special treat.
I've seen people eat quickly without really thinking about what they're eating. I've also seen people eat greedily like when people eat birthday cake or popcorn. They don't think about what they're tasting.
4. Each word describes something important that's taking place, and we know what kind of soup it is, so there is a picture for the reader. Them eating soup, but there are two empty chairs at the table. In my mind, the soup is pink because of the roses and the cream.
I've never had cream and rose-petal soup, but I have had creamed soups, so I know what they're like. I've also smelled roses, so if they taste like they smell (and some things do), I have an idea what the soup might taste like.
5. The words "traps," "Gamemakers," "hidden," "liven," and "slower" are words that are specific.
I picture the tributes walking through mine fields. They aren't sure what's going to pop up and surprise them.
I've played games like Hide and Seek where people have jumped out at me. It's scary not knowing what's coming up but knowing that something is going to come up.

Part II
1. The first sentence is specific. The readers know how loud the crowd was. In the second sentence, the reader has to guess at how loud it is.
2. The reader knows what kind of soup it is…and it sounds like an odd soup! The reader also knows that Peeta is missing from the table.

Part III
Answers may vary. Sample answers
Haiku 2
Train ride with rich foods,
Confronting Haymitch for help
Arrive – Capitol.
Haiku 3
Parade – flaming capes
Rooftop secrets of Avox,
Katniss feels such guilt.
Haiku 4
Practicing snares, knots.
Demonstration disaster.
Peeta's confession
Haiku 5
Katniss perceived trick,
But assents to strategy.
Enters arena.
Vocabulary possibilities
Aghast
Reaping the children
Horrified, aghast at Games
Pit child against child.
Assent
They assent to go
Into an arena of
Death. Just one winner.
Breached
Cannot breach the Games
Uncertain about future
Katniss hopes and plans.
Entourages
Cinna and Portia
Entourages for tributes
Make them beautiful.
Perceived
She perceived safety
At the reaping, but Prim's name
Was chosen at first.
Reenactments
After the Games end,
Reenactments draw tourists.
Vacations with death.

Page 67: Chapters 11 – 12 Comprehension Check Questions
Answers may vary. Sample answers
Chapter 11

1. It's a golden horn filled with supplies that will help the participants survive. She sees water, medicine, clothes, and other supplies. Close to the cornucopia, there are lots of supplies, but as you go further away, there are fewer supplies.
2. She wants to run to the Cornucopia to get the bow and arrows, but she also wants to follow Haymitch's advice.
3. Katniss runs for the orange backpack. She and another boy fight for it, but he's stabbed in the back. She turns and runs. A knife is thrown at her, but it lodges in her backpack.
4. At nightfall, the "death recap" is projected onto the sky. Eleven tributes are dead.
5. She hears Peeta talking and realizes he's made an alliance with the Careers.
6. There is a forest, and she knows she can survive in a forest.
Chapter 12
1. She needs to find water.
2. Peeta has teamed up with the Careers. They're hunting as a pack. Katniss thinks Peeta is leading them to her.
3. I don't agree with her because I think Peeta has been honest about his feelings all along. I think he's just trying to survive.
4. I think she is right that she's already very close to water, and he doesn't need to send it to her.
5. A fire is racing toward her.
6. She understands how the Games work. She's trying to play with the audience. She's aware that she's on camera (or potentially on camera) all the time.

Pages 68-69: Chapters 11 – 12 Standards Focus: Point of View – The World According to Katniss
Answers may vary. Sample answers
It lets you know who is telling the story. You can understand the bias of the narrator.
1. First person
2. *Answers may vary. Sample answers:*
"That's how long we're required to stand on our metal circles before the sound of a gong releases us" (148).
"At the edge of the woods I turn for one instant and survey the field" (151).

The world is a hostile place. She doesn't trust anyone except for Gale. She believes she must do everything herself and can't rely on others.	cherished memories include… Time she spent in the woods with her father. Time she spent with Gale. Being with Prim.
the Capitol is… full of silly, selfish, shallow people who have no idea what it's like to be poor or hungry.	feelings are … something she doesn't want to show. She thinks crying makes her look weak.

the Games are... cruel and horrible, but there is nothing she can do about them.	the Gamemakers are... stupid and more interested in what they have to eat and drink than the tributes.
Peeta is... an enemy. He's trying to get the upper hand by making up the love story aspect. He's not to be trusted.	life is ...a constant battle for survival.
District 12 is ... home. A place she loves and wants to return to.	family is ... a responsibility, a job.

1. He doesn't feel loved or cherished.

2. He tells Katniss that his mother thinks Katniss will win because she's a fighter. Katniss remembers that Peeta came to school with a bruise on his face after the bread-burning incident.

3. He hates them as much as Katniss does, but he wants to die with dignity and remain true to himself.

4. He tells Katniss this when they're on the rooftop the night before the Games begin.

5. They joined forces with him because he's good with a knife, and they think he'll be able to lead them to Katniss.

A resident would think that the Games are wonderful. They are entertaining and exciting. The resident might not do anything but watch the Games on TV. It's the highlight of the year.

After the gong went off, I ran to the closest item I could see – a knife. I grabbed it. At the same time, I saw a group of Careers coming toward me. They seemed ready to attack, but I shouted out, "Let's form an alliance."

The leader of the group laughed. "Why should I bother with you, Lover Boy? You're of no use to us."

This guy wasn't too bright. He knew who I was, but he didn't know what I could do to help him. "You want to get Katniss, right? She's going to be a hard one to catch, but I know her. I know how you can find her. Everyone wants to take her down, and I can help you do that."

He thought about it for a second, and then said, "Okay, you can join us. But as soon as you stop being useful, I get to kill you."

Pages 70-72: Chapters 11 – 12: Assessment Preparation: Reflective Writing
Answers may vary. Sample answers

What she thinks about the Cornucopia *She thinks there were good things there that she wishes she had, but she saw the blood bath, so she's glad she got away.*	What she feels about Peeta joining the Careers *She's angry*
What she worries about now *She's got to find water.*	What her plan is *Get out of the tree and find water*
What is she angry about *She can't believe that Peeta has joined the Careers and that he's helping them hunt her.*	What does she feel lucky about *She's lucky she found a good hiding place in the tree.*

A diary would be more personal. It might contain information that you wouldn't want others to know. It contains your feelings where a paper might just contain facts.

Sample student diary: I've survived the first day, but not without a few shocking events along the way. First, I cannot believe Peeta! That rat! He acted completely differently during training, but he was plotting all along to hunt me down. He probably started making alliances with the Careers before we even left the Capitol. I wouldn't put it past him. He's

such a fake! The Cornucopia was worse than I thought it would be. I knew from watching the Games in the past that it was bad, but I didn't want to watch kids get killed. That boy who was fighting me for the backpack...I don't think I can ever forget that. But I'm strong, and I can handle these things. I have to. I promised Prim.

So my focus is to find water. That's the most important thing right now. I just need to find water; then I'll be okay.

Page 73: Chapters 13 – 14 Comprehension Questions

Answers may vary. Sample answers

Chapter 13

1. First the fire and smoke are forcing Katniss to move forward. Then, there are fireballs that are launched at her. She cannot stop to rest. A fireball hits her calf and burns her.
2. Katniss's hands are burned and her calf is badly burned.
3. Cato tries to climb the tree, but he can't. Then Glimmer tries, but she can't climb as high as Katniss can. She's up at the top of the tree. They can't get her, but she can't get away either.
4. She's safe in the tree, but she can't get away. She'll eventually need to get down for water or food. She's trapped. They can just wait until she has to come down to fight them.
5. The audience wants to be entertained, and they think the best entertainment is when someone dies. The Gamemakers want to make sure the Games are entertaining.
6. Rue must like Katniss or at least she feels bad that Katniss is in this predicament. Perhaps she wants to form an alliance with Katniss.

Chapter 14

1. They hunt after anyone who disturbs their nest, and their venom can be deadly; a few stings can kill a person. Their venom can cause people to hallucinate.
2. She keeps going in spite of being burned. She doesn't give up. She crawls up the tree to cut down the tracker jacker nest, she returns to the tree to retrieve the bow and arrows even after she's been stung.

3. He was really pretending to be in alliance with the Careers. He really does care about Katniss. He doesn't want to kill anyone.
4. Katniss has already been through so much, the fire, the search for water, discovering Peeta has betrayed her, but she kept on going. The fact that she climbed the tree and taunted the Careers and then clearly had a plan to attack them with the tracker jackers probably showed the sponsors she was not giving up. That's why they decided to help her.
5. She would probably like a beekeepers mask or a better saw to get through the branch. She would certainly appreciate a bow and arrows.
6. She will probably hallucinate, but she is also vulnerable. There is a chance that Peeta might be able to help her and protect her.
7. She had to do something to get rid of the Careers otherwise they would have figured out a way to kill her. It probably was the best idea at the time, but it was dangerous.

Pages 74-76 : Chapters 13 – 14 Standards Focus: Conflict in the Arena

Answers may vary. Sample answers

She battled with another tribute for a backpack, she lost a loaf of bread, she had a knife thrown at her, she couldn't find water, she learned that Peeta had betrayed her, she was awakened in the night to a wall of fire, she choked on the smoke, her leg was burned by a fireball, she was chased up a tree by the Careers, she was stung by tracker jackers, she experienced hallucinations from the tracker jacker stings.

Character vs. character	Character vs. nature	Character vs. society	Character vs. self
Katniss vs the boy. She fights with him over the backpack. Katniss vs. the Careers. As she is in the tree, Katniss must figure out how to survive.	Katniss vs the arena. Katniss struggles to survive when she's looking for water. Katniss vs the woods. In District 12 Katniss has to search the woods for food in order to keep her family alive. Katniss vs the fire. Katniss has to run and get away from the fire. Katniss vs the tracker jackers. Katniss has to	Katniss vs the Capitol. This isn't a very clear conflict, but Katniss obviously doesn't want to participate in the Games, but she must. Katniss vs society/the Games. When Katniss thinks she can manipulate the audience, she plays up to the camera. She's always aware that she's on camera.	Katniss vs. Katniss. She has a short temper and acts without thinking. She feels guilty and indebted to Peeta for his kindness. Katniss vs Katniss. She has to force herself to go back to Glimmer's body to get the bow and arrows. She has to force herself to keep running away from the fire and from the Careers even though she's in pain.

	try to survive their stings; she has to be brave enough to cut down the nest.		

Answers may vary. Sample student answers: Character name: Haymitch, Peeta, Gale

Character vs. character	Character vs. nature	Character vs. society	Character vs. self
Haymitch vs. Katniss. They are in a battle of wills.		Gale vs. the Capitol. Gale is angry about the Games and rants about his feelings when they're in the forest.	Peeta vs. self. Peeta wants to stay true to himself and not let the Games change him.

Slogan: Katniss: The Girl on Fire—Still Smoldering
Statements: She can't be smothered. She's overcome thirst, fire, and tracker jacker stings. She keeps thinking, planning, and surviving. Support a tribute who is burning brightly.
Image: a flame and a picture of Katniss.

Page 77-78: Chapters 13 – 14 Assessment Preparation: Using Vocabulary Words
Answers may vary. Sample answers
Greasy Sae
Stanza 1
I am crafty and old.
I consider the incompetent customers who believe what's in my soup.
I persevere by surviving the only way I know how.
I precariously sell my soup in the Hob.
I will be sated when I have enough food to eat every day.
I am crafty and old.
Stanza 2
A balm will be something I could barter with.
I quell people's fear about what they eat. I tell them it's beef.
I worry I will be in a stupor when I run out of food and cannot survive.
I conspiratorially plan to purchase the animals that Katniss and Gale poach from the woods.
As I watch the mayhem, I think about all I've experienced in my life.
I am crafty and old.
Stanza 3
I am honing my knife so I can cut up the game for my soup.
I struggle to survive the difficult life of District 12. My bravado keeps me going.
I plot to keep making soup.
I wait for the Games to abate as I wait in the Hob.
I am crafty and old.

Page 80: Chapters 15 – 16 Comprehension Check
Answers may vary. Sample answers
Chapter 15
1. Rue found Katniss in the forest. She was hungry and Katniss had food. Rue had leaves that helped soothe the tracker jacker stings.
2. She was able to tell Katniss who was still alive, where the Career camp was and what it was like. She also told Katniss about the leaves that would help the tracker jacker stings. She also told Katniss about the berries that are safe to eat.
3. She brings food that she's collected; she brings knowledge about the leaves that help the stings. She also explains the night vision glasses to Katniss and shares information about how long Katniss was unconscious and who died. Rue also shares information about her district, which gives Katniss perspective on her own life.
4. He's no longer with the Careers.
5. Rue doesn't have many skills. She is small and weak. She won't be able to fight very well. Haymitch might think Rue would slow Katniss down.
6. The glasses give them an advantage to see at night. Even though some of the Careers have glasses as well, it will be an advantage to have them at night.
7. She wants them to be on equal footing. Katniss can survive on her own, but the Careers would have trouble doing that. She also wants to be on the offensive instead of just running away and hiding.
Chapter 16
1. She tore a hole in a bag of apples that was suspended over the pile. They'll fall down at slightly different times and start the series of explosions.
2. Katniss will use the mockingjay song to signal that she's okay.

3. He was able to booby-trap the supplies. He knew how to work with explosives.
4. Cato. He obviously wants revenge and is determined to get it.
5. She learns that Cato cut Peeta. His injury is severe enough to kill him.
6. She is the tribute Katniss and Rue couldn't remember. She is able to climb up to the supplies, steal a few items, and then sneak away.
7. I agree that it's a good idea to attack. Katniss is good at hunting, so her strategies and instincts are probably correct. Plus, she's not running away.

Pages 81-83: Chapters 15 – 16 Standards Focus: Character Map

Tributes	District	Descriptions and your thoughts on the character
Boy	District 1	
Cato	District 2	He seems to be the leader of the Careers. He wants to kill Katniss
Girl	District 2	
Boy	District 3	good with explosives
Foxface girl	District 5	Sneaky, good at hiding
Boy	District 10	
Rue	District 11	Small and can jump from tree to tree
Tresh	District 11	
Katniss	District 12	Clever and has a plan.
Peeta	District 12	Wounded but still alive.

1. Katniss
2. Rue

1. Cato
2. Boy from District 1
3. Girl from District 2
4. Boy from District 3

What advantages and disadvantages to the teams have? Use the chart below to analyze them.
Answers may vary. Sample student answers are given.

Tribute (s)	Advantages	Disadvantages
Careers	They have access to water and supplies (until they get blown up). They have each other, so they can protect one another. There are more of them, so each person probably gets more rest since someone can act as a guard.	Once they lose all their supplies, they're going to get hungry. They could get weak from hunger and not be such threatening opponents. They cannot really trust each other since they all know they'll have to kill each other in the end.
Katniss and Rue	They both know how to survive on just a little food. Even Rue knows how to gather food supplies. They are both good tree climbers. They both seem to really care about each other.	They are outnumbered by the Careers. Their supplies and weapons aren't as plentiful. They don't have easy access to water.
Foxface	She is sneaky, so the Careers probably don't even know that she's been stealing from them. She has figured out a way to survive.	She is alone, so she has to rely on herself for survival. Without a partner, she's probably more vulnerable.

1. The boy from District 10, Peeta, and Tresh are unaccounted for.

2. One of them was killed (the cannon went off). They may be in the forest or in the area behind the Cornucopia.

3. I think it'd be better to be on your own. I wouldn't want to form an alliance and then end up killing the others in my group or worse yet, having to watch my back every minute.

Pages 84-85: Chapters 15 – 16 Assessment Preparation: Who Is the Audience?

Answers may vary. Sample answers
Television, high-speed trains, lavish food, strange hair color, tattoos.
Personal computers, cell phones, video games.

Katniss to Prim after she awakens from the tracker jacker stings.	Hi, feeling better! Don't worry about me. Those stingers looked worse than they felt.
Katniss to Gale after Katniss realizes Peeta saved her life	When will I stop owing him? Why did he do that?
Katniss to Haymitch when she's searching for water	Can't you see that I'm dying of thirst! Are you drunk? Help me! I thought that was your job!
Katniss to her mother after she's burned in the fire	I know there are plants around that could help me, but I don't know what they look like. Can you send me a picture?

1. The messages were more forceful to Haymitch because Katniss and Haymitch have a rocky relationship already. The message to Prim was upbeat and hopeful, so she won't worry.

123 Rich House
Capitol, Panem

Jan. 1, 2210

Dear President Snow,

    As you know, my daughter Katniss is in the arena. She has endured the onslaught of the Career tributes once. She outsmarted them with the tracker jacker nest, but it was a horrible ordeal for her. I cannot believe you can allow these Games to continue. The noxious fire was appalling; what is going to happen next?

    I beg you, as a prominent man, please end these Games.

    Sincerely,
    Mrs. Everdeen

Pine tree
Arena

Jan. 2, 2210

Sweetheart,

    I see that things are going well for you. Good job with the tracker jacker nest. I was so impressed I had an extra ration of grain sent to your family.

    You will find that the sponsors will be obliging only if you continue your impressive actions. Just remember not to rendezvous with Cato. He is someone you do not want to make an alliance with.

    Stay alive,
    Haymitch

Pine tree
Arena

Jan. 2, 2210

Dear Katniss,

I'm glad we're allies now. Every night, the cold has wracked my body – even though I have socks for my hands. I was warm for the first time last night. Please be careful when you hide in the copse near the lake. Cato is looking for you. He never acts tentatively.

Your friend,
Rue

Page 87: Chapters 17 – 18 Comprehension Check

Answers may vary. Sample answers

Chapter 17

1. It is completely destroyed by a series of explosions.
2. She temporarily loses hearing, but the hearing in her left ear appears to be permanently damaged.
3. She is trapped in a net.
4. He obviously has a short temper. When he's angry, he doesn't think; he just acts.
5. Katniss is really ready to fight. She's been through enough, she knows who her competition is, and she's ready to meet him. She is feeling strong.

Chapter 18

1. She covers Rues body with wildflowers. She also sings to her while she's dying. She gives Rue the three-fingers to the lips goodbye.
2. There can now be two winners from each district.
3. She builds a fire and hopes the Careers come; she doesn't want to get out of the tree; she feels lethargic.
4. Perhaps there is pressure from the people of the Capitol to allow for two winners. Maybe they are playing up the romance.
5. They must have held Rue in high esteem because it is an expensive gift. They

appreciated Katniss's kindness to her at her death.
6. She has a motive to find him and save him. Prior to that, they were still enemies who would have to fight to the death. If she can find Peeta, they can work as a team.

Pages 88-89: Chapters 17 – 18 Standards Focus: Map of the Setting/ Visualization

Answers may vary. Setting descriptions will vary. Sample answers are given.

Katniss finds water and the wall of fire chases her; then Katniss climbs the tree with the tracker jacker nest.

1. The tributes don't know what the arena will be like. The setting itself could be the cause of a tribute's death.
2. The setting must keep the tributes together and prevent them from running away from the arena where they will not be visible on camera. The setting needs to provide enough surprises to keep the audience entertained.
3. They control the weather, the length of the day and night, the temperature. They control everything. They are like God.
4. The tributes can't change the setting, but they can make it work to their advantage. They have the night-vision glasses, and Katniss has been able to survive in the forest on the food she's scavenged there. Katniss is able to use her knowledge of the tracker jackers to fashion a weapon.

Pages 90-92: Chapters 17 – 18 Assessment Preparation: Writing Powerful Sentences

Answers may vary. Sample student answers are given.

Sentence	Number of words	Purpose of the sentence
"For the most part, the only communication the tributes get from outside the arena is the nightly death toll" (244).	19	Explains the reason Katniss sits up to listen after the trumpets blare.
"But occasionally, there will be trumpets followed by an announcement" (244).	10	Explains what happens after the trumpets.
"Usually, this will be a call to a feast" (244).	9	Explains the usual meaning of the trumpets.
"When food is scarce, the Gamemakers will invite the players to a banquet, somewhere known to all like the Cornucopia, as an inducement to gather and fight" (244).	27	Explains what it means when they call the tributes to a feast.

Sentence	Number of words	Purpose of the sentence	Reason for the sentence length
"Claudius Templesmith's voice booms down from overhead, congratulating the six of us who remain" (244).	19	Gives information – not just congratulating the six tributes, but reminding the reader how many are left.	It's longer because it has more explanation and description.
"But he is not inviting us to a feast" (244).	9	This information contradicts what Katniss expects.	It's shorter because it's contains surprising information.
"He's saying something very confusing" (244).	5	The sentence encourages both Katniss and the reader to pay attention. Why is it confusing?	Katniss is confused, so she's taking in just a bit of information at a time.
"There's been a rule change in the Games" (244).	8	This is new information.	It's startling and surprising.
"A rule change!" (244)	3	Repeating information because she's surprised.	She's surprised, so she repeats the information.
"That in itself is mind bending since we don't really have any rules to speak of except don't step off your circle for sixty seconds and the unspoken rule about not eating one another" (244).	34	This sentence explains to the reader that there really aren't any rules, so it's surprising that they'd announce a rule change.	The long sentence explains why the announcement is so surprising to Katniss.

Sentence	Number of words	Why are these sentences so short?
"The news sinks in" (244).	4	Finally, Katniss is beginning to understand that she is not imagining that the rule has changed.
"Two tributes can win this year" (244).	7	She's breaking down the information bit by bit. Here is the first part of the information.
"If they're from the same district" (244)	6	Here is the second piece of information she needs to understand.
"Both can live" (244).	3	She understands the rule.
"Both of us can live" (244).	5	She repeats it because she finally realizes both she and Peeta could go home.

Answers may vary. Sample student answers are given.

1. Why hasn't she searched for Peeta up until now? Doesn't she love him?
I can't see what's going through her mind, but I know she didn't want to be in a situation where she'd have to kill him. She probably stayed away from him because she didn't want to see him suffer from his wounds, and she didn't want to kill him.

2. How are you going to decide what to send her as gifts from the sponsors?
It depends on what she needs. Of course, she's got to earn the silver parachute. It's up to the sponsors as well. They can suggest what they want her to receive.

3. Why should sponsors back Katniss? She doesn't even know where Peeta is.
Katniss has shown she's a fighter. Who else had the guts to confront the Careers by blowing up their supplies? She's gone on the defensive. She's not going to quit. In spite of burns, stings, lack of food and water, Katniss has kept on going. She's not going to stop now.

4. Who is already sponsoring Katniss and Peeta?
I can't name names, but there are some big players behind them. Of course, sponsors want to back a winning team, and Katniss and Peeta are going to be a winning team.

5. What kind of advice would you give them now if you could?

I'd stick to the first piece of advice I ever gave them. They need to stay alive. However they can. Katniss is innovative and will see opportunities to win.

6. Where do you expect the final action of the Games to take place?

I hope it happens in the forest. That's where Katniss is most comfortable, and I don't know how badly Peeta is injured. He may not be much help to her in the final battle.

Page 108: Chapters 19 – 20
Comprehension Check
Answers may vary. Sample student answers are given.
Chapter 19
1. Katniss tracks him up the stream and notices blood on a rock. Peeta camouflaged himself in the bank of a river.
2. He's badly injured. His leg is deeply cut and infected.
3. She's used to killing animals and dressing them, but she can't stand seeing wounded people. You would think there's little difference between the two. Plus, her mother

has been treating sick and injured people all Katniss's life, so she should be used to it.
4. She goes looking for him and she knows he's alive. She doesn't want to return to District 12 without him because she knows the people of District 12 wouldn't forgive her. She knows she has to make an effort to find him and save him, so they both can win.
5. The sponsors want romance. They are being rewarded with the broth by kissing.

Chapter 20
1. Medicine for Peeta's leg.
2. She uses the syrup sent by silver parachute to knock him out. He won't be able to follow her.
3. He'll die. He has blood poisoning.
4. She got her sister something she loved. Katniss knew how happy it made Prim. It was the result of a good day of hunting.
5. Perhaps there would be no fun in that. They would be giving him too much help, and they wouldn't get to see Katniss fight. The medicine might have been too expensive.
6. I agree that she had to go to see what was in the backpack. If she didn't knock him out, she couldn't go, and Peeta would die.

Pages 109-111: Chapters 19 – 20 Standards Focus: Inner Thoughts
Answers may vary. Sample student answers are given.

Katniss's thoughts	Proof that they are thoughts
"Whatever doubts I've had about him dissipate because if either of us took the other's life now we'd be pariahs when we returned to District 12."	Katniss uses the first person pronoun "I." She is also imagining what life would be like back in District 12.
Peeta has been playing the star-crossed lover role all along.	Katniss doesn't say this out loud, but the reader doesn't know where Peeta has been all this time and what he's been saying and doing.
"For two tributes to have a shot at winning, our 'romance' must be so popular with the audience that condemning it would jeopardize the success of the Games."	She's analyzing the Gamemakers and how the audience is viewing the Games. She's guessing based on past experiences with the Games.
"All I've done is manage not to kill Peeta."	She uses the "I" pronoun and reflects on what she hasn't done.

1. She doesn't know where to put Peeta so he'll be safe. She doesn't know how to treat his wound. She is worried about her own safety. She is afraid to leave him. She wants to go to the feast, but is worried about Peeta following her. She's worried Peeta is going to die.
2. She doesn't want him to know how bad his wounds are, that she is grossed-out by his wounds and worried about him having to take off his clothes, that she is worried about being found, that a kiss equals a gift from the sponsors.

3. The true story of Prim and the goat, how the trading works in the Hob and her past experiences of trying to sell a deer, and that she is kissing Peeta in order to get something from her sponsors.
4. I feel sorry for her because I know what she's thinking. I understand her more because I can see that she's struggling with what she should do. I feel more sympathy for her belief that she had to betray Peeta by drugging him.
5. She's worried about Peeta dying. She has a softer side that shows when she talks about

Prim and her goat. She has a sense of humor – Peeta can make her laugh.

6. She still thinks that Peeta is acting, but I think that he really loves her.

7. He probably doesn't want Katniss to know how much pain he is in because he doesn't want her to worry. He probably also doesn't want her to know that he knows he has a good chance of dying from his wounds.

Answers may vary for the Thought Bubbles activity.

Answers may vary. Sample student answer:
Dear Diary,

At least now Katniss has found Peeta. There's a slim chance that he won't die before the Games are over, but I'm not sure I'd bet on that. Based on how his leg looks, he's not going to make it unless Katniss goes to the feast.

Sure, I wanted the sponsors to just send them the medicine, but where is the entertainment factor in that. These sponsors are so righteous with their money and gifts, yet they wouldn't last two minutes in the arena. They want to be entertained by the suffering of the tributes. They make me sick! I still have to smile and be polite to them because, otherwise, there'll be no medicine for Peeta. I know I've got to keep the sponsors happy and the gifts coming. That's what's going to save those two.

Is it any wonder I drink? The stress of this job is getting to me. But as long as we can keep sponsors happy and Peeta alive, they have a chance.

Pages 112-114: Chapters 19 – 20: Assessment Preparation: "Showing Not Telling"
Answers may vary. Sample student answer:

Words that describe or explain:	The narrowed topic is:	Vivid details include:	Sensory language includes:	Figures of speech:
Scowl, dry lips, test his cheek, I give him more fever pills, he drinks one and then a second quart, I tend to his minor wounds, I steel myself and unwrap…	Katniss is checking on Peeta after she's been asleep.	Scowl, dry lips, hot as a coal stove, burns, stings,	Dry, hot, feel, drinks, burns, stings	Yes. Simile – "Hot as a coal stove."
Why is this passage a good example of "showing" writing? Answers may vary. Sample student answer: I can easily imagine the scene. Katniss staring at Peeta until he finishes the water. I can also imagine how high his fever is getting.				

Words that describe or explain:	The narrowed topic is:	Vivid details include:	Sensory language includes:	Figures of speech:
I can tell the day will be hotter, the water is cool, I'm tempted to call out, I will have to find him with my eyes and one good ear	Katniss is walking upstream trying to find Peeta.	Sun burns off the morning haze, water is cool and pleasant, bare feet	Burns, hotter, cool, bare, call, eyes, ear	no
Why is this passage a good example of "showing" writing? Answers may vary. Sample student answer: I can imagine Katniss walking up the stream and the contrast between the heat of the sun and the coolness of the stream.				

Part II: Identify "Showing" Writing sample answer: "His undershirt is so plastered into his wounds I have to cut it away with my knife and drench him again to work it loose. He's badly bruised with a long burn across his chest and four tracker jacker stings, if you count the one under his ear" (254).

Words that describe or explain:	The narrowed topic is:	Vivid details include:	Sensory language includes:	Figures of speech:
His undershirt is so plastered into his wounds, he's badly bruised, four tracker jacker stings	Description of Peeta's wounds	Plastered, cut it away, drench him, work it loose, bruised, long burn across check, four tracker jacker stings	Plastered, cut, drench, bruised, burn, stings	no
Why is this passage a good example of "showing" writing? I can imagine Peeta's condition and what Katniss has to do to treat his wounds. I can see Katniss cutting away the undershirt.				

Page 116: Chapters 21 – 22:
Comprehension Check Questions
Answers may vary. Sample answers
Chapter 21
1. Foxface is the first to dash out and grab her backpack. Katniss goes next. Clove ends up tackling Katniss and pins her to the ground. Clove is going to kill Katniss slowly, but Thresh grabs Clove and kills her. He then lets Katniss go.
2. The backpacks contain something vital. If a tribute takes another backpack, he or she has put someone at a disadvantage.
3. Katniss tells him she and Rue were allies, and she was with her when she died. Thresh doesn't kill her because they're even. He returned the favor for Katniss.
4. Thresh took both backpacks, and Cato will want his backpack before going after Katniss.
5. It's a syringe filled with medication. Katniss gives Peeta the shot, and he's feeling much better.
6. She was able to get the backpack, her wounds are superficial, she wasn't killed, Peeta is much improved.
Chapter 22
1. They kiss.
2. He is similar to Katniss in that he believes that a favor should be returned. He obviously

thought Rue was special or maybe he felt some loyalty toward her because she was from his district. He isn't a heartless killer like the Careers. He does have some compassion.
3. It's pouring rain, so they're stuck in the cave. They don't have anything to do; they can't hunt or go out. They have to sit and talk to each other.
4. Katniss wants to keep her feelings private. She realizes that everyone is watching her, and her feelings are exposed. Even though she knows that in order to get food from her sponsors she has to show her feelings, she wants them to stay private.
5. I agree that our feelings should be private. It's nobody's business what we're thinking. We shouldn't be judged or given gifts because we share private feelings. That cheapens those feelings and makes them some kind of entertainment.
6. They need to find better shelter because the cave leaks, they have to find food because they're going to run out. They need to figure out where the other tributes are. Katniss needs to take care of her forehead, and Peeta needs to continue to get better. They have to be alert to what is going on and their surroundings.

Pages 117-120: Chapters 21 – 22: Standards Focus – Dialogue
Answers may vary. Sample student answers are given.

	Yes	No	My reason for believing this is…
It advances the plot.	X		It tells us that Thresh is giving Katniss a chance. He's letting her get away because of what she did for Rue.
It sounds like the speaker.	X		It certainly sounds like Katniss.

It sounds natural.	X		It sounds like something someone would really say. Thresh sounds like he might not be educated.
It has give and take.	X		Thresh is asking questions and Katniss is answering them.
It varies in sentence length.	X		There are short and long sentences.
It breaks up the exposition.	X		Yes. After the passage, Katniss is back in the woods running away. She doesn't have anyone to talk to.

Anything else you notice about the dialogue? Thresh sounds like he might not be well educated. He doesn't talk a lot. He uses short, choppy sentences.

Answers may vary. Sample student answer:

	Yes	No	My reason for believing this is…
It advances the plot.	X		It tells us that Peeta has a sharp memory about when he first saw Katniss.
It sounds like the speaker.	X		It sounds like Peeta.
It sounds natural.	X		It sounds like something someone would really say.
It has give and take.	X		Katniss interrupts the conversation at the appropriate time.
It varies in sentence length.	X		There are short and long sentences.
It breaks up the exposition.		X	This is part of an ongoing conversation they're having.

Anything else you notice about the dialogue? This sounds like a very natural conversation because Katniss keeps interrupting Peeta with questions.

Answers may vary. Sample student answer:

"Where's your boyfriend, District Twelve? Still hanging on?" she asks.

Well, as long as we're talking I'm alive. "He's out there now. Hunting Cato," I snarl at her. I scream at the top of my lungs, "Peeta!" ….

"Liar," she says with a grin. "He's nearly dead. Cato knows where he cut him. You've probably got him strapped up in some tree while you try to keep his heart going. What's in that pretty little backpack? That medicine for Lover Boy? Too bad he'll never get it" (284 – 285).

	Yes	No	My reason for believing this is…
It advances the plot.		X	It really doesn't give any new information. Nothing new is revealed.
It sounds like the speaker.	X		It certainly sounds like Katniss – bluffing. It sounds like I imagine Clove would talk.
It sounds natural.	X		It sounds like something someone would really say.
It has give and take.	X		At the beginning of the passage, Katniss is responding to Clove. She gets her talking.
It varies in sentence length.	X		There are short and long sentences.
It breaks up the exposition.	X		The omitted paragraph is exposition telling what Clove is doing.

Anything else you notice about the dialogue? Clove sounds cruel.

Use quotation marks at the beginning and the end of the spoken words; a new paragraph starts when the speaker changes; when Peeta is quoting his father, he uses single quotation marks.

"Are you going to eat that last donut?" Hugh asked.

"I was thinking about it," said Ralphie as he rubbed his stomach. "Powdered sugar donuts are my favorite."

"Well, I only had one donut today," Hugh said. "And yesterday I heard your mom say, 'Hugh, you eat too many donuts.' So I think it's only fair that you should let me have that last one."

"Okay," Ralphie said, "you're right. I need to cut down. Go ahead and help yourself. After all, I did eat the other eleven."

Pages 121-122: Chapters 21 – 22: Assessment Preparation: The Silver Parachute – Using Well-Chosen Details
Answers may vary. Sample answers
Writing should include vivid details, sensory language, description/explanation, figures of speech, and a narrowed topic.

Finally, it was my turn to share my "show and tell" item. Even though I had to sit "criss cross applesauce, hands in your lap" while I watched the other kids, I squirmed with excitement. I bounced up to the front of the room. I twirled around in a circle as my dress swooshed out around me like the parachutes we played with in gym class. Then, after a dramatic pause, I faced the class and stood on my tiptoes to show off my new, pink ballet slippers.

1. "Sitting on my sleeping bag is a small plastic pot attached to a silver parachute….The pot easily fits in the palm of my hand. What can it be? Not food surely. I unscrew the lid and I know by the scent that it's medicine. Cautiously, I probe the surface of the ointment" (188).
2. page 276. Katniss receives the sleeping syrup for Peeta. It "floats" by her, she tears off the "silver fabric." It's a tiny vial. Katniss takes "a deep sniff."

The silver parachute fluttered down and landed with a loud thump. It was attached to a rectangular block wrapped in gold foil. At first, I thought it might be a brick, but it was too fat to be a brick. The block was about the same size as *The Hunger Games* novel on my desk, but it had a particularly inviting aroma. It smelled like creamy chocolate. I unwrapped the gold foil and confirmed my suspicion: chocolate!
Answers may vary. Sample student answer:

"Hey, look at what just landed on Mary's desk!" shouted Billy.

"Oh who cares? It's just a gold brick," said Carlos yawning.

"Not more silver parachutes!" sighed Mrs. O'Donnell plaintively. "This is the third silver parachute that's been delivered this week in my English class. Really, is class that boring?"

"Actually, Mrs. O," Ben said with an exasperated look, "you don't want us to answer that question, do you?"

"Hey! Look what's in the gold brick," shouted Mija.

"I thought I smelled chocolate," said Matthew. "I'm famished."

"Yes," said Manuel, "I'd love a big bite of chocolate right now. I've always considered chocolate to be an asset in English class."

"Pass some to me!" shouted Sarah. "Don't make me throw a tantrum! I want chocolate. Now!"

"Thank you," said all the students together. "We love silver parachutes!"

2. Asset: Susie's terrific spelling skills were an asset in helping her win the spelling bee.
3. Infusion: The scented candle infused the room; the wonderful smell of apple pie filled the air.
4. Emanating: The fire warmed everyone crowded around the campfire as heat emanated from the crackling flames.
5. Irreparable: Jimmy's smashed bike couldn't be fixed since the irreparable damage was caused by the steamroller.
6. Ominous: The ominous dark clouds were threatening to ruin the party with a torrential downpour.
7. Staunch: Casey couldn't staunch the flow of water from the dam even though he tried to stop it with sandbags.
8. Vaguely: We answered Cynthia's questions about the party vaguely since we didn't want to give away the details of the surprise.
9. Plaintively: The child cried plaintively when her dad refused to give her an ice cream cone.
10. Famished: The famished students would have eaten everything in the kitchen.
11. Irreverent: Henry's irreverent behavior toward his teacher resulted in a weekend class in manners.
12. Tirades: His tirades over breakfast cereal must stop; a tantrum is a horrid way to start the day!

13. Exorbitant: Due to the shortage of chocolate, the exorbitant price of my favorite candy means <u>it costs too much</u> for me to enjoy it.

14. Exasperated: Because they were <u>frustrated</u> by constantly reminding everyone who they were, the twins were exasperated that no one could tell them apart.

Page 124: Chapters 23 – 24
Comprehension Check Questions
Answers may vary. Sample answers
Chapter 23
1. He's noisy and scares away the game.
2. She eats the poisonous berries that Peeta picked.
3. He could have set snares, he could have served as a lookout, and he could have tried to go fishing.
4. She was right to be angry because that is what they'd agreed on. There is so much as stake that it's important for them to know where the other is and that he or she is safe.
5. Foxface didn't know much about surviving on her own in the wild. She basically stole food from others. She assumed that the berries were safe because Peeta had collected them.
6. Katniss realizes that Foxface not only stole some of the cheese, but she also stole some of the berries. Peeta had unknowingly collected the berries and Foxface ate them, so it is because of Peeta's actions that Foxface died.

7. Now their only opponent is Cato. They will have to face off against Cato, and he is a strong, and probably well-supplied, enemy.
Chapter 24
1. Perhaps they can drop them and Cato will eat them.
2. The Gamemakers want Katniss and Peeta to go to the lake to have the final battle with Cato.
3. She thinks they should be well fed since they're going to face Cato. She also says that this will be their last meal until they return to the Capitol.
4. She realizes that, like herself, he can lose his temper when he's angry. Katniss has shown this same quality when she's been angry; however, Katniss doesn't come completely unglued, so they're not alike, but they both have trouble controlling their anger.
5. He could pop out of the forest at any time. Katniss and Peeta assume that he is injured from his battle with Thresh, but don't know for sure. They can't let their guard down or relax because he could appear at any minute.
6. Instead of running toward Katniss and Peeta to fight them, he is running away from something. His behavior is opposite of what they expect. He's on the retreat instead of the attack.

Page 125: Chapters 23 – 24 Standards Focus: Foreshadowing
It adds to the enjoyment of the story, it makes the story more believable, it makes the story more engaging, it helps the reader develop a better picture of the characters

Sample student answers:

Foreshadowing	What does this foreshadow?	Why is it important later in the novel?
"You can lift hundred-pound bags of flour" (90).	That Peeta is strong enough to endure a deadly wound. He's physically strong enough to fight the Careers.	He has to fight Cato. He also has to hide himself after he's wounded.
"He can wrestle," I tell Haymitch. "He came in second in our school competition last year, only after his brother" (90).	Peeta will be fighting other tributes.	He fights Cato in order to keep him from catching Katniss.
"Peeta, she's right, never underestimate strength in the arena. Very often, physical power tilts the advantage to a player" (91- 92).	Peeta's physical strength allows him to survive his injuries. In spite of being stung, he goes back to the tree to check on Katniss and protect her from Cato.	Peeta's strength keeps him alive.
I hear Peeta's voice in my head. *She has no idea. The effect she can have.* Obviously meant	This foreshadows Peeta's feelings about Katniss.	Katniss is constantly trying to figure out what Peeta means. She distrusts that he might like her.

to demean me. Right? But a tiny part of me wonders if this was a compliment. That he meant I was appealing in some way. It's weird, how much he's noticed me. Like the attention he's paid to my hunting" (93).		She's convinced that he is trying to manipulate her.
"Then we move on to camouflage. Peeta genuinely seems to enjoy this station, swirling a combination of mud and clay and berry juices around on his pale skin, weaving disguises from vines and leaves" (95).	This foreshadows Peeta's ability to hide himself in the mud.	This is important because being able to camouflage himself saves him.
"We do pick up some valuable skills, from starting fires, to knife throwing, to making shelter" (96).	This foreshadows the survival skills they'll need in the arena.	This is important because they need to start a fire and make shelter.
"Despite Hamitch's order to appear mediocre, Peeta excels in hand-to-hand combat" (96).	Again, this foreshadows his fight with Cato.	It's important because the reader has to believe Peeta can take care of himself against the Careers.
"One day, Peeta empties our breadbasket and points out how they have been careful to include types from the districts along with the refined bread of the Capitol" (97).	This foreshadows the gift of bread that Katniss receives from District 11.	It is important because later in the book Katniss receives a gift of bread from District 11. She realizes that it is based on Peeta's lesson this day.

Sample student answers:

"Rue is a small yellow flower that grows in the Meadow. Rue. Primrose. Neither of them could tip the scale at seventy pounds soaking wet" (99).	This foreshadows the relationship between Rue and Katniss.	This is important because it shows how Rue and Prim are alike. The reader can understand how Katniss feels about Rue and why she feels that way.
"Like me, she's clever with plants, climbs swiftly, and has good aim. She can hit the target every time with a slingshot. But what is a slingshot against a 220-pound male with a sword?" (99)	This foreshadows how she will be killed.	This is important because it shows that Rue is skilled, but still no match for the other tributes.
"At Rue's suggestion, we lay out all our food to plan ahead....I roll an unfamiliar berry in my fingers. 'You sure this is safe?'" (203)	This foreshadows how Katniss is suspicious about foods in the forest. It also foreshadows the importance of the berries.	This is important because Foxface dies because she doesn't know how to be suspicious of the berries.

Sample student answers:

"At first one, then another, then almost every member of the crowd touches the three middle fingers of their left hand to their lips and hold it out to me. It is an old and rarely used gesture of our district, occasionally seen	This is foreshadowing as to how Katniss says good-bye to Rue.	It is important because it explains the meaning of the symbol and why it is so powerful to the people of District 12.

at funerals. It means thanks, it means admiration, it means good-bye to someone you love" (24).		
"To this day, I can never shake the connection between this boy, Peeta Mellark, and the bread that gave me hope....I feel like I owe him something, and I hate owing people" (32).	This foreshadowing Katniss's mixed feelings about Peeta and her understanding of Thresh.	It's important because Katniss knows how Thresh feels about letting her go. It's also important because Katniss can never stop feeling a connection to Peeta.
"The woods became our savior...Plants are tricky. Many are edible, but one false mouthful and you're dead. I checked and double-checked he plants I harvested with my father's pictures. I kept us alive" (51).	This foreshadows the berries and the importance of knowing whether the food is safe or not.	It is important because that is how Katniss keeps Peeta from eating something poisonous. She protects them both from death by eating something that looks safe but isn't.
"My father buys her squirrels. He always comments on how the arrows never pierce the body. She hits every one in the eye. It's the same with the rabbits she sells the butcher. She can even bring down a deer" (89).	This foreshadows how good an aim Katniss has.	It's important because when Katniss blows up the Careers food, she has to get the shot exactly right.
"She said, 'She's a survivor, that one.' She is," says Peeta (90).	This foreshadows the determination and skill Katniss shows in the arena.	It's important because she's not only able to keep herself alive, she can also keep Peeta alive.
"She has no idea. The effect she can have" (91).	This foreshadows Peeta's feelings about Katniss and how oblivious she is to them.	It is important because she doesn't realize how Peeta feels about her. She thinks it's all an act.
"I sweep the edible plants test without blinking an eye" (96)	This foreshadows the berries that Katniss recognizes.	It's important because they could easily mistake the berries for edible ones.
"I take my initial position and skewer the dummy right through the heart. Then I sever the rope that holds the sandbag for boxing, and the bag splits open as it slams to the ground." (101)	This foreshadows Katniss as she blows up the Career's supplies.	It is important because she knows she can do it and it gives her an idea.

1. It lays the groundwork for the characters' behavior. I can believe that Peeta can fight Cato when I know Peeta is a good wrestler and is strong.
2. I thought the poisonous berries were the most important. I also thought knowing that Peeta was good with decorating cakes was helpful in understanding how he could hide in the mud and not be seen.
3. She wanted to make sure the reader knew Katniss would be able to survive. That she had a lot of experience surviving.
4. She wanted the reader to know Peeta was strong and did have some skills. He wasn't going to be helpless in the arena.

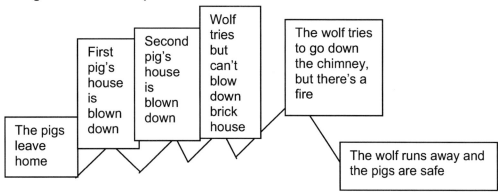

Climax: It will be when Katniss and Peeta have the battle with Cato.
1. These were the events of the novel that I thought were the most exciting. I could picture them the best as I was reading. I couldn't stop reading at these points in the novel.
2. The characters (and reader) know that eventually there will be a final battle to the death. There can only be one winner (and later in the story, two).

3. They're responsible for making sure the Games are entertaining. They create problems like the fire or the temperatures or the rain. They also have created something that will provide a frightening conclusion to the novel – whatever is chasing Cato.
4. The story is exciting and it makes me want to keep reading. The novel becomes a "page turner" and I can't stop reading. I want to keep reading to find out how the story is going to end.

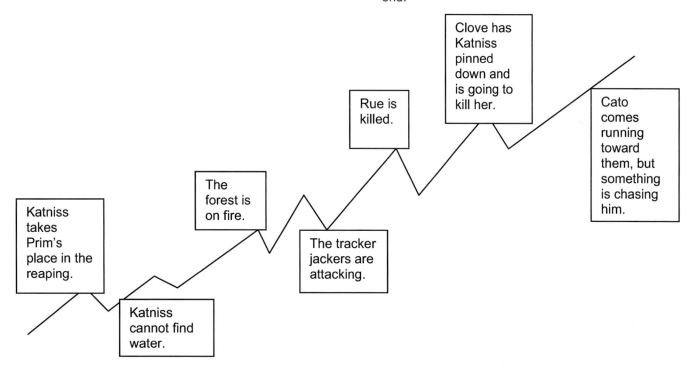

Part II: Analyze your Diagram:
Answers may vary. Sample answers:
2. We still don't know what the end of the story is.
3. They keep making changes, so we never know what is coming next.

4. It becomes more and more exciting when the story is changed up so often.

Pages 132-135: Chapters 23 – 24 Assessment Preparation: Inferring

Answers may vary. Sample student answers are given.

Chapters 5 – 6
Capitol Citizen
Did you see the parade? It was amazing! Who are these two from District 12? I may have to bet on them. They were on fire! Literally!

Chapters 7 – 9
The Gamemakers
Impressive show of skills from the tributes! How about that interview drama? The arena will have surprises for those lovebirds.

Chapter 10
Effie Trinket
Let the Games begin! My tributes will do their best. They are better than any I've had in the past. I've updated my resume for next year!

Chapters 11 – 12
Clove
Nearly had District 12 girl at the Cornucopia. Stupid backpack. I'll have another chance when she won't be so lucky. Plenty of knives!

Chapters 13 – 14
Second Capitol Citizen
Fire, tracker jackers, no water! These are the best Games EVER! Peeta saved Katniss. That girl acts like he's her enemy.

Chapters 15 – 16
Gale in the Seam
Rue's not the best ally, but she reminds me of Prim. Bow and arrow skills never looked better – what a great explosion!

Chapters 17 – 18
Citizen3
Anyone see the lines for betting? Wild! Real players and fighters this year. Too bad about District 11, but Peeta has a chance now.

Chapters 19 – 20
Mrs. Everdeen
Blood poisoning is fatal. There's no choice but to use the syrup. They've fallen in love in the arena? Can this be true?

Chapters 21 – 22
Cato District 1
I'll get revenge for Clove. She should have had that girl. No one is better with a knife than her. I'll be the winner now.

Chapters 23 – 24
The Gamemakers
We've saved the best for last. The accidental poisoning was dramatic, but we know you want more! Tune in for the next surprise!

2. Noncommittal means – neutral
The part of speech – adjective

3. Emaciated means – starved
The part of speech – adjective
4. Sustained means – kept going
The part of speech -- verb
5. Surreal means – unexpected combination
The part of speech – adjective
6. Dobby peevishly answered Harry Potter. Adverb
7. The dinosaur had difficulty extricating itself from the tar pits. Verb
8. The sparkling diamonds in the museum display mesmerized me. Verb
9. The dissonant chords of the song made my ears hurt. Adjective
10. The knight was wielding a sword when he approached the castle.

Page 137: Chapters 25 – 27: Comprehension Check Questions

Answers may vary. Sample answers
Chapter 25
1. They look life wolves, but they can stand on their hind legs. They have the physical characteristics of the tributes who have died.
2. They climb onto the Cornucopia.
3. Katniss gets her bow and arrow ready, and Peeta throws his knife in the water. She is on the attack, and he is refusing to kill her.
4. She doesn't trust Peeta. She still believes that the love story is a story and not true. She would be able to kill him.
5. They threaten to eat the poison berries so no one is the winner, but the Gamemakers change their minds and allow them to both win.
6. I agree with their decision because it put the responsibility for the outcome of the Games back on the Gamemakers. They have to make a quick decision or they'll lose both tributes.
7. They both have shown a lot of bravery throughout the Games. They have done difficult things and not shied away from them.

Chapter 26
1. She still acts like she's in the arena. She acts like a wild animal.
2. All of her scars are removed, and she's made into a new person.
3. He wants to remind the audience that the tributes are just children, and children should not be in a battle to the death. He is protesting the Games in his own way.
4. They want everything on television. They want to have the honest reaction televised. If they see each other, it won't be an authentic "show."
5. She is not in danger from the other tributes; she's in danger from the Capitol. They will be

looking for her to slip up or make a mistake so they can punish her.

Chapter 27
1. They watch a replay of the Games.
2. She feels like she's a prisoner.
3. He has an artificial leg.
4. She is leaving behind who she became in the arena and who the Capitol wants her to be. She wants to go back to being herself and not playing the role of the tribute.
5. I don't think so. She'll have a new house, and she'll be wealthy. She won't need to hunt any more, and she'll have to explain to Gale what her relationship with Peeta was about.
6. I think that she should stay with him because they went through so much together. I really feel like I know more about Peeta than I know about Gale.

Pages 138-143 : Chapters 25 – 27 Standards Focus: Symbolism
Answers may vary. Sample student answers are given.
Name of your fairy tale: "Hansel and Gretel"

	Name/description	What could it symbolize?
Character(s) in your tale	Hansel and Gretel The witch	Innocence, trust Greed, evil
Setting of the tale	The woods A house made of candy	Danger Greed, gluttony
Villain	The witch	Greed, gluttony
Hero (if there is one)	The children	Intelligence, innocence, ability to learn from mistakes
Is there a struggle for something?	The children struggle not to be eaten	There is a struggle between good and evil, between gluttony and moderation, between trusting and thinking (believing the witch and figuring out a solution)

1. When you first read the story, you think it just means what it says, but you can analyze it and all of a sudden the story means more than you think it means on the surface.
2. It opens up the story. It makes it more enjoyable to think of it in different ways.
1. people's names, the arena, chariots that carry the tributes in the parade, the rich foods, and shimmering city
2. They probably think they symbolize wealth, intelligence, art, and civilization
3. Wealthy Romans lived lives that were often gluttonous and wasteful. They were concerned about their own entertainment at the cost of other's lives. They kept slaves.
4. They act like the Romans because they are gluttonous and think of a fight to the death as entertainment. They are only concerned with their own pleasure.
5. Accept answers that can be analyzed.

Symbol	Analysis of the symbol
The mockingjay pin	The pin symbolizes rebellion
Cinna	He symbolizes rebellion and strength.
Prim	Her full name is Primrose – the name of a flower. She doesn't have the stamina and strength that Katniss has. Prim symbolizes gentleness and fragility.
Peeta	Peeta sounds like "pita" the bread. Since he's a baker's son and the boy with the bread, his name symbolizes bread – a source of nourishment, sustenance.
A silver parachute	A parachute symbolizes salvation from a fall out of an airplane. In the arena, the parachute symbolizes a form of salvation as a gift.
Fire	Symbolizes destruction when the fire chases Katniss, but also strength and power. Katniss and Peeta were on fire in the parade.
Water	Symbolizes life and healing.
TV cameras hidden everywhere	Symbolizes the private made public. Symbolizes the watching eye of the government.
Tracker jackers	Symbolize the evil intent of the Gamemakers.
The muttations	Symbolize the evil intent of the Gamemakers. The fact that they used dead tributes in the mutts shows their total disregard for human life.

Effie Trinket	A trinket is a small item of little value. That seems to be Effie – not very substantial. She may symbolize the general attitude of the people of the Capitol.

1. It is a horn overflowing with food.

2. I think of Thanksgiving and an abundance of food.

3. Instead of being filled with foods that sustain life, it's filled with supplies that are designed to ultimately kill someone. Rather that offering plenty and goodness to all, in order to get any of the cornucopia goodies, the tributes have to partake in a blood bath.

4. I think of lots of food and plenty to eat. I think of being so full that I can't move.

5. There is no food. She receives only a tiny backpack. It doesn't seem to be an event of excess in any way.

6. I think of sports, or board games, or playground games. Things we play where no one gets hurt.

7. Rather than being a game where people compete but don't die and the players have fun, these Games are deadly and don't appear to be fun at all.

8. It shouldn't be entertaining to see someone kill or be killed.

9. People have a distorted view of what is entertaining. Competition is certainly exciting to watch – like the Super Bowl or World Series, but watching children kill each other shouldn't be the way people are entertained. That is wrong. The country and leaders are twisted.

10. When we think of the odds being in your favor, we think of it in a positive way. It is clear that Effie thinks getting chosen in the reaping is having the odds be in your favor. The irony is that no one wants the odds to be in their favor in this case.

11. There are themes of gluttony and oppression. The theme is that children should be allowed to be children – not exploited by adults.

12. She might be pointing out that we're all obsessed with TV and watching what other people are doing. We want all the little personal details. She may also be saying that we don't value children enough or that they are exploited. Most of all, I think she is trying to make a statement about the dehumanization of people through the media.

Pages 144-147: Chapters 25 – 27 Assessment Preparation: Relationships Between Ideas – Subordination, Coordination, and Apposition

Intro: The writer added a list of verb phrases.
Part I:
1. The first conjunction is: so
It joins: clauses
The relationship between the items joined: the first clause describes the horn and the second clause describes how she's able to get a hold on it.
The second conjunction is: and
It joins: words – ridges and seams
The relationship between the items joined: it describes what they are able to get their feet into in order to climb the horn.

2. The conjunction is: but
It joins: phrases – "not only the leg" "the knife in his hand"
The relationship between the items joined: both his leg and the knife are causing Peeta to have difficulty climbing.

3. The conjunction is: and
It joins: words – the verbs "cries" and "releases"
The relationship between the items joined: Cato does both things at the same time.

4. The first conjunction is: and
It joins: phrases – the victor, his or her support team
The relationship between the items joined: It shows that the two rise together.
The second conjunction is: or
It joins: words – pronouns his, her
The relationship between the items joined: It shows an either/or relationship.

1. Subordinate clause: Before I can get this out
Relationship between the clauses: The mutts attack, but Katniss doesn't have time to say anything. She has thought about what the mutts mean, but she doesn't have time to verbalize her thoughts.

2. Subordinate clause: If the stiffness in my limbs is this bad
Relationship between clauses: The first clause is assessing how Katniss feels; the second clause compares (or tries to compare) it to Peeta.

3. Subordinate clause: As I stoop to pick it up
Relationship between clauses: First Katniss stoops, and then they hear the voice.

4. Subordinate clause: Before I am even aware of my actions
Relationship between clauses: Katniss's actions are so automatic that she's not even aware of what's she's doing. The first clause indicates

how quickly it happens, and the second clause indicates what she does.

1. Appositive: a good-sized mutt with silky waves of blond fur
What does it rename: It tells the reader which mutt it is and what it looks like.
2. Appositive: our packs
What does it rename: what the supplies are
Subordinate clause: when we fled from the mutts
Relationship between clauses: It shows the time sequence of them losing their packs.
3. Appositive: Peeta may end up losing his leg
What does it rename: It clearly states what the risky business is.
Coordinating conjunction: but
It joins: clauses
The relationship between the items joined: The two choices Katniss has to make – his leg or his life
4. Appositive: the subtle shift of the moon
What does it rename: It renames or clarifies how she can see the passage of time in the sky.

Pages 148-156, Create a Survival Game, Create a Museum Display, and Movie Connections: *Projects will vary widely.*

Pages 157-158: Quiz: Chapters 1 – 2
Answers may vary. Sample answers
1. will be representing District 12 in the Hunger Games.
2. a great hunting companion
3. This is her first year in the reaping. Her name has only been entered once.
4. a former Hunger Games winner from District 12
5. She is the Capitol representative for District 12.
6. the son of a baker
7. Madge has only entered her name once a year, but Katniss and Gale have taken the tesserae, so they have a greater chance that their name will be drawn.
8. The government is cruel to the people – they restrict their rights, don't care for the health and well being of the citizens, and they implemented the Hunger Games as a way to intimidate citizens.
9. radical
10. deterrent
11. poaching
12. reaping
13. maniacally
14. preposterous
15. predicament

16. adjacent
17. protocol
18. dissent
19. haggling
20. plummets

Pages 159-160: Chapters 3- 4 Quiz
1. d. is taken to the Justice Center.
2. a. cookies from Peeta's father.
3. a. if Haymitch is drunk, he can't help Katniss and Peeta.
4. b. She feels indebted to Peeta for being nice to her.
5. d. He is willing to help them if they listen to him.
6. mentor
7. deteriorate
8. pondering
9. detest
10. inexplicable
11. sniveling
12. insurmountable
13. gratified
14. disastrous
15. replicate
16. substantial
17. intensity
18. disgruntled
19. gnarled
20. deteriorated

Pages 161-162: Chapters 5 – 6 Quiz
1. they are on fire.
2. She can order any food she wants, the windows zoom in and out, she can program her closet, it is plush.
3. there is privacy. Their conversation won't be heard.
4. She recognizes her as one of the runaways she and Gale saw in the woods.
5. It would mean she'd have to admit to being in the woods which is illegal. She'd also acknowledge that the Capitol might not be the safest place to be.
6. People have everything they need; they are preoccupied with fashion, food, and entertainment; they don't have privacy or freedoms because they are "watched."
7. This is the beginning of the events that will eventually lead to her death. The people are cheering for her, but they are waiting to be entertained by her ultimate death.
8. vulnerable
9. flamboyant
10. sustenance
11. tangible

12. adversaries
13. despicable
14. exclusively
15. barbarism
16. affectations
17. ironic
18. mandatory

Pages 163-164: Chapter 7 – 9: Quiz
1. amiable
2. surly
3. potential
4. impulsiveness
5. ludicrous
6. banal
Answers may vary. Sample student answers are given.
7. d. unrequited. His feelings toward Katniss are not returned.
8. c. hostile. He's angry at Katniss because she is unresponsive to his suggestions for the interview.
9. e. prestigious. A high score can mean sponsors.
10. f. fixated. She was focused on Cinna rather than the audience.
11. a. leniency. She wants the Avox to forgive her for not helping her in the woods.
12. false
13. true
14. true
15. false
16. false
17. false
18. true
19. false (NOTE: He does not ask to be separated from Katniss until after they get their scores and then only for coaching for their personal interviews.)
20. Peeta confesses he has a long-standing crush on Katniss. I think it will affect the rest of the novel because in the arena there can only be one winner. Katniss and Peeta may have to fight to the death.

Pages 165-166: Chapter 10 Quiz
Answers may vary. Sample student answers are given.
1. She's upset because she thinks he's made her look weak.
2. It makes her memorable because she's popular in the district, but she's not aware of it. They've both become popular because of the love story surrounding them.
3. Haymitch isn't drunk and laughing. He means it as a sincere piece of advice. Now, Katniss and Peeta have had training and may feel they are better prepared than when they were on the train.
4. He doesn't want to become a monster or lose his identity because he's fighting for his life. In spite of being in a horrible situation, he wants to be himself, not what the Capitol wants him to be. He wants to stand up to the Capitol and show them that he is a real person not a toy or piece of entertainment.
5. Katniss trusts and admires Cinna. She values his opinions and his confidence in her.
6. a. hopes for a promotion to a better district at next year's Games.
7. c. she acts impulsively without thinking.
8. b. star-crossed lovers who can never be together.
9. a. will become a vacation spot.
10. b. must be approved by a review board.
11. The protesters breached the fence when they knocked it down.
12. An entourage followed the popular singer; there were many people to help take care of the details of the trip.
13. Phillipa was aghast when she realized she'd left her homework at home; her friends were shocked because she never forgot her work.
14. I perceived that the teacher would return the tests because I knew she spent the weekend grading papers.
15. My uncle enjoys participating in Civil War reenactments each summer when he goes to Gettysburg and pretends to be a soldier in the war.

Pages 167-168: Chapters 11 – 12 Quiz
1. scarcity
2. lapdogs
3. gall
4. void
5. rejuvenating
6. dispersed
7. dynamic
8. hoist
9. imprudent
10. botched
11. condenses
12. a. an orange backpack and a sheet of plastic.
13. c. Peeta has joined the Careers.
14. b. the Careers think she is stupid.
15. c. wonders why Haymitch won't send her water.
16. b. She has fallen into mud.
17. a. purify it.
18. d. a fire.

19. b. she knows she can survive on her own.
20. d. hydrated, endangered, surprised.

Pages 169-170: Chapters 13 – 14 Quiz
1. mayhem
2. conspiratorially
3. abate
4. bravado
5. persevere
6. sated.
7. quell
8. stupor
9. incompetent.
10. balm
11. honing
12. precariously
13. True
14. True
15. True
16. False
17. False
18. False
19. True
20. True

Pages 171-172: Chapters 15 – 16 Quiz
1. b. giving her leaves to heal her wounds.
2. a. Cato
3. d. she plans to attack the Careers.
4. a. still feels weak and shaky.
5. b. why Peeta saved her life.
6. c. song as a signal.
7. b. they see smoke.
8. c. it isn't guarded.
9. b. is able to steal from the Careers.
10. a. tentatively
11. b. wracked
12. c. obliging
13. d. noxious
14. c. rendezvous
15. a. forages
16. c. ordeal
17. b. onslaught
18. c. prominent
19. d. copse
20. c. ration

Pages 173-174: Chapters 17 – 18 Quiz
1. a. broken
2. b. next
3. c. splitting apart
4. a. able to be heard
5. a. lack of energy
6. b. to impose something unwanted
7. b. defeatedly
8. a. abruptly

9. b. plain and boring
10. c. unconcerned
11. d. too much
12. b. joy
13. She has stayed hidden and watched what the Careers did.
14. She was cared for while she was dying. Her body was strewn with wild flowers. It was evident that she was cared for and appreciated.
15. The Career tributes will have to hunt for their food. They'll be hungry. They'll lose the advantage over the other tributes.
16. She relies on her hearing as much as she relies on her other senses. It's like she's blind. She now has a huge disadvantage.
17. She now understands what Peeta meant when he was talking on the roof. She doesn't want to be a part of the Games. She also wants to win and feels that she could win.
18. She can find Peeta, and they can work as a team. She has renewed hope that they could win together.
19. It shows that Katniss has done something special for District 11. It is a way for them to show her that they appreciate what Katniss did for Rue.
20. The mockingjay repeats Rue's song, so they can use it as a signal that she is okay. The mockingjay continues to repeat the song after Rue is dead.

Pages 174-175: Chapters 19 – 20 Quiz
1. c. tracks Peeta and tries to imagine where he might be.
   d. notices bloodstains along the river and on a rock.
2. a. Katniss treats Peeta'a tracker jacker stings with the leaves Rue taught her about.
   b. Katniss has to risk the dangers of the feast to save Peeta.
   g. Katniss thinks about how her mother and Prim treat injured people.
3. b. Katniss has to risk the dangers of the feast to save Peeta.
   e. Katniss drugs Peeta with the sleeping syrup.
4. b. Katniss has to risk the dangers of the feast to save Peeta.
5. f. Katniss makes a shelter for them beside the river.
6. a. Katniss treats Peeta'a tracker jacker stings with the leaves Rue taught her about.
   b. Katniss has to risk the dangers of the feast to save Peeta.
   g. Katniss thinks about how her mother and Prim treat injured people.

7. g. Katniss thinks about how her mother and Prim treat injured people.
8. b. Katniss has to risk the dangers of the feast to save Peeta.
9. b. Katniss has to risk the dangers of the feast to save Peeta.
   e. Katniss drugs Peeta with the sleeping syrup.
10. ratcheting
11. scrupulously
12. loathe
13. evade
14. pariahs
15. incoherence
16. potent
17. tethered
18. peruse
19. wheedles
20. ruse

Pages 177-178: Chapters 21 – 22 Quiz

1. asset
2. exorbitant
3. famished
4. exasperated
5. arduous
6. plaintively
7. emanating
8. irreparable
9. infusion
10. ominous
11. staunch
12. irreverent
13. tirades
14. vaguely

Answers may vary. Sample student answers:
15. Clove is intent on killing Katniss. She doesn't miss the opportunity to taunt Katniss as well as discuss how she's going to kill her. Clove seems to be enjoying her capture of Katniss. Thresh wants more information about how Katniss knew Rue. He also is thoughtful about how he can repay Katniss for her kindness toward Rue.
16. Once Peeta is feeling better from the medicine, he's able to take care of Katniss. He seems more protective. He helps her with her wound and forces her to sleep and eat. He does many of the things Katniss did for him.
17. First, they both can win, so they can work as a team to protect each other and fight against one enemy. Second, the more romance they show, the more gifts they seem to be getting from their sponsors. Third, they both genuinely want the other to survive. Peeta even tells Katniss not to die for him.

Pages 179-180: Chapters 23 – 24 Quiz

1. False
2. True
3. True return the signal to whistle.
4. False
5. True

Answers may vary. Sample student answers:
6. They might say she was resourceful. She was able to survive on what others had done and not get caught. They might also say she was too trusting in relying on other tributes' knowledge of what was safe to eat rather than knowing that for herself. They might say she was smart because she knew how to survive and stay hidden.
7. She recognizes the poison berries and saves them from eating them, she hunts, she thinks about what Cato will think when he hears the cannon and sees their fire.
8. He is strong and well prepared for the Games, but he has a violent and unpredictable temper. He is merciless and cruel. Katniss doesn't think he's particularly smart, though.
9. They should expect it to be difficult and long. At the end of the chapter, Katniss discovers that Cato is wearing body armor, so Katniss's arrows may not have any effect on him.
10. a. savoring
11. c. peevishly
12. c. noncommittal
13. d. surreal
14. d. extricating
15. a. sustained
16. c. emaciated
17. b. surly
18. a. mesmerized
19. c. dissonant
20. a. wielding

Pages 181-182 : Chapters 25 – 27 Quiz

1. True
2. False
3. True
4. False
5. True
6. True
7. False
8. d. feverishly tries to reach Peeta.
9. a. callously
10. c. sophisticated
11. d. insidious
12. b. glowering
13. c. stalemate
14. a. debut
15. arbitrary
16. contrived
17. garish

18. segue
19. disproportionate
20. avenging

Pages 183-184: Part One: Final Test
1. True
2. True
3. False
4. False
5. True
6. False
7. True
8. False
9. True
10. False
11. False
12. False
13. False
14. True
15. False
16. f. Effie Trinket
17. a. Gale
18. g. Peeta
19. d. Cinna
20. e. Haymitch
21. Two tributes between the ages of 12 - 18 are chosen from each of the twelve Districts of Panem. Those twenty-four tributes will fight in a battle to the death. The winner receives prizes.
22. If a child between the age of 12 – 18 needs more rations of food for his or her family, the child can put his or her name into the reaping an extra time for each member of his/her family.
23. The Capitol is lavish and rich. People are obsessed with food and fashion. People in District 12 are just trying to stay alive. They are two extremes.
24. She explains what happened when the Districts rebelled. She explains how the Hunger Games came about.
25. Katniss is short tempered and impulsive. She doesn't forgive easily. Her positive qualities include being fiercely loyal, driven to pay debts, and practical.

Pages 185-189: Part One Vocabulary Test
1. sic
2. deterrent
3. plummets
4. preposterous
5. despicable
6. sustenance
7. haggling
8. tangible
9. hostile
10. sniveling

11. adjacent
12. gnarled
13. ironic
14. barbarism
15. fixated
16. amiable
17. insurmountable
18. mentor
19. gratified
20. substantial
21. adversaries
22. impulsiveness
23. reaping
24. poaching
25. flamboyant
26. b. maniacally
27. a. protocol
28. c. dissent
29. a. radical
30. d. predicament
31. b. lucky
32. b. boredom
33. a. one of a kind
34. c. happy
35. d. daydreaming
36. c. returned
37. a. unexplained
38. c. disintegrated
39. c. hate
40. a. exposed
41. d. cut
42. a. unable to be recovered
43. False
44. False
45. True
46. False
47. False
48. True
49. True
50. False
51. True
52. potential
53. defiantly
54. ludicrous
55. sullen
56. prestigious

Pages 190-192: Part Two Final Test
1. Caesar Flickerman
2. Haymitch
3. Peeta
4. Katniss
5. tracker jackers
6. silver parachute
7. Cato
8. Rue

9. Claudius Templesmith
10. Foxface
11. desirable
12. Katniss and Peeta can never be together; lovers whose relationship will fail because it's destined by the stars
13. a backpack and sheet of plastic
14. Rue
15. two tributes from the same district can win
Answers may vary. Sample student answers are given.
16. Rue works in the orchards. The mayor is brutal toward anyone who steals. The people don't get to keep any of the crops they pick. They have mockingjays there, and Rue sings to them.
17. She finally understands what Peeta means about being a person. She responds by placing flowers around Rue to show that she is a valued person.
18. Katniss and Peeta can both win. There is hope that they won't have to face each other in a fight to the death.
19. She has the ability to survive in the wild. She finds water, battles fire, uses tracker jackers as a weapon, and destroys the Careers food supply.
20. She's going to find Peeta and make sure they win so they can go home together.
21. False
22. True
23. False
24. False
25. False

Pages 193-196: Part Two Vocabulary Test
1. condenses
2. rejuvenating
3. assent
4. breached
5. imprudent
6. hoist
7. entourages
8. void
9. gall
10. perceived
11. aghast
12. reenactments
13. botched
14. lapdogs
15. dispersed
16. balm
17. quell
18. sated
19. mayhem
20. onslaught
21. stupor

22. conspiratorially
23. precariously
24. persevere
25. dynamic
26. scarcity
27. abate
28. honing.
29. incompetent
30. bravado
31. a. shaken
32. b. harmful
33. c. noticeable; standing out
34. a. cautiously
35. d. trouble
36. a. a portion
37. b. searches for food
38. d. willing to do favors
39. c. meeting place
40. d. a group of trees or bushes
41. a. halfheartedly
42. c. healed
43. b. suddenly
44. a. ordinary and plain
45. d. calm
46. False
47. True
48. False
49. True
50. False
51. True
52. True

Pages 197-199: Part Three Final Test
Answers may vary. Sample student answers are given.
1. Cato
2. muttations
3. Peeta
4. Claudius Templesmith
5. Haymitch
6. Katniss
7. Clove
8. Thresh
9. camouflaging himself in the riverbank
10. show the audience some romance
11. wolf; dead tribute
12. a little girl
13. Cato is threatening him. He has a wound in his leg and he could bleed to death.
14. They allow two winners from each district.
15. They dry up the stream, cause a torrential rain storm, create the "feast," bring in the mutts, cause the extreme temperatures both day and night.
16. The Gamemakers have no regard or respect for those who are killed in the arena. They are

just using them to entertain the audience and horrify the tributes.

17. The reader already knows how poisonous the berries are because they killed Foxface.

18. She knew she couldn't leave the arena without Peeta. She knew she could never return to District Twelve if she killed him or he died. She'd spend the rest of her life trying to figure out how she could have changed things.

19. He truly loves Katniss and can't imagine life without her.

20. The Capitol is angry that she defied them and forced them to accept their terms. They don't believe her motivation to do so was sparked by love.

21. In Part 3, the berries are a symbol of defiance. Katniss and Peeta can eat them and die, thus robbing the Capitol of a victor for the Games.

22. False
23. False
24. True
25. True

Page 200-204: Part Three Vocabulary Test

1. dissipate
2. pariahs
3. insidious
4. evade
5. scrupulously
6. ruse
7. peruse
8. tethered
9. potent
10. segue
11. wheedles
12. incoherence
13. arduous
14. asset
15. infusion
16. emanating
17. irreparable
18. ominous
19. keen
20. vaguely
21. a. sorrowfullly
22. c. very hungry
23. b. disrespectful
24. d. first appearance
25. a. excessive
26. c. frustrated
27. b. unequal
28. d. neutral
29. a. showing annoyance
30. b. dreamlike
31. False, True

32. False
33. True
34. False
35. False
36. False
37. True
38. False
39. True
40. a. callously
41. b. avenging
42. c. stalemate
43. a. tourniquet
44. b. feverishly
45. d. garish
46. d. contrived
47. a. arbitrary
48. d. sophisticated
49. a. benign

Answers may vary. Sample student answers are given.

50. The surgeon had to staunch the bleeding so the patient didn't bleed to death.

51. The two-year-old was prone to tirades because he was spoiled and his mother gave him his way whenever he had a tantrum.

52. The fans went berserk with their screaming and yelling when the rock star took the stage.

53. At Thanksgiving we enjoyed savoring the delicious food, so we took our time eating.

54. We lingered at the dinner table for three hours.

55. Francis loathes homework; he'd rather clean the house than complete his schoolwork.

56. The mechanic was ratcheting the bolt on the engine when the alarm went off.

Pages 205-210: Final Exam

Answers may vary. Sample answers

1. President Snow
2. Cato
3. Katniss
4. Peeta
5. Effie Trinket
6. Caesar Flickerman
7. Prim
8. Haymitch
9. Rue
10. Gamemakers

11. The reader needs to know the history of Peeta and Katniss. They also need to know about the Games – how they came about and why they're important. Additionally, the flashback helps the reader learn about Gale, and Katniss's conflicted feelings about him.

12. One archetype is the star-crossed lovers. It's an archetype because it's common in literature,

for example *Romeo and Juliet*. It's important in the novel because it's like a type of shorthand that readers can understand – they know what a star-crossed lover is and that the relationship is doomed. That makes it even more compelling.

13. She knows that she can't return to District 12 without him. They both have to survive. She also knows that they have a chance to survive the Games. Katniss believes that they can win.

14. I think he really loves Katniss and he knows the risk that she's taking by going to the feast. He would rather die himself than have Katniss die at the feast.

15. Except for Peeta and Katniss, they all probably need food and weapons. Perhaps they need supplies like a sleeping bag or blanket. Like Peeta, they may also need first aid.

16. The point of view is first person from Katniss. It helps the story because the reader understands what Katniss thinks and what she's going through. The reader knows her limitations and history. It limits the story because the reader doesn't know what Peeta or any of the other characters think. Katniss only has a limited view of the inner thoughts and experiences of others.

17. One type of conflict Katniss experiences is character vs. nature. Katniss experiences this in both her life in District 12 where she has to hunt and gather her own food and when she's in the arena. Katniss has to hunt, find shelter, stay healthy, and stay alive. Two good examples of this are when Katniss searched for water. She couldn't find it but continued to search. Finally, she found it. Another conflict with nature was when Katniss was trying to find shelter for Peeta. She had to find and camouflage the cave.

18. Suzanne Collins uses foreshadowing to hint at events that are to come and to also explain why something that happens in the novel is believable and consistent with the behavior and actions of a character. For example, Peeta decorates the cakes at his family's bakery. He does a great job at the camouflage station during training, and ultimately that foreshadowed skill is what he uses to hide when he's injured. It saves his life.

19. One symbol in the novel is bread. Bread, symbolizing life or nourishment, is used throughout the novel. Peeta's name even sounds like "pita" a type of bread, and he's a

Pages 211-217: Final Exam: Multiple Choice
1. a. was once North America.
2. b. punishment for an uprising against the government.

baker. Katniss recalls how his gift of bread saved her family. Additionally, bread is a gift to Katniss after Rue dies. Katniss enjoys the soft rolls she has in the Capitol. Peeta points out the different types of breads that each district bakes. People have long associated bread with nourishment, life, and health.

20. The novel is similar to the myth in a few ways. First of all, tributes are sacrificed as a form of punishment. Additionally, a hero in both the myth and the novel overcome the challenge. In the myth, it is Theseus. In the novel, Katniss and Peeta overcome the challenge.

21. False
22. True
23. True
24. True
25. False
26. False
27. True
28. True
29. False
30. True
31. d. are popular with the crowds.
32. c. Katniss and Peeta are together all the time.
33. b. has a short temper.
34. c. to die on his own terms.
35. c. Peeta has made an alliance with the Careers.
36. a. get away from the Cornucopia and find water.
37. d. The Careers trap Katniss in a tree.
38c. her sponsors like her strategy in dealing with the tracker jackers.
39. d. going to destroy the Careers' food.
40. d. singing to her until she dies.
41. a. show the audience that she loves him.
42. c. give each tribute something he needs.
43. b. thought it was better entertainment to send Katniss to the feast.
44. c. has been planning how to kill Katniss.
45. a. understand what it means to owe someone a favor.
46. a. mutations created by the Capitol.
47. d. they believe Katniss and Peeta will eat the berries.
48. a. Peeta was acting.
49. d. the forest.
50. b. The purpose of the feast.

3. b. takes Prim's place in the reaping.
4. d. saved Katniss's family from starvation.
5. c. Madge
6. a. he's responsible for their lives in the arena.

7. a. how she learned to survive in the woods.
8. c. impress Haymitch with their violent response to his drinking.
9. a. is the stylist responsible for Katniss's costumes.
10. d. are popular with the crowds.
11. b. she recognizes an Avox.
12. b. how she knows the Avox.
13. c. Katniss and Peeta are together all the time.
14. a. realizes the Gamemakers are not interested in her.
15. b. has a short temper.
16. c. Peeta's request to be coached on his own.
17. c. is openly hostile.
18. d. Peeta tells Caesar that he loves Katniss.
19. b. how Peeta's confession gives her an advantage.
20. c. he wants to die on his own terms.
21. b. gather supplies and weapons at the Cornucopia.
22. c. Peeta has made an alliance with the Careers.
23. a. get away from the Cornucopia and find water.
24. c. fire.
25. d. The Careers trap Katniss in a tree.
26. a. eventually saves Katniss.
27. c. muttations.
28. c. her sponsors like her strategy in dealing with the tracker jackers.
29. a. thinks Peeta saved her life.
30. b. has information about the Careers.
31. d. going to destroy the Careers' food.
32. a. the supplies are booby trapped.
33. c. has lost her hearing.
34. b. killed by a boy from District 1.
35. d. singing to her until she died.
36. b. is depressed.
37. c. two tributes from the same district can win.
38. a. show the audience that she loves him.
39. c. give each tribute something he or she needs.
40. b. think it is better entertainment to send Katniss to the feast.
41. c. has been planning how to kill Katniss.
42. a. understand what it means to owe someone a favor.
43. b. Peeta begins to heal and take care of Katniss.
44. d. has loved Katniss since he heard her sing.
45. c. need food.
46. b. steals their food.
47. c. something is chasing Cato.
48. a. mutations created by the Capitol.
49. b. Katniss shoots Cato in the hand.
50. c. There can now be only one winner.
51. d. they believe Katniss and Peeta will eat the berries.
52. a. President Snow is angry with her.
53. a. Peeta was acting.
54. d. the forest.
55. b. The purpose of the feast.

Page 218-230 Vocabulary Final Test
1. reaping
2. plummets
3. dissent
4. adjacent
5. preposterous
6. haggling
7. maniacally
8. protocol
9. poaching
10. deterrent
11. radical
12. predicament
13. imprudent
14. dynamic
15. scarcity
16. quell
17. abate
18. stupor
19. incompetent
20. conspiratorially
21. true
22. true
23. true
24. false
25. false
26. true
27. false
28. true
29. true
30. true
31. false
32. false
33. false
34. true
35. true
36. true
37. false
38. true
39. false
40. true
41. amiable
42. exclusively
43. barbarism
44. ironic

45. adversaries
46. mandatory
47. demean
48. oblivious
49. surly
50. debut
51. b. exciting
52. c. full
53. a. intentionally
54. d. happy
55. a. cowardice
56. c. whole
57. c. full
58. a. reasonable
59. a. healthy
60. b. friendly
61. a. cut
62. b. focused
63. d. mercy
64. a. to incite to attack
65. c. unable to be recovered
66. b. possible capacity
67. a. rebelliously
68. c. laughable
69. c. fascinated
70. d. respected
71. a. harmless
72. condenses
73. gall
74. lapdogs
75. dispersed
76. hoist
77. assent
78. breached
79. aghast
80. perceived
81. unrequited
82. entourage
83. reenactments
84. botched
85. rejuvenating
86. precariously
87. tentatively
88. avenging
89. stalemate
90. tourniquet
91. feverishly
92. a. noxious
93. b. persevere
94. d. sated
95. b. soothing
96. c. dulling
97. c. mayhem
98. a. attack
99. a. wracked
100. d. prominent

101. d. ordeal
102. c. a portion
103. b. searches for food
104. a. willing to do favors
105. d. meeting place
106. d. a group of trees or bushes
107. b. stubbornly
108. c. next
109. b. splitting apart
110. a. gradually
111. c. luxurious
112. b. distressed
113. d. able to be heard
114. b. not enough
115. a. impose something that isn't wanted
116. d. hopelessness
117. b. sluggishness
118. c. to scatter
119. b. outcasts
120. c. hate
121. d. random
122. d. evade
123. c. scrupulously
124. a. ruse
125. a. peruse
126. a. tethered
127. c. potent
128. b. ratcheting
129. d. wheedles
130. a. incoherence
131. d. arduous
132. b. asset
133. c. infusion
134. c. emanating
135. b. irreparable
136. a. ominous
137. c. staunch
138. a. vaguely
139. b. plaintively
140. c. irreverent
141. a. tirades
142. b. keen
143. c. exasperated
144. c. savoring
145. d. noncommittal
146. a. peevishly
147. b. surreal

Answers may vary. Sample student answers:
148. The farmer was extricating the tractor by pulling it out of the mud.
149. The marathon runner sustained his long run by eating a power bar that gave her energy.
150. The magician mesmerized the children by performing amazing tricks; they could have watched him for hours.

151. The beginner band played the dissonant piece that made us want to cover our ears.

152. Salvador was wielding his favorite pen when he came to class. He always brought it to class when there was a test.

153. We didn't mean to break the lamp, but I inadvertently knocked it over.

154. The glowering witch was staring at the intruders.

155. I couldn't find purchase on the mountain because my feet kept slipping over the rocky surface.

156. The landlord callously evicted the tenants; he didn't care that they had nowhere to go.

157. Florence enjoys wearing garish socks that practically glow in the dark.

158. Mark's contrived story about what happened to his science experiment was clearly made up.

159. The sophisticated students showed great maturity.

160. Clyde went berserk and acted crazy when he heard his favorite song on the radio.

161. There were such a disproportionate number of dogs in the pet store that I thought they only sold dogs.

162. The aroma of the burnt toast lingered in the air for several hours.

163. An insidious trap was waiting just inside the door.

164. We made a smooth segue between the discussion about chocolate and discussion about cookies.

Pages 231-235 Multiple Choice Vocabulary Test
1. b. searches for food
2. a. willing to do favors
3. d. meeting place
4. b. stubbornly
5. c. next
6. a. gradually
7. d. able to be heard
8. b. not enough
9. a. to impose something unwanted
10. d. depression
11. b. sluggishness
12. c. to scatter
13. b. outcasts
14. c. hate
15. d. random
16. b. exciting
17. c. full
18. a. intention
19. d. happy
20. a. cowardice
21. c. whole
22. c. sated
23. a. reasonable
24. a. healthy
25. b. friendly
26. a. cut
27. b. focused
28. d. mercy
29. c. unable to be recovered
30. b. possible capacity
31. a. resistantly
32. c. laughable
33. c. fascinated
34. a. respected
35. a. harmless
36. a. foul-smelling
37. b. persist
38. d. sated
39. b. soothing
40. a. attack
41. d. evade
42. c. scrupulously
43. a. peruse
44. a. tethered
45. c. potent
46. a. incoherence
47. d. arduous
48. b. asset
49. c. infusion
50. c. emanating